D1122046

The American History Series

SERIES EDITORS

John Hope Franklin, *Duke University*
A. S. Eisenstadt, *Brooklyn College*

Thomas K. McCraw
HARVARD UNIVERSITY

American Business, 1920–2000: How It Worked

HARLAN DAVIDSON, INC.
WHEELING, ILLINOIS 60090-6000

Visit us on the World Wide Web at www.harlandavidson.com.

Library of Congress Cataloging-in-Publication Data

McCraw, Thomas K.
   American business, 1920–2000 : how it worked / Thomas K. Mc-
Craw.
         p. cm.—(The American history series)
   Includes bibliographical references and index.
   ISBN 978-0-88295-985-6 (alk. paper)
      1. Industries—United States—History—20th century.
2. Corporations—United States—History—20th century. 3. United
States—Commerce—History—20th century. 4. Labor—United
States—History—20th century. 5. United States—Economic condi-
tions. I. Title. II. American history series (Wheeling, Ill.)

HC106.82.M39 2000
338.0973'09'04—dc21   99-086083

Cover illustration: Boeing-designed B-17 bombers being assembled at a Douglas Aircraft plant in Long Beach, California, during the height of mobilization for World II. *Courtesy National Archives*

Manufactured in the United States of America
08 7 VP

This book is for Liz and Rob McCarron

FOREWORD

Every generation writes its own history for the reason that it sees the past in the foreshortened perspective of its own experience. This has surely been true of the writing of American history. The practical aim of our historiography is to give us a more informed sense of where we are going by helping us understand the road we took in getting where we are. As the nature and dimensions of American life are changing, so too are the themes of our historical writing. Today's scholars are hard at work reconsidering every major aspect of the nation's past: its politics, diplomacy, economy, society, recreation, mores and values, as well as status, ethnic, race, sexual, and family relations. The lists of series titles that appear on the inside covers of this book will show at once that our historians are ever broadening the range of their studies.

The aim of this series is to offer our readers a survey of what today's historians are saying about the central themes and aspects of the American past. To do this, we have invited to write for the series only scholars who have made notable contributions to the respective fields in which they are working. Drawing on primary and secondary materials, each volume presents a factual and narrative account of its particular subject, one that affords readers a basis for perceiving its larger dimensions and importance. Conscious that readers respond to the closeness and immediacy of a subject, each of our authors seeks to restore the past as an actual present, to revive it as a living reality. The individuals and groups who figure in the pages of our books appear as real people who once were looking for survival and fulfillment. Aware that historical subjects are often matters of controversy, our authors present their own findings and conclusions. Each volume closes with an extensive critical essay on the writings of the major authorities on its particular theme.

The books in this series are primarily designed for use in both basic and advanced courses in American history, on the undergraduate and graduate levels. Such a series has a particular value these days, when the format of American history courses is being altered to accommodate a greater diversity of reading materials. The series offers a number of distinct advantages. It extends the dimensions of regular course work. It makes clear that the study of our past is, more than the student might otherwise understand, at once complex, profound, and absorbing. It presents that past as a subject of continuing interest and fresh investigation.

For these reasons the series strongly invites an interest that far exceeds the walls of academe. The work of experts in their respective fields, it puts at the disposal of all readers the rich findings of historical inquiry, an invitation to join, in major fields of research, those who are pondering anew the central themes and aspects of our past.

And, going beyond the confines of the classroom, it reminds the general reader no less than the university student that in each successive generation of the ever-changing American adventure, from its very start until our own day, men and women and children were facing their daily problems and attempting, as we are now, to live their lives and to make their way.

John Hope Franklin
A. S. Eisenstadt

CONTENTS

INTRODUCTION

Eighty Years
of Relentless Change

The period from 1920 to 2000 was not a very long time—not much longer than the lifespan of the average American today. Yet our ancestors in 1920 lived very differently from the way we live in the twenty-first century. Momentous changes were already underway in 1920, but many daily routines were as much like those of 1840 as those of 2000. Some people were experiencing the exhilaration of driving an automobile, but at least as many still traveled by horse-drawn buggy. (About one of four U.S. households had a car in 1920, compared with more than nine of ten in 2000.) Large numbers of shoppers were buying branded processed foods such as Kellogg's corn flakes, Nabisco crackers, and Crisco shortening; but lots of families were still canning their own vegetables and some were still churning their own butter.

In 1920 half of all Americans lived on farms or in towns of fewer than 2,500 people, and many communities lacked even railroad tracks to connect them with the rest of the country. About 25 percent of the labor force still farmed, compared with only 2 percent at the end of the century. Most Americans in 1920 never traveled more than a few hundred miles from where they were born.

Only a third of the nation's homes had electricity in 1920, compared to nearly all in 2000. In 1920 the tasks of cooking, cleaning, and doing laundry and other housework took between 60 and 70 hours per week. That number soon began to decline, largely because of the advent of the electric refrigerator, washer, dryer, vacuum cleaner, iron, toaster, mixer, dishwasher, and garbage disposal. By the end of the century the number of hours spent on cooking and housework had stabilized at fewer than 25 per week. Obviously, nobody in 1920 had a TV, VCR, video game, CD player, fax machine, computer, or cellular phone. Nobody ate at a McDonald's, Wendy's, Pizza Hut, or other fast-food chain. Nobody made a Xerox copy, carried a pager, flew on a commercial airline, or drew cash from an automatic teller machine. Nobody surfed the Internet, shopped at a mall, or bought food at a supermarket. Because the need for a paying job was so urgent, most people never graduated from high school. Instead they took full-time jobs when they reached their middle teens. Only 1 person out of 30 completed college in 1920, compared with 1 of 4 in 2000.

In 1920 the care of children, the sick, and the elderly almost always took place in the home. The development and use of antibiotics lay far in the future, and deaths from pneumonia, tuberculosis, cholera, diphtheria, measles, influenza, and typhoid fever ran at more than ten times their rates of today. Nor was it easy to control the size of families. Birth control pills had not been invented, reliable condoms were not easily obtained, and abortions were illegal. In many areas sanitary conditions were still premodern. Only 1 in 5 American households even had an indoor flush toilet.

Most of these conditions true for Americans in 1920 still existed for the majority of the world's people eighty years later at the start of the twenty-first century. Even in most "rich" countries, household conveniences came slowly. In 1960, the year John F. Kennedy was elected president, 96 percent of American homes had electric refrigerators, as compared to only 52 percent of West German homes, 41 percent of French homes, and 30 percent of British and Italian homes. Nor, of course, did refrigerators and other modern products just appear automatically. They had to be invented, developed, manufactured, and marketed by the business systems of the world. In many cases, American companies led the way.

American Business and the World

In 1920 the United States was already producing more agricultural and industrial goods than any other country, and its people were enjoying the highest per-capita income. But 80 years later this per-capita income had grown to more than four times the figure for 1920. Measured against human experience over the whole of recorded history, such a level of affluence for so many people had no precedent. Thus, the most significant fact about American business from 1920 to 2000 was its outstanding economic performance. This generalization holds for almost all types of businesses, whether small, medium, or large, and whether high-tech or low. Performance was especially strong during the 1920s, the 1940s through the 1960s, and the 1990s; it was less so during the 1970s and early 1980s, and much less so during the Great Depression of the 1930s.

The American Dream of rags to riches clearly did not come true for everyone, but it did materialize for enough people so that masses of others were motivated to try. The spirit of entrepreneurship exhibited by so many twentieth-century Americans was predicated on the hope that an energetic and hard-working person actually could become prosperous. The potential for business success was far higher in the United States than elsewhere, and the widespread perception of authentic opportunity released immense amounts of economic energy. On a per-capita basis, Americans probably started more businesses, saw more of them fail, and then started more new ones than did the citizens of any other country. Best of all, one person's success did not necessarily mean another's failure.

This was a truth that proved difficult for critics of capitalism to accept. As the German socialist Karl Liebknecht said in 1907, "The basic law of capitalism is you or I, not both you and I." But he was wrong. Even though many individuals and companies failed, American business was and still is a positive-sum game. As consumers' purchasing power increased, more and more entrepreneurs and companies flourished. At its best, a market economy becomes a "virtuous circle," each round of prosperity stimulating the start of another round.

The virtuous circle seldom surrounds a peaceful scene, however. Business can be, and usually is, a stormy affair. The Harvard economist Joseph Schumpeter (1883–1950), one of the keenest analysts of capitalism who ever lived, liked to argue that internal turbulence epitomizes modern business. Capitalism itself, wrote Schumpeter, is a process of transformation "that incessantly revolutionizes the economic structure *from within,* incessantly destroying the old one, incessantly creating a new one." The market shows no mercy, and constant competitive turmoil is one of the defining traits of capitalist economies. Certainly it characterized American business in the eight decades from 1920 to 2000.

Schumpeter's metaphor for this process, a "perennial gale of creative destruction," was more emblematic of the U.S. economy than that of any other country. The sweeping out of old products, old enterprises, and old organizational forms by new ones became a hallmark of the American business system. Schumpeter and others called the agents of creative destruction "entrepreneurs," a French word meaning business adventurers. In the absence of a good English equivalent, the word gained wide currency.

The Story Told Here

This book is concerned mostly with the inner workings of the business system, where creative destruction usually starts. It focuses on the entrepreneur, the company, and the industry. It takes the vantage point of people working within companies rather than the external perspectives of consumers, governments, or other groups. It shows from the inside how businesses operated.

The eighty years from 1920 to 2000 are logically divisible into five periods: the 1920s, the 1930s, the years of the New Deal and World War II, the period 1945 to 1973, and the time from 1973 to 2000. The periods vary in length and some overlap others, but each has a unity that will become evident. The book's main chapters correspond with these periods, but the narratives of each chapter extend to other eras where necessary to present an uninterrupted analysis of a particular industry or person. For example, airplanes were manufactured in all five periods, but the story of aviation is told in the chapter that includes World War II. Similarly, the electronics pioneer David Sarnoff did significant work in four of the five periods, but he appears in the chapter that covers the years 1945–1973, when television first became widely available.

By the start of the twenty-first century, about 4.5 million corporations were doing business in the United States, along with 16.4 million non-farm proprietorships and 1.6 million partnerships. Only a few of these 22.5 million enterprises can be examined in the chapters of this book. The traditionally arranged chronological chapters begin with a survey of social and economic trends. Then, to provide deeper analysis, each chapter eventually comes to focus on an illustrative firm. The companies chosen for these analytical stories are Ford, General Motors, Procter & Gamble, Boeing, RCA, and McDonald's—each of which has an exciting and sometimes riveting history.

American business history also includes some vital aspects not easily covered in the chronological design just described, with its necessarily small sample of illustrative firms. In between the narrative chapters, therefore, you'll find five brief "overview" chapters: one on the financial system, one on industrial chemicals and pharmaceuticals, and one on computers, Silicon Valley, and the Internet. The other two overview chapters trace the business experiences of women and African Americans, two of the many groups who have suffered discrimination but have nonetheless participated in the U.S. business system in significant ways. There could be numerous other short chapters on additional topics, but these five are especially important. Each is examined briefly for the entire 1920–2000 period.

A Matter of Size

With the exception of RCA, which no longer exists as an independent firm, the companies analyzed in the book's major chapters are now big businesses. But each one began small. Most originated as entrepreneurial startups and became big because they had a winning formula.

Their large size is also a function of the kinds of industries in which they operate. In automobiles, airplanes, consumer electronics, oil, chemicals, and a few other industries (most of them requiring large capital investments), firms that survived the competitive struggle over a long period almost always grew to large size. This was true not only in the United States but also in other countries where these kinds of industries flourished. In the great majority of industries, including apparel, furniture, printing, food service, jewelry, and repair of all kinds, even successful companies seldom grew into big businesses. Only a few thousand of the 22.5 million enterprises operating in the United States in the early twenty-first century are truly large. In neither the United States nor any other country does most of the labor force work for a "big business," which is customarily defined as one having more than 500 employees.

Large companies buy from and sell to networks of small and medium-sized suppliers and subcontractors, so businesses of different sizes have close and frequent dealings. In most of these relationships the big firms have the preponderance of power. But big and small are relative terms. Even very big tire firms, for example, have little bargaining power against giant auto companies, which squeeze the prices of "original equipment" tires to the barest minimum. So tire firms must make most of their profits on sales of replacement tires to consumers, not on initial deliveries to auto manufacturers.

Patterns such as these, which have appeared in all industrialized countries, are easier to understand now than they were in 1920. Many of the old political debates on the relative merits of big versus small business therefore look a little curious in retrospect. They resemble ancient but wrongheaded arguments about the nature of the cosmos, and poorly informed debates over medical treatment before the discovery of germs. (Is the sun or the earth the center of the universe? Should we bleed the patient a lot or just a little?)

Is big business better than small business—in efficiency, treatment of workers, and ethical behavior? As a general proposition, the question is incorrectly framed and has no logical answer. It all depends on the nature of the industry, the companies and leaders involved, and many other factors specific to the situation.

The Key Business Problem

In the running of a company of whatever size, the hardest thing to manage is usually this: the delicate balance between the necessity for centralized control and the equally strong need for employees to have enough autonomy to make maximum contributions to the company and derive satisfaction from their work. To put it another way, the problem is exactly where within the company to lodge the power to make different kinds of decisions.

This issue is not confined to business, of course. It applies to any organization. Even in a group as small as the family, it arises every day. And the way in which it does or does not work itself out can be a stubborn problem—or a vivid memory to anyone recalling the frustrations of childhood. Must the family eat together every night? Should the adults choose what kinds of clothing may and may not be worn to school, or is it better to leave that decision to the children? Should the parent or the adolescent child set the appropriate hour of curfew?

No single rule will guarantee the best result every time, or in all families. But in every situation a decision does have to be made by someone. As with families, so with businesses. Constant decision making lies at the heart of management. But who decides? On what basis? In whose interest? Economists like to speak of these questions as involving "decision rights," and to embed the questions in a framework they call "agency theory." In this framework, "principals" try to get "agents" to do certain kinds of tasks, with managers working to align incentives so that everyone strives toward the same goal.

In military organizations, the issue of decision rights and relationships between principals and agents has even more pitfalls than it does in families. Military hierarchies are so rigidly defined that even a small deviation from the rules can lead to prosecution and court-martial.

The business world stands on this issue about halfway between the family and the military. Its balance between centralized and decentralized decision making has to be continually evaluated and adjusted so that incentives remain properly aligned. The better a business firm is organized, the more naturally decision rights gravitate to the spot where the best information is available about the specific decision that has to be made.

This book illustrates the historical struggles with decision rights and relative centralization through stories of extraordinarily capable entrepreneurs and the organizations they led: Alfred P. Sloan, Jr., at General Motors during the 1920s, Neil McElroy at Procter & Gamble in the 1930s, Ferdinand Eberstadt at the government's Controlled Materials Plan during World War II, David Sarnoff at RCA in the 1950s and 1960s, and Ray Kroc and his franchisees at McDonald's in the late decades of the century.

The American Business Achievement

In most academic books on American history, assertions of high achievement have been out of fashion for four or five decades, and with good reason. For a period of over 150 years, from about 1800 until the 1960s, American history was usually taught as an uninterrupted march of progress. George Washington never told a lie, slavery would have died out without the need for a bloody civil war, women had it better in the United States than elsewhere, and the United States never fought an unjust foreign war. All of these teachings were highly questionable, and perpetuating them ill served the interests of students and the nation as a whole.

Starting in the 1960s, the pendulum of interpretation swung the other way. History began to be taught with fuller coverage of the ugly aspects of American experience, including the plagues of racism, sexism, and imperialism. In the case of business, many critics properly pointed out that capitalist success of the American sort had an obnoxious underside in its unbridled pursuit of money. A society obsessed with business was not likely to be refined or genteel, and American capitalism at its worst promoted a vulgar egocentrism that emphasized the materialistic self to the detriment of the spiritual. It elevated individual rights at the expense of familial and community duties. It tended to make some people fabulously rich while others remained poor. Its endless advertising assailed the senses and affronted the soul.

The degree to which economic progress was *inevitably* accompanied by these negative aspects is not well understood, even by experts. The issue remains a matter of controversy. But the really bad news about the material condition of human beings applies not to the United States but to those large parts of the world where mass living standards still teeter on the edge of subsistence. Against this background, the stark fact of American business success in improving the material life of millions of people is beyond dispute. Despite its negative side few informed people would wish to reverse it.

This book analyzes how the American business achievement from 1920 to 2000 came about. We begin with motor vehicles, the key consumer durable of the so-called Second Industrial Revolution.*

---

*The idea of separate industrial revolutions is not explicitly emphasized in the text of this book but underlies its whole approach. For North America and Western Europe, the following dates apply; for most other areas of the world, the same phenomena appeared at somewhat later dates: In the period of the First Industrial Revolution, which lasted from about the 1760s to the 1840s, steam engines powered by coal began to replace human and animal energy, and people began to work by the clock for the first time in history. Large factories arose in textiles and a few other industries, and the mass-produced output of those industries became much less expensive to consumers.

In the era of the Second Industrial Revolution, stretching from the 1840s to about the 1950s, transportation and communication were radically altered, first by the railroad, telegraph, telephone, and radio, and then by the automobile, truck, and airplane. Electric motors and internal combustion engines furnished vital new sources of power for factories, vehicles, and equipment. Mass marketing was added to mass production. Big businesses appeared, giving rise to sophisticated new forms of management.

A Third Industrial Revolution began in the 1940s and 1950s and is still changing the course of business and everyday life. Its main features have been an emphasis on information technology and knowledge work, and a shift to services as a source of employment for more people than the combined total of all other sectors (agriculture, mining, construction, and manufacturing). In the Third Industrial Revolution, science-based businesses such as electronics, synthetic chemicals and pharmaceuticals, and computer hardware and software have led economic growth.

CHAPTER ONE

The 1920s: Motor Vehicles and Modern Management

A defining mark of advanced capitalist economies is the proliferation of new items offered to consumers. By the end of the twentieth century, at least 20,000 new American products per year were being "rolled out" for sale, as businesspeople like to put it. But even this figure of 20,000 is deceptively low, because a much larger number of other new items, after being test-marketed by major companies, were not chosen for large-scale distribution.

The replacement of old products by new ones happens rapidly. During just one decade, from 1980 to 1990, about 85,000 new products were introduced into U.S. grocery stores. On any given day, large American supermarkets now offer more than 40,000 items for sale. But today's 40,000 differ from yesterday's, and tomorrow's will be different still. Most new products drop quickly from sight, casualties of consumer verdict. The mass of consumers is like a giant jury, listening to constant messages from advertisers, trying out different products, and continually passing judgment in the marketplace.

This jury has determined that a few types of items are near-necessities. And some of the producers and marketers of these items—companies such as Procter & Gamble and McDonald's—have achieved iconic status within business and also in popular culture. Their names have become familiar all over the world.

During the first half of the twentieth century, the industry that best symbolized the genius of the American business system was motor vehicles, and cars in particular. The car came to be regarded almost as a necessity, just as television would later on. Both came to rank near food, clothing, and shelter as perceived essentials of modern life.

The production of inexpensive cars depended on a prosperous mass market, and preferably a growing one. In 1900, as cars first appeared on the scene, the United States was already the richest market in the world, and it was growing fast. Over the course of the twentieth century, the population of both the U.S. and the world more than tripled. In no other period of history had that kind of absolute growth occurred, and the increase itself was a condition of the progress of American business as epitomized by the manufacture and sale of cars.

An insignificant industry in 1900, motor vehicles became by the 1920s the largest in the United States. The industry's connections with suppliers of glass, rubber, and steel, plus its close relationship with road-building and oil production, made the car the most important single product of the twentieth century. By the 1970s about one-sixth of all American business firms were participating in some way in the manufacture, distribution, service, or operation of cars and trucks.

During the 1920s, the car became the center of the national consumer economy, and until the successful Japanese challenge of the 1970s and 1980s, it remained a pre-eminently American-made product. In the middle 1920s, about 80 percent of all cars in the world were located in the United States, where there was one automobile for every 5.3 people. By comparison, in both Britain and France there was one for every 44 people. (Seven decades later, toward the close of the century, these ratios were as follows: in the United States, one car per 1.7 people, in Western Europe one per

2.5, in Japan one per 3.0, in Mexico one per 12.5, in China one per 680.) For many people everywhere, driving came to be a means of escape, a way to express personal freedom. The word "automobile" itself expresses the appealing idea of autonomous mobility. The first cars were built in Europe during the 1880s and 1890s, and by 1899 about 30 American companies were producing an annual total of 2,500 automobiles. Like most new industries, this one was led in the United States by a few bold entrepreneurs—such people as Ransom Olds, James Packard, the Dodge brothers, and Walter Chrysler. The two greatest giants in the industry were Henry Ford, who soon became the best-known manufacturer of anything anywhere, and Alfred P. Sloan, Jr., who built General Motors into the world's largest industrial corporation.

Henry Ford (1863–1947)

Ford grew up on the family farm in Dearborn, Michigan. Even as a boy he was an incurable tinkerer, and he amused himself by taking clocks apart and putting them back together. At the age of sixteen, he began working in a Detroit machine shop, then moved on to a dry-dock firm, a machinery company, and an electric utility, where he became chief engineer. Ford's first car was an impractical "quadricycle" he built in 1896. His first two automaking companies failed, but his third, launched in 1903 as the Ford Motor Company, succeeded brilliantly. His Model T, brought out in 1908, quickly revolutionized the entire industry.

A handsome, fit-looking, self-confident man, Henry Ford had good reason to regard himself as an oracle of mass production. In 1903, a time when cars were still being built in small numbers of diverse and expensive models, he said to one of his partners, "The way to make automobiles is to make one automobile like another automobile, to make them all alike, to make them come from the factory just alike—just like one pin is like another pin when it comes from a pin factory or one match is like another match when it comes from a match factory." Not long after his start in the business, he vowed to "build a motor car for the great multitude . . . constructed of the best materials, by the best men to be hired, after the simplest designs that modern engineering can devise . . . so low in price that no man making a good salary will be unable to own one—and enjoy with his family the blessing of hours of pleasure in God's great open spaces." A good friend of Ford's observed that "Standardization is his hobby. He would have all shoes made on one last, all hats made on one block, and all coats according to one pattern. It would not add to the beauty of life, but it would greatly reduce the cost of living." Ford himself went a step further, arguing that standardization did add to the beauty of life by making diversity possible: "Machine production in this country has diversified our life, has given a wider choice of articles than was ever before thought possible— and has provided the means wherewith the people may buy them. We standardize only on essential conveniences. Standardization, instead of making for sameness, has introduced unheard-of variety into our life. It is surprising that this has not been generally perceived." Whether right or wrong in this statement, Ford was expressing the paradoxical nature of standardization. The phenomenon itself became a defining trait of many American products for the rest of the twentieth century.

As for the Model T, it was standardized in the extreme—a simple, reliable, and durable machine that could be repaired by its owner. When Ford decided that he had finally put together the right kind of car, he stopped working on other models. All of his company's efforts now went into making and improving the T. This was a singular moment in the history of the automobile industry, and it began a 20-year dynamic of rising sales and declining prices. Whereas the first Model T of 1908 sold for $850, the four millionth, which rolled off the line in 1920, could be purchased for $440. By the early 1920s the Ford Motor Company was producing more than half of all motor vehicles manufactured in the world. The ten millionth Model T, produced in 1925, sold at the remarkably low price of $290, and it was a much better car than were earlier versions. Such a cycle of increased output, reduced prices, and improvement of the product had never before appeared for such a "big-ticket" item.

A major step in Ford's miracle of production was the perfection of the moving assembly line. In early 1914, this development cut the time necessary to assemble a Model T chassis by about 85 percent: from twelve and a half hours to one and a half. Writing for an engineering magazine in 1915, two visitors to the Ford factory described the assembly line and went on to speculate about the larger meaning of what Henry Ford had done:

Beyond all doubt or question, the Ford Motor Company's plant at Highland Park, Detroit, Michigan, U.S.A., at the time of this writing is the most interesting metalworking establishment in the world—because of its size (something over 15,000 names on the payroll); because it produces one single article only (the Ford motor car) for sale; because the Ford Motor Company is paying very large profits (something like $15,000,000 a year); and because, with no strike and no demand for pay increase from its day-wage earners, the Ford Company made a voluntary and wholly unexpected announcement January 5, 1914, that it would very greatly increase day-pay wage [to five dollars, more than twice the prevailing rate] and would at the same time reduce the day-work hours from nine to eight.

The combined magic of the assembly line and the five-dollar day made Henry Ford famous all over the world. He seemed to represent the potential humaneness of industrialization. Higher wages, shorter hours, a fabulous product designed to liberate masses of people from isolation—these achievements made him an international hero. His actual motives in introducing the five-dollar day had more to do with reducing the labor turnover in his plants than with any humanitarian urge. By 1914, his company needed to hire more than 50,000 workers each year to maintain a force of 15,000. This 300-percent turnover rate derived from the pressures and boredom of assembly-line work. The five-dollar day could not change those conditions, but it did partly compensate people for the monotony of their tasks. The reduction of working hours also helped, and in the 1920s Ford went a step further and shortened the workweek from six days to five without a commensurate decrease in pay.

All of these changes received wide publicity. The company courted journalists, and Henry Ford himself was always good copy. By the middle 1920s, he had become the most famous American in the world. The term "Fordism" entered many languages as shorthand for standardized mass production. As the

French analyst R. L. Bruckberger wrote in the 1950s, "What Marx had dreamed, Ford achieved." With the assembly line and the five-dollar day, he had made a reality of the "vast role that mechanization can play in emancipating human society."

Ford's celebrity brought with it daily opportunities to speak out on subjects he knew nothing about. One of his biographers, David Lewis, lists some of Ford's outlandish comments, such as "This globe has been inhabited millions of times, by civilians having airplanes, automobiles, radio, and other scientific equipment of the modern era." In 1919 Ford proposed that horses, cows, and pigs be eliminated. "The world would be better off without meat." In 1925 he said that starches and sweets were incompatible with human digestion, and in 1927 he added chickens to his list of things not to be eaten. For many years, he challenged visitors to footraces, and he especially enjoyed outrunning young newspaper reporters. He was still running footraces at the age of eighty. A friend of Ford's once wrote, "His mind does not move in logical grooves. It does not walk, it leaps. It is not a trained mind. It does not know how to think consecutively. . . . He does not reason to conclusions. He jumps at them." Ford employed large numbers of African Americans, but he was deeply prejudiced against Jews, and his company-sponsored newspaper the *Dearborn Independent* regularly published anti-Semitic articles.

In his approach to business, Ford held to two basic principles. He would produce high-quality cars and sell them as inexpensively as possible. He was fond of asserting that every dollar chopped off the price of a Model T attracted at least a thousand new buyers. Many customers, he said in 1916, "will pay $360 for a car who would not pay $440. We had in round numbers 500,000 buyers of cars on the $440 basis, and I figure that on the $360 basis we can increase the sales to possibly 800,000 cars for the year—less profit on each car, but more cars, more employment of labor, and in the end we get all the total profit we ought to make."

He plowed most of his profits back into the business. In defending his low-dividend policy against a lawsuit brought by the Dodge brothers, who were minority stockholders, Ford said from the witness stand that "the only thing that makes anything not sell is because the price is too high." He himself had come into his immense fortune "incidentally," by producing a great product and giving employment to thousands of people.

Although Ford was probably the world's wealthiest individual, remarks such as these appealed to everyday people, who seemed to admire and trust him as the embodiment of the common man, as someone much like themselves. It was often said that Ford's fortune of more than a billion dollars had been earned "cleanly," unlike the wealth of "Robber Barons" such as John D. Rockefeller and Andrew Carnegie. Ford himself made no secret of his disdain for some of the trappings of capitalism. He spoke harshly of "financeering." He detested stockholders, whom he described as "parasites."

In 1919, to rid himself of any stockholder influence, he bought up all the outstanding shares of his company and took it private. This was a profound and ominous step. At a single stroke, it put the gigantic Ford Motor Company under the absolute control of one erratic "Genius Ignoramus," as biographer David Lewis calls Ford. And at just that moment the company was about to confront a formidable competitor, the emerging General Motors Corporation.

Alfred P. Sloan, Jr. (1875–1966)

Henry Ford had grown up on a midwestern farm. The man who became his great rival was a city boy from the East. The son of a prosperous merchant, Alfred Sloan had lived first in New Haven, Connecticut, then at the age of ten had moved with his family to Brooklyn. At Brooklyn Polytechnic Institute he made a splendid academic record, and he continued to shine academically at the Massachusetts Institute of Technology, where he studied electrical engineering. Sloan finished his MIT degree in three years, having worked "every possible minute, so that I might be graduated a year ahead." He had been, in his own words, "a grind."

When Sloan left college ("I was thin as a rail, young and unimpressive"), he took a job at the Hyatt Roller Bearing Company, a small New Jersey firm with 25 employees and $2,000 in monthly sales. The company was going through difficult times, and Sloan's father helped to finance its survival and then its expansion. As the firm began to market products to more and more manufacturers, Sloan Jr. came to know the car industry well. He sold roller bearings to Ransom Olds, Henry Ford (his best customer), and the colorful William C. Durant.

"Blue-eyed Billy" Durant, a business visionary, had put together the General Motors Corporation in 1908, the same year in which Ford introduced the Model T. Durant was a wheeler-dealer who enjoyed buying and selling whole companies. Under his leadership, General Motors continued to grow, but it remained a loose group of functionally separate firms, several of which competed with each other. Buick, the best of the lot, made money that Durant then dissipated among the less successful companies. This policy angered Buick's superb leaders, Charles Nash and Walter Chrysler, both of whom walked out and later set up their own firms. As Alfred Sloan put it, "Mr. Durant was a great man with a great weakness—he could create but he could not administer."

Despite this shortcoming, Durant had perceived the vital point that the industry's future lay in combining within one big firm all the diverse elements involved in the production of cars: parts and engine manufacturers, body companies, chassis works, and assemblers. Only through this kind of "vertical integration," as it came to be called, could a reliable flow of mass-produced output be achieved. The industry could then exploit its potential economies of scale—that is, a declining cost of products as output increased. Henry Ford, who became almost obsessive in his own commitment to vertical integration, expanded from within. Durant did it by buying other companies and adding them to General Motors.

This policy of acquiring related firms took him to the door of Alfred P. Sloan, Jr. Durant wanted to include Hyatt Roller Bearing in a group of accessory companies he was putting together under the name United Motors. By this time (1916) Hyatt had grown into a prosperous enterprise with 4,000 employees. Sloan and his family now owned most of the company, and they agreed to sell it to Durant for $13.5 million, half to be paid in United Motors stock. Durant decided that the president of United Motors should be Sloan himself.

Two years later, in 1918, Durant merged United Motors with General Motors and made Sloan a vice-president and member of the GM Executive Committee. Then, in 1920, a stockholders' uprising forced Durant out. Pierre du Pont, a major investor in the company and one of the shrewdest business executives in the country, took the GM presidency himself and made Sloan his chief assistant. Now 45 years old, Sloan was operating at the peak of his abilities, but he still faced daunting problems. Internally, General Motors remained an organizational mess, and Durant's maneuvers had put the firm in bad financial shape. Worst of all, as Sloan later wrote, the economic depression of 1920–21 was threatening to kill it: "The automobile market had nearly vanished and with it our income."

With some difficulty, GM weathered the short depression, and in 1923 Sloan became president of the company. He turned out to be a different kind of businessman from either Billy Durant or Henry Ford. Whereas Durant and Ford wooed the press and welcomed media coverage, Sloan shunned personal publicity. Nor did he have much of a private life. He seemed uninterested in any subject except the welfare of General Motors. And in one of the most brilliant performances in the history of business, he proceeded to turn GM around and build it into the world's largest company.

As a writer in *Fortune* described Sloan, "[He] displays an almost inhuman detachment from personalities, [but] a human and infectious enthusiasm for the facts. Never, in committee or out, does he give an order in the ordinary sense, saying, 'I want you to do this.' Rather he reviews the data and then sells an idea, pointing out, 'Here is what could be done.' Brought to consider the facts in open discussion, all men, he feels, are on an equal footing. Management is no longer a matter of taking orders, but of taking counsel." An associate of Sloan's once said that he had a lot in common with the products he had made at Hyatt Roller Bearing: "self-lubricating, smooth, eliminates friction and carries the load."

General Motors versus the Ford Motor Company

During the depression of 1920–21, Henry Ford had started building an enormous new manufacturing complex at the River Rouge near Detroit. At the same time, he was taking over ownership of his company after purchasing all outstanding shares of its stock. These steps strained even Ford's bank account, and he decided to squeeze additional funds from local dealers throughout the country. At the nadir of demand for cars, he directed his 6,400 dealers to take 90,000 new cars and pay him cash for them. The price of refusal was loss of the Ford franchise. Alfred Sloan, by contrast, sympathized with GM's retailers. Through a subsidiary called General Motors Acceptance Corporation, he made it easier for dealers to finance bulk purchases, and much easier for customers to buy cars at retail. Ford was reluctant to sanction installment buying.

As Sloan recalled in his autobiography, the car business was changing fast during the early twenties. Management tools remained primitive, even at General Motors:

There was no awareness of the importance of the used-car market. There were no statistics on the different cars' market penetration; no one kept track of registrations. Production schedules, therefore, were set with no real relationship to final demand. Our products had no planned relation to one another or to the market. The concept of a line of products to meet the full challenge of the market place had not been thought of. The annual model change as we know it today was still far in the future. The quality of the products was sometimes good, sometimes bad.

Long in advance of Henry Ford, Sloan saw that the industry was becoming a trade-in business. (Eventually three units out of every four sold were used cars.) Sloan sensed that a big shift in taste was occurring, and that consumers now saw car purchases as signals of their own progress up the income scale. He responded by developing a complete product line. Starting with Chevrolet, which was designed to compete with Ford's Model T, Sloan established a series of nameplates that included—at progressively higher prices to imply higher social status—the Pontiac, Oldsmobile, Buick, and, at the top, the Cadillac. GM came to call its product policy "a car for every purse and purpose." By the middle twenties, GM's cars were equal and often superior to Ford's, not only in styling but in basic engineering and production qualities as well.

Henry Ford's product policy remained much simpler: keep building a better version of one car in one color (black), and keep cutting the cost. Very successful in earlier years, the policy led to disaster during the 1920s and 1930s. Whereas in 1921 Ford's share of the domestic car market had stood at 56 percent, by 1925 it had dropped to 40 percent. During this same period, General Motors' share jumped from 13 to 20 percent.

By 1929 the two firms stood neck and neck, each selling at the colossal rate of almost a million and a half cars per year. Then Ford took another big fall, and by 1937 GM's market share had shot up to 42 percent while Ford's plummeted to only 21 percent. The Chrysler Corporation was now in second place at 25 percent. Just a short time earlier, Ford's company had been undisputed king of the industry and Chrysler had not even existed.

The key years in this fateful shift were the middle and late 1920s, when a series of events caused Henry Ford at last to abandon the Model T. One of these was the "closed-car" movement. Most Model T's, with their very light chassis, could accommodate only a cloth roof, if they had any roof at all. Model T's often remained open to the elements, and people were becoming tired of getting dusty and wet as they drove. Whereas in 1919 only 10 percent of new cars had been "closed" (built with metal roofs) by 1927 the figure was 85 percent. Another change was the proliferation of new models in assorted colors, a policy adopted not only by General Motors but also by Chrysler. The effect of this explosion of models and colors was multiplied still further by the advent of annual model changes. Together, all of these developments amounted to a revolution in styling and marketing—and Alfred Sloan led it.

Henry Ford responded to the welter of changes by closing his plants and designing a new car, the Model A. This was a radical step for so large a company, because it stopped all income without stopping all expenditures. As Sloan later wrote, few people in the industry had anticipated "so catastrophic and almost whimsical a fall as Mr. Ford chose to take in May 1927 when he shut down his great River Rouge plant completely and kept it shut down for nearly a year to retool, leaving the field to Chevrolet unopposed and opening it up for Mr. Chrysler's Plymouth." Ford's Model A, once it appeared, was a much better car than the T, but it was still just one car, not a full line of products. Nor did the A go through annual model changes. Not until 1933 did Henry Ford bring out new models each year, and not until 1938 did he begin to offer the Mercury, a mid-sized car designed to compete with GM's Pontiacs, Oldsmobiles, and Buicks. The Mercury had only indifferent success. So did Ford's Lincoln, which had competed ineffectively with Cadillac since its introduction in 1929.

As these changes were unfolding, the Ford Motor Company's once stellar management team slowly disintegrated. Its best young executives, fed up with Henry Ford's autocratic methods, simply quit. Many of these people were hired by Sloan at General Motors. Henry Ford turned 70 in 1933, but long before that he had become a rigid, peevish, and arbitrary chief executive. Had his company's cars not been of high quality and his brand name so famous, his company might have gone under during the Great Depression of the 1930s.

During the 1930s and 1940s, Sloan deliberately held GM's domestic market share under 45 percent, perhaps because he did not want to attract hostile attention from antitrust authorities. This policy of Sloan's contributed to the survival of the Ford Motor Company during its worst years. Then, during the Second World War, Ford did a lot of defense business. The company was finally rescued in the late 1940s by young Henry Ford II, grandson of the founder. Henry II hired executives from General Motors, copied GM's organizational structure, and installed statistical controls designed by a group of "Whiz Kids" who had worked for the Army Air Corps during the war. The Whiz Kids included Robert S. McNamara, who later became president of Ford and secretary of defense under Presidents Kennedy and Johnson, and Arjay Miller, who headed Ford before becoming dean of the Stanford Business School.

Meanwhile, there was no question about who had won the contest for market leadership. Beginning in 1925 and continuing for 61 consecutive years, General Motors' profit performance exceeded Ford's. This was an extraordinary record of competitive supremacy, unmatched in American business history for big-ticket consumer products and perhaps any other kind of product.

Lessons of the Car Wars

What can be learned from this battle? For one thing, that "first-mover advantages" of the kind enjoyed by Henry Ford are powerful but do not constitute a formula for permanent leadership. Almost nothing is permanent in business, and the market punishes those who don't adapt. General Motors itself absorbed tremendous wounds during the closing decades of the twentieth century, when it became almost as rigid and ingrown as the Ford Motor Company had been 50 years earlier.

During the 1920s, Henry Ford had grasped part of the lesson of relentless change in business, but not all of it. Certainly he understood the principle of creative destruction on the manufacturing side. "Not a single item of equipment can be regarded as permanent," he wrote. "Not even the site can be taken as fixed. We abandoned our Highland Park plant—which was in its day the largest automobile plant in the world—and moved to the River Rouge plant because in the new plant there could be less handling of materials and consequently a saving. We frequently scrap whole divisions of our business—and as a routine affair."

But as clearly as Ford understood the imperatives of production, he turned a blind eye to those of marketing. He refused to see that marketing, in all its phases, from product policy to styling to advertising, is as important to business success as manufacturing. He had little respect for the tastes of consumers, whom he correctly regarded as fickle. Irrespective of what they seemed to believe they wanted, Ford thought he knew what they needed. He could not bring himself to admit that in a market economy the consumer really does reign supreme, and that for an organization to act otherwise is to invite disaster.

What are the lessons of the car wars with regard to decision making? As emphasized earlier, the key problem within any organization of whatever size—a family, church, school, business, army, or country—is how to allocate authority. Should a particular decision be made at the top, in the middle, or at the bottom?

If all decisions are made at the top, then sooner or later two things will happen. First, the quality of decision making will deteriorate, because no single person, not even a Henry Ford, can know enough to make the right choice on every issue. There is too much to know, and conditions change. Second, employees not directly in touch with the top will become bored with routine, their potential contributions lost to the organization.

If, on the other hand, all decisions are pushed to the lowest level, then authority will degenerate. Cooperation will become impossible. Anarchy will prevail.

So the pivotal challenge of modern management is in finding the right *balance* between centralization and decentralization, and in continually adjusting the mix as circumstances change. The critical levers are the use of information and the fixing of decision rights at the point where the best information is available on the issue being decided. For this reason the design of the organization becomes crucial.

Henry Ford, who resisted even thinking about such matters, debunked the whole idea of organizational design. Sometimes his scorn became gleeful:

There is no bent of mind more dangerous than that which is sometimes described as the "genius for organization." This usually results in the birth of a great big chart showing, after the fashion of a family tree, how authority ramifies. The tree is heavy with nice round berries, each of which bears the name of a man or of an office. Every man has a title and certain duties which are strictly limited by the circumference of his berry. . . . And so the Ford factories and enterprises have no organization, no specific duties attaching to any position, no line of succession or of authority, very few titles, and no conferences.

This kind of policy is not necessarily inappropriate. In Ford's time it could bring good results in small organizations, and it still can today, especially in entrepreneurial startups. But once a company grows beyond a couple of hundred employees, organizational design cannot be ignored. And successful firms in automobiles and a few other capital-intensive, mass-production industries almost invariably become large. General Motors eventually employed more than three-quarters of a million workers.

The tradition in business before the 1920s, at Ford and most other companies, was to organize divisions not according to *prod-*

uct (the Model T, the Ford truck, the engine, the sparkplug) but according to *function* (purchasing, manufacturing, selling). The responsibility of executives in charge of these functions stretched across all of the company's products.

When things went bad under such a system, it was hard to pinpoint the sources of problems. And if an entire industry suffered a downturn like the automobile crisis during the depression of 1920–21, nobody knew how to respond. It was this situation, in part, that gave Alfred Sloan his idea about reorganizing General Motors. As he later wrote, the depression brought "just about as much crisis inside [the firm] and outside, as you would wish for, if you like that sort of thing."

In response to the crisis, Sloan developed a new organizational design that became known as the "multi-divisional structure." Whereas the Ford Motor Company had one boss (Henry Ford) and a mostly undifferentiated mass of underlings, Sloan devised for GM a system with dozens of product divisions within the company, each organized under a semi-autonomous chief executive. This person had what came to be called "bottom-line responsibility" for the operations of the division, and therefore had to be concerned with both manufacturing and marketing a particular product. With this heavy responsibility came broad authority, which was decentralized throughout the company, division by division.

In creating GM's multi-divisional structure, Sloan worked out a way to deal with human relationships that was just as ingenious for business organization as Ford's assembly line had been for production. What Ford did for physical machines, Sloan did for human beings. Just as Ford's greatest innovation was the systematic assembly of separate mechanical parts into one Model T, Sloan's was the fusion of separate human talents into one organizational whole.

Viewed in retrospect, the idea of having semi-autonomous product divisions within one big company sounds simple. (So does the assembly line.) But in the 1920s it was an intellectual breakthrough of the first order. Sloan himself, as bright as he was, had to struggle to reach the right solution. In a long internal GM document dated 1921 and labeled "Organization Study," Sloan and his associates wrote the following:

1. The responsibility attached to the chief executive of each [divisional] operation shall in no way be limited.
2. Certain central organization functions are absolutely essential to the logical development and proper control of the Corporation's activities.

Years later, as he was working on his autobiography, Sloan looked back on these two sentences and realized that "the language is contradictory." A typical business executive "usually asserts one aspect or another of [organization] at different times, such as the absolute independence of the part, and again the need of co-ordination, and again the concept of the whole with a guiding center." The puzzle of centralization versus decentralization "is the crux of the matter"; and "interaction," therefore, "is the thing." Centralization had to be mixed with decentralization according to the issue being decided.

The multi-divisional structure made such a mixture possible. Among its other virtues, the new structure in effect turned one large company into groups of smaller-scale entities. In so doing, it provided incentives for numerous managers to work together in a spirit of cooperation as they moved up the corporate ladder. Wherever possible, Sloan exerted his own influence by persuasion rather than by fiat. He put in place a series of cross-divisional committees and saw to it that high-ranking executives served on multiple committees of different makeups. In this way he indirectly forced all managers of importance within the company to communicate regularly with each other.

He did this with resolute attention to the key puzzle he was trying to solve: "How could we exercise permanent control over the whole corporation in a way consistent with the decentralized scheme of organization? We never ceased to attack this paradox." Good management, Sloan concluded, must reconcile two opposing forces. It must combine "decentralization with coordinated control."

The coordinated control came primarily through financial reporting and capital allocations. Sloan worked hard on these issues, and GM soon became one of the most sophisticated of all American companies in its use of financial ratios and budget targets. Within its factories, GM made continual adjustments along the production lines, based on what the numbers were telling top managers at headquarters. As Sloan summed up his approach, "From decentralization we get initiative, responsibility, development of personnel, decisions close to the facts, flexibility. . . . From coordination we get efficiencies and economies. It must be apparent that co-ordinated decentralization is not an easy concept to apply." Over the next several decades, and particularly after World War II, GM's multi-divisional structure (also pioneered by Du Pont) was emulated by hundreds of other companies throughout the world.

Sloan's autobiography, the source of many of the quotations above, is one of the two or three most important books on business management ever written. But it does not represent the last word on the subject, because conditions change and there is no last word. As Sloan himself knew, the essence of management is persistent attention not only to what goes on inside an organization but also to altered circumstances in the external environment: changes in consumer preference, the rise of new technologies, swings in the business cycle, shifts in government policy, and new patterns of international trade. Sloan knew that constant attention to these changes was essential.

The only alternative was chaos—which is what reigned at the Ford Motor Company during the 1920s and 1930s. Information flows at Ford grew confused and irregular. Managers could not seem to identify problems or pinpoint responsibilities. Budgeting procedures fell so far behind that overburdened accountants began using scales to weigh piles of invoices rather than adding up the numbers written on each sheet. The company had become a victim of its own success. It had grown too large to manage in the way Henry Ford insisted on managing it.

Alfred Sloan, by contrast, continually adapted, adjusting his company's structure in response to external and internal pressures. Under his direction, as *Fortune* put it, General Motors "escaped the fate of those many families of vertebrates whose bodies grew constantly larger while their brain cavities grew relatively smaller, until the species became extinct . . . because Mr. Sloan has contrived to provide it with a composite brain commensurate with its size."

In historical retrospect, the contrast between Henry Ford and Alfred Sloan illuminates a characteristic irony in American business and in the national culture as a whole. Many strands of American tradition romanticize the solitary hero and underrate the necessity for cooperation through structured organizations. Individualism is cherished, while "bureaucracy" remains a dirty word. In this sense Henry Ford, with his unschooled solo genius and bombastic opinions about everything, was the more typically "American" personality. That is probably why his name appears before Sloan's on many a list of great business executives. (Ford was also the first billionaire crackpot, another recognizable American type.) But it was Sloan, the quiet, persuasive, decentralizer—the trained engineer and systematic organization man— who better epitomizes many and perhaps most American business triumphs of the twentieth century.

CHAPTER TWO

Overview: The Financial System

The turnaround of General Motors during the 1920s owed much to the company's staff of financial experts. For one thing, they helped Alfred Sloan set up the General Motors Acceptance Corporation, which provided vital credit to GM's dealers and retail customers. More broadly, at corporate headquarters they made astute use of financial ratios such as inventory turnover, net profit on sales, and return on investment.

These kinds of ratios provide quick photographs of a firm's condition, and year-to-year trends in the numbers turn the photographs into movies. Ratios become even more useful when managers compare numbers for their own firms with those recorded by other companies in similar industries.

Unlike Alfred Sloan, Henry Ford disdained the use of mathematical ratios as management tools. In particular, Ford detested all aspects of "financeering," and his misgivings typified the bewilderment and suspicion of numerous other Americans.

The Functions of Finance

All businesses, of whatever size, share some basic financial problems: how to meet the payroll and other current expenses, how to get and maintain credit, and how to raise the occasional large sums necessary to develop new products and build new facilities. These problems are timeless, and companies need a constant diet of financial information in order to manage the problems effectively.

Investors have similar requirements. Owner-investors, individual shareholders, and financial institutions such as banks, insurance companies, and pension funds need reliable information in order to make intelligent decisions about where and how much to invest, and what specific form their investments might take—whether stock ("equity"), long-term bonds, or short-term loans.

A basic function of financial systems in capitalist economies is to channel funds from investors (savers) to companies (users), then to distribute appropriate amounts of the companies' earnings back to the investors. The system transfers capital across time, as in the issuance and repayment of a 10-year corporate bond, and also across space, as funds move from one region or country to another.

Each transfer may require intermediate steps. One vital step is the pooling of large amounts of money from household savers by banks, insurance companies, and mutual funds (which are investment pools containing many different stocks or bonds or both). Companies can then draw on these accumulated pools of money by borrowing, or by selling their own stocks and bonds. After that, as money moves back to investors, the transfer process includes the disaggregation of corporate earnings so that dividends on stocks and interest payments on bonds and loans can be disbursed.

Over the course of the twentieth century, one of the most important trends in American business was an immense increase in the amounts of money handled by the financial system. Both investments and earnings grew by huge multiples, and the system for channeling these funds back and forth became much more efficient. This increased efficiency derived in large part from a steady growth in the amount of information available to managers inside companies as well as to investors outside. On the inside, the development of ratio analysis and other tools by accountants and financial managers brought a new abundance of information on nearly all aspects of the company. On the outside, a second force emerged when regulatory agencies began to insist on standardized accounting procedures and the public disclosure of hitherto privileged information. Still a third force was the rapid progress of information technology itself—from the pen and ledger to the computer and spreadsheet.

By about the 1960s, the vast new storehouse of information created by these interacting forces lay at the fingertips of managers, investors, and a rising cadre of financial analysts who used it to help individuals and institutions make investment decisions. The new wealth of data made it possible to achieve better management by executives inside companies, greater confidence by outside investors, and a higher degree of analytical sophistication at all levels.

Players from both the public and private sectors had developed the new financial tools and pushed for their standardization across the business system. During the first half of the twentieth century, the Securities and Exchange Commission, the Federal Reserve System, and other public agencies had acted in concert with an assortment of private bodies, which included the American Institute of Certified Public Accountants, the Financial Accounting Standards Board, the New York Stock Exchange, and the National Association of Securities Dealers (NASD, which set up the NASDAQ exchange). Over the years, coordinated public and private efforts built a complex infrastructure that helped make American capital markets the world's largest and most advanced.

In snowball fashion, the availability of more information attracted additional investors, and the pools of money available to businesses grew larger year by year. Growth was interrupted by the Great Depression of the 1930s, but it was also very much bolstered by new regulations that came directly out of the government's response to that catastrophe.

Meanwhile, the depth and scope of the capital markets steadily increased. One early milestone was a greater public acceptance of common stock as a suitable investment, which began during the 1920s and took a big leap forward 60 years later, during the 1980s. A second was the need to finance permanently high government expenditures, which began in the 1930s, then surged ahead with the coming of World War II, the Cold War, and the welfare state. A third milestone was the rise of pension funds in the 1950s and their mushroom growth over the next several decades. A fourth was computerized securities trading, which began in the 1970s and reached a peak at the end of the century.

Still a fifth milestone was the emergence of mutual funds in the 1960s and their proliferation during the 1980s and 1990s. Many employers' retirement plans gave each participating worker the opportunity to invest the amount accumulating for retirement benefits in one or more mutual funds chosen by the worker. Whether investing through a retirement plan or by way of direct purchase, even individuals with modest amounts of disposable income could diversify their holdings through the vehicle of mutual funds. In doing so they often faced less risk than they would by purchasing shares of a single company's stock. Those who felt comfortable tolerating *more* risk in the hope of a higher return could select a speculative mutual fund over a conservative one. The wide array of different funds provided investors at all income levels with a myriad of choices.

As the new money pools began to grow very large during the 1980s, they came to represent an important new source of capital that mutual-fund managers might invest in businesses of various kinds. Traditionally, investment banks—firms such as Goldman Sachs, Lehman Brothers, and Morgan Stanley—had restricted their own underwriting of corporate debt instruments to "investment grade" bonds that they issued on behalf of safe, well-established companies. Wealthy individuals as well as insurance companies and other financial institutions were the usual purchasers of these bonds. Because the bonds involved little risk to the buyer, they carried relatively low rates of interest.

But with the growth of mutual funds and similar money pools, the sum of available capital began to exceed the total amount that could be invested under the old pattern of small risk and small return. In this new context, innovative financiers began to look outward and to imagine a different pattern altogether: widespread issuance not only of low-risk investment grade bonds, but also of high-yield and high-risk bonds. Because of the higher risk, the new instruments came to be called "junk" bonds.

Michael Milken of the investment bank Drexel Burnham Lambert pioneered the issuance of junk bonds and their sale to mutual funds and other institutional investors such as insurance companies and savings and loan associations. During the 1980s, Milken arranged high-yield developmental financing for such intrepid entrepreneurs as William McGowan of MCI Communications and Ted Turner of Turner Broadcasting. In each case the deals benefited almost all parties concerned.

The availability of junk bonds also made possible the hostile takeover movement of the 1980s. Through "leveraged buyouts" financed with junk bonds, the control of giant companies such as RJR Nabisco could change hands overnight. (The "leverage" here referred to a new practice of using the acquired firm's own assets as partial collateral for the junk bonds that were sold to raise the sum needed to buy a controlling interest in it.) The whole process proved to be lavishly profitable for the "corporate raiders" who, with the assistance of Milken and other new-model investment bankers, carried out these kinds of takeovers.

As is often the case with novel methods of finance, the pioneers found themselves operating in gray areas of the law, and sometimes they crossed the line into clear illegality. Several financiers, including Milken himself, were prosecuted under the securities laws and sentenced to jail. Milken's firm, Drexel Burnham Lambert, was forced into bankruptcy and went out of business. But in the meantime, the advent of new capital pools and high-yield bonds had made major funding available to a far broader spectrum of American business.

Some writers on American finance have suggested that these developments effected a "democratization" of opportunities and rewards once reserved for the privileged few. Others assert that "democratization" cannot be the appropriate word. Their argument is that a disproportionate share of the vast profits from financial manipulations went to a select handful of financiers, thereby accelerating a national trend toward greater inequality of wealth and income.

However one interprets the meaning of these developments from the 1960s through the 1990s, three salient facts stand out: first, by the end of the century tens of millions of people were taking part in the financial system as investors, far more than at any time before; second, the pools of available funds were now much deeper and more diverse; and third, a few thousand speculators and investment bankers had become very, very rich.

Wall Street and the Stock Market

Investments in stocks and bonds could bring big returns, but playing the market could also be like casino gambling. This dual character of the market was recognized quite early. The opportunities for corruption by insiders were substantial, which is one reason why Henry Ford and many others grew so distrustful of Wall Street. Then, too, very little of the daily buying and selling of stocks actually provided funds to the companies whose shares were being traded. Instead most of that activity comprised a "secondary market" that merely shifted ownership of the shares from one person or institution to another.

The issuance of stock did provide some direct financing for companies, particularly in the case of "initial public offerings," or the first sale of stock by a company to the public. But stocks were seldom the main source of capital for most companies. Instead, firms financed their operations through two other routes: retained earnings, which were far and away the most important source of funds for large companies; and borrowing via bank loans, corporate bonds, and other financial instruments.

For the century as a whole, equity investors' real returns from stock dividends plus appreciation ("real" because adjusted for inflation) averaged roughly 7 percent per year. (For the late 1980s and all of the 1990s they averaged a lot more than that.) As against this 7 percent, annual returns from government and high-grade commercial bonds, which have always been regarded as safer investments, averaged only 2 percent. So over the long term, the market nicely rewarded many investors in stocks.

The market also provided continuous quotations of share prices, which by the end of the century appeared in newspapers and online reports for nearly 10,000 companies in the United States. These continually updated share prices were, and still are, important for at least three different reasons.

First, they supply instantaneous reports on a company's prospects. Because the selling price of a stock depends on buyers' estimates of the future income and value of a firm, a stock price is analogous to the collective evaluations of a patient's health by a group of physicians. The price for which a stock is selling registers the market's beliefs about the present and future performance of the company. Sometimes these beliefs are borne out by events and sometimes not, as is the case with diagnoses by doctors.

Second, share prices as aggregated in such indexes as the Dow-Jones Industrials, the Standard & Poor's 500, and the NASDAQ composite, offer a window on the state of the national economy. The Dow-Jones, which was established in 1884 to track the securities of railroads and in 1897 for industrial firms, comprises 30 stocks considered among the most solid of the 3,000 or so listed on the New York Stock Exchange.

Although share prices and market indexes are good yardsticks, their movement often exaggerates underlying business trends. In September of 1929, for instance, the Dow-Jones Industrial Average climbed to 381, but by July 1932 it had dropped by almost 90 percent to 41. It then crept upward over the next four decades, dipping during occasional recessions. In 1980 the Dow stood at just under 1,000, rising to 2,500 in late 1987. After a severe but brief dip, it then began a rapid ascent to heights that by prior standards seemed phenomenal, surpassing 11,000 in 1999.

For many individual companies, the ups and down were even more dramatic. During the 1920s the share prices for RCA and other electronics firms gyrated wildly, and toward the close of the century the same thing happened for startup Internet firms.

Despite these extreme examples, share prices do remain one of many useful signals about the condition of the national economy. Others include well-known macroeconomic indicators such as the rates of interest, inflation, and unemployment, plus the deficit or surplus in the federal budget and levels of consumer confidence indicated by polls.

A third reason for the importance of share prices is that as securities markets grew more "democratized" they became major repositories of the national wealth. At the start of the twentieth century, only about half a million Americans owned stocks. By 1929, after the greatest bull market in history up to that time, this figure had increased twentyfold, to about 10 million. By the end of the century, after the even bigger bull market of the 1990s, stocks were owned by more than 100 million Americans, most of them having indirect ownership through investments in mutual funds and retirement funds. By that time about 9,000 mutual funds were doing business in the United States, some 6,000 having been started during the 1990s alone.

The passage in 1974 of the landmark Employee Retirement Income Security Act (ERISA) had powerful effects on securities markets. ERISA compelled all companies that chose to have retirement plans to put aside, in a trust fund separate from the assets of the company, money to meet pension payments to current and future retirees. This new legislation promoted the growth, over time, of huge capital pools that by law had to be invested productively. The stock market turned out to be the preferred destination for most of these funds because it usually brought the highest returns.

The largest of all pension funds, the California Public Employees Retirement System (CALPERS), made immense investments in equities. Eventually it began to wield power as a stockholder to influence the policies of corporations in which it held major blocks of shares. Beginning in the 1980s, the increasing strength of CALPERS and other institutional investors such as mutual funds signified a relative shift in decision rights from managers to shareholders, forcing tougher financial discipline in numerous American companies.

Meanwhile, the volume of trades on the New York Stock Exchange, which had averaged fewer than 3 million shares per day before the 1960s, shot up to almost 160 million shares per day by 1990. Because of the new role of institutional investors, the average number of shares per trade rose from 224 in 1965 to over 20,000 in 1990. Many transactions were "block trades" made on the basis of computerized investment programs in a nearly continuous response to evolving market data.

Then, during the 1990s, the total number of shares bought and sold annually more than *quadrupled*. Enormous sums were shifted out of low-risk savings accounts, certificates of deposit, and bonds, and into the shares of publicly held companies. By the year 2000, about 25 percent of all U.S. household wealth was invested in stocks, as compared with only 10 percent during the 1980s.

In the closing decades of the century, venture capitalists began to take a conspicuous role in American finance. These sophisticated investors put up cash in return for a portion of the stock (or stock options) of numerous firms in biotechnology, computer software, and other high-tech industries. Many of these companies were startups. Most were young firms in need of capital for product development. If a firm became successful enough, its initial public offering (IPO) could realize millions of dollars for both the venture capitalists and the entrepreneurs who had founded the company. Through this route many entrepreneurs still in their twenties or early thirties made substantial fortunes.

Abundant venture capital became a key ingredient for the surge in high-tech industries that fueled American economic growth during the 1990s. Much more money was available for startups in the United States than elsewhere, for a variety of reasons: a favorable tax climate, lenient corporate and personal bankruptcy laws, and a decidedly entrepreneurial national culture. By the mid-1990s about as much venture capital was being invested in Massachusetts as in Great Britain; more was available in California than in continental Europe. Of all American venture-capital investments in the late 1990s, about 37 percent went toward startup companies, compared to only 12 percent in Europe.

The pattern of investments in high-tech stocks brought significant changes to the nature of the stock market. During most of the twentieth century, a company that ranked high in sales and employment was likely to have a correspondingly high "market capitalization" (total value of its stock). These relationships seemed to connect Wall Street and its paper assets with the "real" economy of fixed assets, and with the manufacture of steel, automobiles, and other tangible goods. Such products were emblematic of the Second Industrial Revolution, which was based on machine massproduction and cheap transportation.

During the information-based Third Industrial Revolution, the market capitalizations of some high-tech companies came to have much less correlation with either their sales, fixed assets, or number of employees. For example, at the end of the twentieth century America's two largest firms, General Motors and Ford, had combined annual sales of $306 billion, employment of 940,000 people, and market capitalization of $134 billion. By contrast, the two leading software firms, Microsoft and Oracle, had combined sales of $22 billion and employed 63,000 people—about one-fourteenth the sales and employment of the two auto giants.

But Microsoft and Oracle had a combined market capitalization of $462 billion, nearly 3.5 times that of the car companies. The figure for Microsoft alone was $418 billion, reflecting that company's tight hold on the standards for computer operating systems and its advantageous position relative to opportunities raised by the Internet. What these new financial relationships implied for the future was not very clear. But they signalled a break with the past and caused puzzlement for securities analysts and the buying public. Several government officials, including Chairman Alan Greenspan of the Federal Reserve System, warned that share prices for stocks of high-tech companies had become dangerously overvalued.

Although the clear trend from 1920 to 2000 was one of growth and optimism in the economy, the most important single episode in the history of Wall Street remains the stock market crash of 1929. This traumatic event heralded—though it did not cause, as is commonly believed—the worst economic crisis in the nation's history. We next look at how companies fared during the Great Depression of 1929–1941.

CHAPTER THREE

The 1930s: Depression, Consumers, and the Case of Procter & Gamble

Because the Great Depression was so severe, most history books treat the 1930s as a catastrophic decade for the American business system. That judgment is largely accurate, but not entirely.

Unemployment, which had stood at about 3 percent in 1929, soared to 25 percent in 1932, the highest figure up to that time and still a record. Whole sectors of the economy went into precipitous decline: mining, agriculture, construction, finance. Vital industries shriveled: banking, lumber, cement, steel. Millions of families became poor, and a small number of people actually starved to death.

The crisis hit every part of the nation's economy, but it hit the financial sector especially hard. When the depression began in 1929, more than 25,000 banks were in operation. Within a few years, this number had dropped by 40 percent, to 15,000. Because there was no mandatory deposit insurance, these bank failures took away the life savings of millions of people. They suffered not just a material setback but a psychological trauma as well.

During the first four years of the depression, real Gross National Product dropped by 31 percent. Investment fell by an almost unbelievable 87 percent, as people ceased building new houses and businesses stopped buying new equipment. The stock-market crash, bank failures, crises in major industries, and widespread unemployment brought a series of strong actions by the federal government under President Franklin D. Roosevelt. (Those actions are a story for a later chapter, "The New Deal and World War II.") Workers gained significant new influence during the 1930s, because of changes in federal law and the increasing power of labor unions. Whereas only 7 percent of the nation's workforce had been unionized in 1930, that number more than doubled by 1940, and tripled by 1945. (The rate of unionization continued to climb after World War II, and in 1960 reached almost 24 percent. After the 1960s union membership began a gradual decline because of the replacement of many union jobs by automation, the rise of industrial competition from abroad, a growing anti-union sentiment at home, and the general shift of the workforce from manufacturing to less easily unionized jobs in the service sector.)

The 1930s, then, were a time of landmark growth for unions. They showed unprecedented strength in negotiations with big firms in the automobile, steel, and coal industries. The fruits of organized labor's great victories of that period, symbolized by successful strikes for higher wages and the right to organize, live on today in federal law and in the folklore of the labor movement.

Although hundreds of thousands of small companies went bankrupt during the thirties, even more new firms emerged during the decade to take their places. Most of these new companies were located in labor-intensive sectors such as food service and small retailing. In 1929, for example, there were about 1.5 million stores in the United States, and by 1939 almost 1.8 million. Many were tiny establishments of the Mom and Pop variety, a high proportion of which quickly perished. But the continual appearance of new establishments of all kinds was testament to the resiliency of the business system even during the nation's worst depression.

The Types of Firms That Prospered

Some enterprises founded during the thirties were well-planned entrepreneurial companies in relatively new industries. A number of these startups became very prosperous, eventually joining

Fortune's list of the 500 largest American companies. Among them were Hewlett-Packard, Polaroid, Texas Instruments, Owens-Corning Fiberglas, Continental Airlines, US Airways, Roadway (freight), and Ryder Truck.

Several existing firms that were still small at the beginning of the decade had expanded significantly by its end. IBM, for example, mushroomed because of the demands for data processing that grew out of new government programs. After the passage of the Social Security Act in 1935, the federal government had to maintain a file on almost every employee in the country. This need generated a big market for the electro-mechanical punch-card systems manufactured by IBM. Thomas J. Watson, Sr., IBM's paternalistic chief and one of the greatest businessmen of the twentieth century, had refused to lay off numerous workers despite the economic downturn of the early 1930s. In the midst of the lean years, Watson had continued to manufacture punch-card equipment in spite of diminishing demand. Consequently, he was ready with a stockpile of machines when government orders began to pour in. By the end of the 1930s, IBM was poised for a spurt of even faster growth in connection with the demands of World War II.

Some important new chain retailers and food processors were established during the thirties: Publix Super Markets, Giant Food, Bruno's Food Stores, Albertson's Supermarkets, Smith's Food and Drug Centers, Long's Drug Stores, Payless Cashways, Dillard's Department Stores, Tyson Foods, and Sara Lee. These companies, too, made it into the *Fortune* 500.

The preceding decade, the 1920s, had been a bonanza for chain retailers. In that boom period, the number of chain grocery stores in the United States grew from fewer than 8,000 to more than 30,000. A&P, the largest chain, went from about 4,500 stores to about 16,000. Several other grocery chains added outlets at an even faster rate, Kroger increasing from 800 stores to 5,000, Safeway from under 200 to over 2,600. Also in the twenties, the number of J.C. Penney's department stores rose from about 300 to 1,500, and the number of Walgreen's drugstores from 23 to 440.

Chains continued to increase in importance during the 1930s. Because of the proliferation of small retailers, the number of chain stores as a percentage of all stores declined, but their share of total retail *sales* grew by 8 percent. By the end of the decade, almost one consumer dollar of every four spent on any retail purchase went to a chain store. So the trend toward chains as preferred places to shop continued without interruption from the prosperous 1920s through the otherwise depressed 1930s.

The consumer-goods sector of the economy fared much better during the depression than did heavy industry and investment goods, and there was a simple reason why: *different kinds of decisions are involved for consumption as compared to investment.* Decisions to invest are made primarily by business executives. When forecasts for future demand are low, executives usually decide to put less money into production and to let inventories dwindle. Consumption decisions, on the other hand, are made by almost everybody. People must eat every day, and they have many other needs that can't easily be postponed. So, whereas investment dropped by 87 percent during the first four years of the depression, consumption declined by only 19 percent. Many people went from year to year without buying new houses, new cars, or even new clothes. But they did not stop eating or doing the laundry or washing dishes.

Nor did they cease to seek entertainment. Throughout the depression Americans flocked to movie theaters, where tickets cost an average of 20 cents apiece. (During the 1930s a typical working person in the United States earned less than $1,000 per year.) Each week about 80 million movie tickets were sold, resulting in a per-capita rate about seven times as high as the rate at the end of the century. After an early dip during the worst years of the depression, the film industry maintained a healthy level of profits throughout most of the 1930s, in part because it was vertically integrated.

A few holding companies such as Metro-Goldwyn-Mayer owned or controlled studios, distributors, and theater chains, coordinating them in a way that shut out many independent artists and theater owners—practices later judged illegal under U.S. antitrust law. But during the heyday of the motion picture industry, these big companies maintained strict controls over production budgets and kept actors, directors, and writers under tight contracts. During the 1930s the Hollywood studios churned out 5,000 feature films, an enormous multiple of the rate of releases in the early twenty-first century. Most 1930s films were made on a shoestring budget, but many were superbly entertaining nonetheless. In the view of numerous critics, several 1930s films, such as *The Wizard of Oz* and *Gone With the Wind* (both expensive productions at the time but cheap by today's standards) have never been surpassed as representatives of the art form.

Even though consumers had much less disposable income during the thirties than they had enjoyed in the twenties, most could still afford to go to the movies—and buy many items that by now were regarded as necessities. About 10 million families even managed to purchase new refrigerators. These Frigidaires, Norges, Kelvinators, and Kenmores were expensive, but they made daily food shopping unnecessary and therefore saved people lots of time. Indoor flush toilets, manufactured by companies such as Crane, Kohler, and Standard, could be found in 60 percent of American homes by 1940, as compared with 51 percent in 1930 and 20 percent in 1920. And as volumes of sales increased, the price of refrigerators and other household conveniences declined.

Procter & Gamble

The experience of the country's leading consumer-products company illustrates the characteristic of the Great Depression in which consumption declined by much less than investment. It also demonstrates that a well-run firm can prosper even in the worst of times. "P&G," as Procter & Gamble came to be called, had been founded in 1837 in Cincinnati by two immigrants: William Procter, a candlemaker from England, and James Gamble, a soap-boiler from Ireland. Their new company prospered, and by 1859 it had 80 employees and annual sales of more than $1 million.

One hundred and forty years later, toward the end of the twentieth century, Procter & Gamble had over 100,000 employees and annual sales of about $40 billion. It was the world's largest producer of branded household goods, and one of the biggest advertisers as well. Its brands led the field in 19 of the 39 market categories in which the company participated, and the average market share for all its brands stood at the exceptionally high figure of 25 percent.

The key event in P&G's early history came in 1878, when an employee forgot to turn off his soap-mixing machine when he left for lunch. While he was gone, the mixer beat additional air into the soap. Soon the company began receiving requests for this new "floating soap," and Harley Procter, who had succeeded his father William as head of the firm, realized that a unique marketing opportunity lay at hand. At this time almost all soap was made in bars, and Harley believed that his company could exploit the advantages of a floating bar. People sitting in a bathtub or washing clothes in a basin could easily find their soap atop the water rather than having to fish around for it underneath the surface.

Harley Procter proceeded to change the product's name from P&G White Soap to Ivory, a word he took from Psalm 45 of the Old Testament. He then persuaded the company's board of directors to spend an unprecedented $11,000 in advertising the virtues of Ivory. The first ad, published in 1882 in a weekly religious magazine, was targeted to consumers, not to wholesalers or retailers as was the usual practice. Beginning in the 1890s, Procter promoted Ivory under the slogans "It Floats" and "99 and 44/100 percent pure." (He had commissioned a chemical analysis that disclosed the information, unimportant except for purposes of marketing, that Ivory contained slightly fewer impurities than most other soaps.) In 1896, P&G ran the first color ad that ever appeared in a U.S. magazine. The company hired its first advertising agency in 1900, to promote both Ivory and Lenox, a yellow laundry bar. In ads Ivory was pictured with babies, as a suggestion that it was mild to the skin. Later this skin-friendly claim led the company to market Ivory as a dishwashing soap too.

Meanwhile, during the 1880s, Procter & Gamble built "Ivorydale," a new factory located in a Cincinnati suburb. In 1901, P&G integrated backward into the pressing of cottonseed oil, a principal ingredient in soap. In 1903 and 1904, it built new plants in Kansas City and at "Port Ivory" on Staten Island in New York. P&G now began to export in large volume, and by the 1930s the company was marketing 200 branded items worldwide, including 140 soaps.

Throughout the twentieth century, P&G's chief competitors were Colgate-Palmolive and Lever Brothers, the subsidiary of a British firm. All three companies advertised heavily because they needed mass markets in order to realize the economies of scale in production and distribution that made low prices possible. Soaps were simple to produce, and most were chemically almost identical. But to manufacture bars in big quantities and sell them for a few pennies each was not simple at all. Branding and efficient advertising became essential to success. Once the leading brands were established, the expense of introducing a new one posed a formidable entry barrier for would-be competitors.

Lever Brothers offered tough competition for Ivory, with its Lux Soap and Lux Flakes laundry soap. Colgate weighed in with soaps called Cashmere Bouquet and Palmolive. Procter & Gamble itself, building a portfolio of brands step by step, introduced Ivory Flakes in 1919 to compete with Lux; then, in 1927, P&G purchased from a St. Louis manufacturer both Oxydol laundry soap and Lava, a hand soap containing pumice for better scrubbing action. Both became strong brands, and Oxydol turned into one of the company's biggest moneymakers. Dreft, the first synthetic detergent for all-around household use, was added to the line in 1933. Drene, P&G's first liquid shampoo (1934), proved too potent, stripping so much oil out of consumers' hair that the company had to mix in a conditioning agent.

The Character of the Firm

By the 1930s Procter & Gamble had developed a curious corporate culture, many aspects of which were still in evidence decades later, at the close of the century. P&G in the thirties was a stodgy, tradition-bound, parochial firm—stiff and formal, almost military. Job applicants were given batteries of exams, including psychological tests. Male P&G managers, even at middle and low levels, wore dark suits and white shirts. All promotions were made from within, and people taking entry-level management jobs were assumed to be signing on for an entire career. The company discouraged unionization and segregated its cafeteria by gender. P&G cut its costs in systematic fashion. It would pay for washing salespeople's automobiles only once per month, and every employee with a car, including the traveling salesforce, was instructed to park on the street rather than in fee-charging lots. Elevators at the Cincinnati headquarters could not be used for trips of fewer than two floors. Security was tight. The company fancied itself as having many secrets and zealously guarded plans for advertising campaigns, new product introductions, and statistics on sales and profits.

Throughout the 1930s P&G's founding families continued to hold most of the voting stock. Top management remained so entrenched that the company resembled a medieval fiefdom, and over the 41 years from 1907 to 1948, only two men served as CEO. The first, "Colonel" William Cooper Procter, a descendant of the founder and an officer in the Ohio National Guard, was a shy, humorless, but rock-solid character with a social conscience. Like Alfred Sloan at General Motors, he almost never gave a direct order, preferring to manage by persuasion. His protégé and successor, Richard Redmont "Red" Deupree, was an extroverted, cheery-eyed manager with a keen instinct for marketing.

The company's culture reflected the personalities of both Procter and Deupree. Even though P&G remained a hidebound organization, it was acknowledged to be the nation's most innovative marketer of consumer products and one of the quickest firms in any industry to respond to external changes. P&G was also well known for its corporate conscience. In 1886 it had become one of the first large firms in the United States to grant employees a half-day off every Saturday. Under Colonel Procter's leadership it pioneered in disability and retirement pensions (1915), the eight-hour day (1918), and, most important of all, guaranteed work for at least 48 weeks per year (1920s). This last policy was extremely unusual in American business. In an era without government unemployment benefits, it made P&G an attractive place to work, almost by itself.

Except under conditions of economic depression, secure year-round employment might have been easy for Procter & Gamble to manage, in that the market for soap and other household goods was steady as opposed to seasonal. But other aspects of the business made it quite difficult. In particular, fluctuations in the price of raw materials caused problems because they indirectly broke up the seasonal regularity of wholesale purchases of P&G's products. Before the 1920s, wholesalers, who distributed most of P&G's brands, would stockpile consumer products during periods when raw materials were cheap and P&G's wholesale prices for finished goods were therefore low. Wholesalers would then draw down their inventories when the prices P&G had to pay for cottonseed oil and other raw materials went up. Thus P&G's shift to guaranteed year-round employment required that the company reorganize its distribution system. In 1920, it started bypassing wholesalers and selling directly to retailers. For a variety of reasons this kind of thing happened in many other industries as well, and the declining power of wholesalers became a noticeable trend in American business throughout the twentieth century.

As Procter & Gamble entered the 1930s, its executives, like most other businesspeople, were very concerned about the deteriorating state of the national economy. But P&G withstood the depression well. In the early years President Red Deupree cut his own salary in half and stopped his annual bonus. P&G kept layoffs to a minimum and temporarily reduced wages by 10 percent. It managed to show a profit even during the worst part of the depression, and in 1937 P&G had its best year since its founding, with $200 million in sales and $27 million in profits. Among its many brands, the big moneymakers were Ivory, Oxydol, and Crisco, a synthetic shortening. P&G had introduced Crisco in 1912 after years of research on the hardening of vegetable oil. The company was confident that consumers would prefer Crisco to lard, which sometimes smelled bad and had inconsistent cooking qualities. P&G flooded the print media with ads, and the name "Crisco" soon became a household word.

In soap, P&G during the 1930s achieved more than twice the U.S. market share of either Lever Brothers or Colgate-Palmolive.

The three together controlled about 80 percent of the American market, with P&G alone at just under 50 percent. Each year during the late 1930s, the company produced about 600,000 tons of soap and 195,000 tons of shortening, both of which it sold in bulk to laundries and restaurants as well as in small packages to household consumers. At that time, the company's annual costs were roughly $90 million for raw materials, $23 million for payroll, and a whopping $15 million for advertising.

Building the Market

Procter & Gamble advertised in almost every way imaginable. It spent about half its ad budget on radio dramas, which became known as "soap operas" because of P&G's sponsorship. For other promotions P&G dreamed up endless contests, many calling for the completion of sentences beginning with phrases such as "I like Ivory Soap because . . ." The company spent lavishly on prizes, which included cash, watches, refrigerators, cars, rugs, radios, vacuum cleaners, and stockings. P&G also conducted door-to-door giveaways of coupons for reduced prices on soap. Beyond providing incentives to consumers, each new campaign offered a convenient excuse for P&G's thousands of salespeople to visit retailers, then brief them on the company's latest marketing initiative and urge them to augment stocks in anticipation of bigger demand.

P&G's competitors adopted many of these same tactics. Lever Brothers, a particularly agile company, invented the initials "B.O." (though not, of course, body odor itself) as something to be remedied by its Lifebuoy soap. In situations like this the modern relationship between mass production and mass marketing attained something close to blissful synthesis. As the economist Joseph Schumpeter once wrote, commenting on the nature of mass marketing in general, "It was not enough to produce satisfactory soap. It was also necessary to persuade people to wash."

In 1936, Lever Brothers introduced a vegetable shortening called Spry, a product designed to compete with P&G's Crisco. After a hush-hush buildup, Lever sprang Spry onto America's consciousness with a nationwide giveaway of one-pound cans. Lever advertised Spry as being "extra-creamed," a meaningless term intended to imply that its texture was more uniform than Crisco's. In a counteroffensive, Procter & Gamble declared Crisco to be "double-creamed." Lever responded that Spry was "triple-creamed," triggering P&G's rejoinder that Crisco was "super-creamed." After several months of competing advertising salvos, Spry reached sales about half those of Crisco, an impressive performance by a new product in so short a time.

But the campaign as a whole helped both companies. Crisco's own sales went up, apparently because the advertising war convinced many more consumers of the superiority over lard of any vegetable shortening regardless of brand. This kind of pattern, in which heavy advertising increased the overall size of the market, occurred again and again with consumer products in the United States.

Neil McElroy's Epiphany

After its successes with Ivory and Crisco, P&G developed a new business technique called "brand management." Because it focused attention on a product rather than a business function, brand management turned out to be similar in its effects to the multi-divisional structure introduced by Alfred Sloan at General Motors. And it had the same powerful tendency to decentralize decision making.

The shift to brand management began on May 13, 1931, with an internal memorandum from Neil McElroy (1904–1972), an athletic young man who had come to P&G in 1925 right after his graduation from Harvard College. While working on the advertising campaign for Camay soap, McElroy became frustrated with having to compete not only with soaps from Lever and Palmolive, but also with Ivory, P&G's own flagship product. In a now-famous memo, he argued that more concentrated attention should be paid to Camay, and by extension to other P&G brands as well. In addition to having a person in charge of each brand, there should be a substantial team of people devoted to thinking about every aspect of marketing it. This dedicated group should attend to one brand

and it alone. The new unit should include a brand assistant, several "check-up people," and others with very specific tasks.

The concern of these managers would be the *brand,* which would be marketed as if it were a separate business. In this way the qualities of every brand would be distinguished from those of every other. In ad campaigns, Camay and Ivory would be targeted to different consumer markets, and therefore would become less competitive with each other. Over the years, "product differentiation," as businesspeople came to call it, would develop into a key element of marketing.

McElroy's memo ran to a terse three pages, in violation of President Deupree's model of the "one-page memo," a P&G custom that had become well known in management circles. But the content of the memo made good sense, and its proposals were approved up the corporate hierarchy and endorsed with enthusiasm by Deupree.

Thus was born the modern system of brand management. It was widely emulated, and in one form or another was still followed in the early twenty-first century by many consumer-products companies throughout the world. Typically, brand managers were energetic young executives marked for bright futures within a company. All of Procter & Gamble's own CEOs after Deupree had brand-management experience. This group included Neil McElroy himself, who headed the company after Deupree retired in 1948, and who in 1957 became Secretary of Defense under President Eisenhower.

Brand management as a business technique was one of the signal innovations in American marketing during the twentieth century. It epitomized the persistent theme of balancing centralized oversight with decentralized decision making based on who in the company had the best information about the decision at hand.

Doc Smelser and the Market Research Department

Neil McElroy's formula for P&G's success was: "Find out what the consumers want and give it to them." Procter & Gamble went to extreme lengths to do both. It hired hundreds of women to bake, wash dishes, and do laundry in their own homes, and then report the results. This kind of market research became the hallmark of P&G's approach to the development of new products and the continuous effort to improve existing ones. For many years, the leader of the market-research effort was D. Paul "Doc" Smelser, a small, feisty, serious man who often came to work dressed in sporty suits and ties. (This was not a tradition at P&G, which was known, as mentioned, for its executives' conservative attire.) The cerebral Smelser had earned a Ph.D. in economics from Johns Hopkins (hence the nickname "Doc"). He started at P&G in a new unit that had been organized in 1923 for the purpose of analyzing the markets for cottonseed oil and other commodities. Doc was fond of walking up to senior executives and asking them, out of the blue, questions such as "What percentage of Ivory soap is used for face and hands and what percentage for dishwashing?" Often nobody knew the answer. Thus Smelser was able to conclude that P&G, as a company, remained ignorant of some basic elements of how its products were being used, and therefore how they should be marketed.

Doc Smelser's embarrassing questions raised big issues, and the company responded quickly. In 1925 it created a formal Market Research Department and put Doc himself in charge of it. For the next 34 years, until his retirement in 1959, Doc built this group into perhaps the most sophisticated unit of its kind in the world. He and his staff of researchers (ultimately several hundred strong) asked a variety of audiences a series of detailed questions. In tabulating the answers, they discovered almost everything that could be learned about how the company's products and competing items were being used, how they might be used, and what consumers liked or disliked about them. Doc was especially well informed about the reach of advertising media. He liked to surprise managers of radio stations by giving them precise statistics about the size of their audience, statistics they themselves did not possess.

One of Doc's best-known innovations was Procter & Gamble's corps of door-to-door interviewers. This group consisted mostly of young women who had graduated from college and therefore possessed "the maturity to travel alone," as one of their supervisors put it. A criterion for the successful applicant was that she be attractive but not inordinately so. Doc wanted members of his force to project a wholesome and nonthreatening image, so as to inspire confidence and elicit candid answers.

Doc's interviewers infiltrated neighborhoods all over the country, going from house to house armed with an imposing array of questions: about laundry, cooking, dishwashing, and every other activity for which P&G marketed a product or was thinking of introducing one. Female interviewers were instructed to wear a conservative dress, high heels, gloves, and a hat. As they knocked on doors and talked with consumers, they were to carry no lists, forms, or writing materials. The visits could then seem more casual, even though all conversations were designed to extract copious and specific data. Interviewers were expected to have total recall, and often would hurry back to their cars to record what they had learned. During Doc's 34 years with P&G, a total of 3,000 women and a fair number of men worked as field researchers.

In the 1960s, the company began to phase out this group. Cheap long-distance telephone rates had made it possible to conduct mass surveys more cost efficiently. By the 1970s, Market Research at P&G was doing about a million and a half telephone or mail-in interviews each year. When the company became a heavy television advertiser, it instituted its "DAR" (Day After Recall) method for measuring the impact and memorability of TV commercials. With the help of its many advertising agencies, P&G used focus groups and many other kinds of opinion-sampling techniques to adapt its products to changing needs and tastes and sharpen its commercial messages.

In time, nearly every consumer-products company had to conduct market research in order to prosper. But Procter & Gamble was the leader, and it remained so into the twenty-first century. The biggest changes at P&G after Doc Smelser's time were in the growing number of the company's brands and the broadening of its markets. As the new century began, about half of P&G's revenues derived from international sales, and the brands it offered constituted a long list of names it had made famous (or was keeping famous, since some had been acquired by purchase). These brands included soap and laundry products such as Ivory, Camay, Safeguard, Tide, Cheer, Bold, Bounce, Cascade, Joy, and Dawn; paper goods such as Bounty, Charmin, Pampers, Luvs, and Tampax; personal care products including Pantene, Head & Shoulders, Oil of Olay, Cover Girl, Secret, and Sure; food and beverage brands such as Crisco, Folger's, Jif, and Pringles; and health care items including Crest, Scope, and Pepto-Bismol. The total advertising budget for these products ran to several billion dollars a year, the majority of it spent on daytime TV commercials.

Toward the close of the twentieth century, Procter & Gamble took steps to update its corporate culture, such as adapting brand-management strategies to the forces of globalization and allowing employees to dress more casually. But overall it remained the same kind of tightly knit, secretive, ambitious, marketing-obsessed company it had always been. One of its corporate goals was to double sales every ten years, an extremely ambitious target for a company that was already one of America's twenty largest.

Soap Operas

Meanwhile the soap opera, invented in the 1930s, had quickly entered the nation's consciousness. Like brand management, it was turning out to be a durable institution. P&G's forays into electronic media had started in the 1920s, with radio programs such as *Sisters of the Skillet* and *Crisco Cooking Talks*. The soap opera made its debut in 1933 with a program called *Ma Perkins*. Ma was a compassionate widow whose extensive friendships brought to her sympathetic attention every type of human predicament. The show ran on NBC radio as *Oxydol's Own Ma Perkins* and attracted a wide audience. Afterward came *The Road of Life,* sponsored by Ivory soap; *The Guiding Light* (Duz laundry detergent, another long-time P&G product); *Young Doctor Malone* (ultimately sponsored by Joy dishwashing detergent, a product introduced in 1950); *Backstage Wife* (Cheer, 1950); and *Life Can Be Beautiful* (Tide, introduced in 1946 and in the year 2000 still the best-selling detergent in history).

By the late 1930s, Procter & Gamble was paying for five hours of programming on network radio every weekday. Most of this vast amount of airtime was devoted to P&G's 19 soap operas, each lasting 15 minutes. All offered lessons of domestic wisdom dispensed by appealing characters wending their way through life's perilous trials. The target audience was women between the ages of 18 and 50, the group that purchased most household goods; but a lot of men tuned in as well. In the late 1940s, P&G began to adapt its soap operas to the new medium of television. The first projects did not turn out well. *Ma Perkins* flopped, saddening her many fans. Another offering, *The First Hundred Years,* failed to last even one year. But P&G struck it rich with the 15-minute serial *Search for Tomorrow,* produced by the advertising firm of Leo Burnett. A few years later, P&G became the first soap-opera sponsor to produce half-hour serials (1956, *Another World* and *Edge of Night*), and, after that, the first to expand to a full hour (*Another World,* 1975). At one point during the mid-1950s, P&G had 13 different serials on television.

As networks themselves often do today, P&G began to raid some of its own successful soap operas for characters to populate new programs. (*Somerset* was spun off from *Another World,* as scriptwriters caused half a dozen characters to move to a new city). During the 1970s, several talented producers and writers left the P&G stable to do spicier shows such as *General Hospital* and *The Young and the Restless.* Now exempted from P&G's strict guidelines for wholesomeness, these soaps became heavily laden with sex. They also contained occasional violence, which usually took place off-screen. Eventually the combination of sex and violence became the winning formula for almost all such programs, including P&G's own.

The company's most enduring soap opera was *The Guiding Light,* which started on radio in 1937, moved to television in 1952, and ran continuously into the twenty-first century. This record far surpassed that of any other serial or program in the history of electronic media. *The Guiding Light* featured the estimable Reverend Dr. John Ruthedge, who imparted comforting messages through his eloquent sermons. Dr. Ruthedge kept a lamp in his window (the guiding light itself) to reassure townspeople that he was at home, available to them. Also at home day and night was Procter & Gamble. Its products were always there for the consumer, who was given scant opportunity to overlook them. The soap opera's contribution to American culture was at best debatable, but its effectiveness as a sales vehicle remained beyond question. According to the editors of *Advertising Age,* P&G's marriage with the soap opera comprised "the longest-running and most successful media strategy in U.S. advertising history."

The Phenomenon of Brands

It's hard to imagine what the history of Procter & Gamble or of modern business as a whole might be like in the absence of brands. The practice of branding is centuries old, but in the way the term is understood today it has a short history of just over a hundred years, and is closely tied to the rise of print and electronic media and the development of self-service shopping. The name of the brand can be the same as that of the company—Coca-Cola, for example; or it can be other brands marketed by the same company—Sprite, Fresca, Diet Coke, and so on.

A form of branding began in the late Middle Ages with craftsmen's trademarks on gold jewelry, silverware, and a few other items. The evolution of these marks into brands started in eighteenth-century England with such names as Chippendale (furniture) and Wedgwood (china). But the modern practice of joining brands with heavy advertising did not begin until the nineteenth century, with products such as Singer Sewing Machines and patent medicines such as Dr. Miles' elixir. The biggest breakthrough came with inexpensive foods and household goods that could be branded and packaged for individual consumers: Nabisco's Uneeda Biscuit, Heinz's Ketchup, Gillette's Safety Razor. Eventually there developed in marketing circles a saying that "brands drive out commodities." That is, once a brand gains a strong foothold, an unbranded product cannot compete as long as the branded item is maintained at high quality and reasonable cost.

By the early twentieth century, Ivory soap and its competitors Lifebuoy and Palmolive had driven out thousands of generic soaps produced locally. They had also displaced homemade soap. The branded soaps were so cheap and reliable that the time and drudgery that families saved from not having to make their own soap came as a much-appreciated relief. The same was true of canned foods offered by Heinz, Campbell, Libby, and other companies. Some brands quickly disappeared, despite heavy advertising and high quality. Others hung on precariously, their market shares rising and falling for no apparent reason. A few went straight to the top and stayed there for decades. Brands that ranked first in their product lines in the 1920s and were still number one at the end of the century included Ivory soap, Wrigley's chewing gum, Coca-Cola soft drinks, Kodak cameras and film, Goodyear tires, Gillette razors, Campbell's soup, Nabisco crackers, and Del Monte canned fruit.

To maintain supremacy over such a long period, any branded product must fulfill several conditions. First, the item itself has to remain useful. (Nobody today knows the brand of the best buggy whip.) Second, the quality of the product must remain high, or it will be overtaken by competing items. Third, because consumers promptly reject a brand that fails to deliver expected value, companies hoping to develop and maintain successful brands must pay close attention to changes in the marketplace. It is important to know who is buying the brand and for what reasons. That is why P&G's Market Research Department under Doc Smelser and others played such a vital role. It was essential to the continuing success of Ivory and Crisco and the development of new brands such as Tide, Joy, and Pampers.

From a business viewpoint, the whole idea of brand management implies that the company's fundamental task is usually not to maximize sales in the short run but rather to develop long-term consumer loyalty. That kind of loyalty not only sustains a strong market for the company's existing products but also facilitates the introduction of new ones.

The goal of brand loyalty is not easily accomplished, in part because not all consumers have the same attitude toward brands. Some develop deep psychological attachments, incorporating brands into their self-images. These kinds of consumers sometimes flaunt the brands they purchase like badges, to announce what types of people they are. Consumers in a second category, which probably comprises the majority who buy branded goods, are simply saving time by choosing items about whose quality they can be confident. Whether or not a branded article is of the highest quality isn't the whole issue, since cost is also a factor. The key here is consistency in value received for money spent. A residual number of consumers, making up perhaps a third of all purchasers, don't seem to care much about brands one way or the other. But enough do care to make it worthwhile for companies to be sensitive to even the subtlest trends in market reaction to their brands. This attention, by itself, is evidence of the continuing growth in the power of consumers throughout the twentieth century.

During the 1970s and 1980s, career-obsessed managers in several American companies began to exploit the brands under their control for short-term profit gains. They did this by raising prices too high (General Motors cars), reducing the quality of the product without cutting its price (Halston clothing), and unwisely "extending" or "stretching" the brand itself (Frito-Lay Lemonade, Crystal Pepsi). During the 1990s, some companies began to assign "brand equity managers" to monitor the behavior of brand managers and prevent them from dissipating brand value through short-term profit-maximization.

Not all extensions or stretchings of brands were ill advised, of course. Procter & Gamble itself stretched Ivory "horizontally" across similar products, from bar soap to Ivory Flakes and Ivory Snow, and on to Ivory Shampoo and Ivory Dishwashing Liquid, all with great success. Many firms carried out effective "vertical" brand stretching to different products and services. The Disney company, for example, moved from cartoons to comic books to theme parks to feature films to toys to retail stores.

It is difficult for people working in companies like Procter & Gamble to judge how far a brand can be stretched, either horizontally or vertically. It's also hard to specify in dollar terms what a particular brand is worth. Similarly, it's impossible to tell at what point advertising expenditures exceed the amount necessary to keep a brand healthy—and become money poured down the drain. There is little question that much of the total spent on advertising serves no useful purpose. But exactly how much is unknowable, and for a company not to spend enough can have serious consequences. During the "leveraged buyout" movement of the 1980s, a more precise notion of the value of brands began to emerge. The occasion was the multi-billion-dollar purchases of companies such as RJR Nabisco, much of whose value was embedded not in physical or financial assets but rather in its brands, such as Ritz Crackers, Oreo Cookies, and A-1 Steak Sauce. So the selling price of such a company's common stock could go up rapidly once the company itself was put "in play," the bidding driven in part by the firm's possession of brands. Many companies began to assign explicit values to their brands, listing them as assets on their balance sheets.

Occasionally, brands have been purchased by another maker of the same product. Electrolux, a Swedish company, produced and sold a variety of kitchen appliances under brands once manufactured and marketed by other firms: Westinghouse, Kelvinator, Frigidaire, White, and Gibson. Then, too, brands are often retained even if companies themselves are acquired, in whole or in part, by their competitors. The French tire company Michelin purchased Uniroyal's and BFGoodrich's tire operations, and the Japanese firm Bridgestone acquired Firestone.

Toward the end of the twentieth century, interest in brands on the part of business managers, consumers, and scholars began to reach a historic peak. In one large-scale study, a British consulting firm devised a formula for measuring the world's "top" brand-based companies, based on an amalgam of name recognition and perceived quality. This study resulted in the following top-ten ranking, the highest seven being American companies' brands: Coca-Cola, Kellogg's, McDonald's, Kodak, Marlboro, IBM, American Express, Sony, Mercedes-Benz, and Nescafé. One conclusion of the consulting firm was that companies contemplating global strategies should not assume that their brands have the same value across cultures, or even that particular brands convey the same meaning to consumers everywhere.

Several prominent brands, such as Kleenex, Scotch Tape, and Jell-O, became over the years almost synonymous with their product categories. In a few extreme cases, if a company did not take sufficient care to protect itself, this kind of success could actually destroy legal rights to a brand name. That happened with such former brands as thermos, linoleum, aspirin, yo-yo, and cellophane—all of which are names that now can be used by generic manufacturers.

Like most other elements of business, brand management will continue to be as much art as science, calling for difficult judgments on the part of producers and especially marketers. Consumers can be persuaded to try new products, but in a competitive economy they can't be exploited very successfully for very long.

As consumers' range of choices became greater, their collective power over decisions made within companies grew commensurately. The ultimate source of such innovations as Doc Smelser's market research and Neil McElroy's brand management was precisely this growth in consumer power. It turned out to be one of the most important trends affecting American business throughout the twentieth century and into the twenty-first.

CHAPTER FOUR

Overview:
Women in Business

By the year 2000, about 70 percent of all retail purchases were being made by women, and since 1920 their influence as consumers had grown faster than that of men. So had their power as employees and executives. Yet women did not stand on an equal economic footing with men in either 1920 or 2000. During the intervening 80 years, and especially the final 30, the United States had made significant progress toward that goal. But at the start of the new century much remained to be done.

Capitalism works best under purely meritocratic conditions, and money knows no gender or color. But any economic system reflects the underlying values of the broader society in which it operates. In many respects, both American business and the workforce have always been divided along lines of gender, race, and ethnicity. These divisions affected the ways in which people thought about business and also influenced the strategies followed by different kinds of companies. Business as a whole neither took the lead in promoting diversity nor lagged behind most of the rest of society.

The business experiences of women reveal the special challenges, opportunities, and tensions that arose from society's divisions. During most of the twentieth century, prejudice and bigotry relegated both women and African Americans to the status of economic niche players. The same was true of many others as well, such as people of Asian and Hispanic descent. More often than not, important business decisions were made for and about these groups rather than by them. But the story goes a lot deeper than this, and it is much more complex and nuanced.

Workforce and Gender

Between 1920 and 2000, the percentage of women in the potential out-of-home workforce who had paying jobs approximately tripled. So women entered the labor market and the business world in a major way, but relatively late in the game. During most of the century, their status in business, as distinct from their numbers, inched forward at a glacial pace. It then accelerated sharply from the 1970s onward.

In the early years of the century, women's jobs had been concentrated in a few areas: teaching, nursing, library work, domestic service, and products and services directed toward other women, such as dressmaking, millinery, and hair and beauty salons. But numerous women were already working in corporate offices too. As early as 1920, women comprised half of the nation's clerical workforce, as compared to only 2.5 percent in 1870. This shift derived in part from the invention of the modern-keyboard typewriter (1872) and the telephone (1876); and also from expansions in the office staffs of large firms during the Second Industrial Revolution. By 1920 over 90 percent of stenographers and typists were female, as well as half of all bookkeepers. Many men who had been bookkeepers moved into the better-paying profession of accounting, which they dominated for the rest of the century.

The number of managers, officials, and proprietors who were women rose slowly, from 4.5 percent of the total in 1900 to 11 percent in 1940. Under the emergency of World War II, millions of women temporarily filled "male" positions in workshops and factories, where they earned better pay than ever before, though less than men performing the same work. During the postwar housing boom, women began to establish a strong presence in fields such as residential real estate, and by 1977 they comprised 44 percent of all brokers nationwide. Then, in the closing decades of the century, women achieved rapid gains in prestigious professions long dominated by men. By the year 2000, women made up far higher percentages of all physicians, lawyers, university professors, and certified public accountants than they had at any time in the past.

This quick progress in the professions owed much to changes in federal law, and the same was true for management jobs within companies. Women benefited especially from legislation passed during the 1960s and spearheaded by African Americans. Title VII of the Civil Rights Act of 1964 banned job discrimination based not only on race, color, national origin, and religion, but also on sex. Congressional opponents of this bill had inserted the word "sex" into its provisions, thinking that by doing so they could kill any possibility of passage. But they proved too clever for their own aims. The bill became law, with inclusion not only of "sex" but also of the momentous phrase "affirmative action."

Entrepreneurship

Throughout the nation's history, there had been many more female entrepreneurs than is commonly believed. In particular, women had operated businesses catering to other women, and this tradition carried over into the twentieth century. Some entrepreneurs whose names became especially well known built thriving enterprises in cosmetics and hair care: Elizabeth Arden, Helena Rubenstein, Madame C. J. Walker, Estée Lauder, and Mary Kay Ash. The last three women eventually took their places among some of the greatest of all American entrepreneurs.

Madame Celeste J. Walker (1867–1919) was a daughter of former slaves. During the late nineteenth century and early twentieth, she built up a hair-care and hot-comb business that earned her a personal fortune of several million dollars, part of which she spent on an elegant mansion in Harlem. Bereft of formal education, Walker proved to be an exceptionally shrewd business manager. By the time of her death, some 25,000 agents were marketing her line of products, primarily to African Americans.

Estée Lauder, who was born in 1908 to Hungarian Jewish immigrants living in Queens, New York, got her start by mixing skin creams in her kitchen and selling them to a beauty parlor. When the parlor's owner set up a salon in Manhattan's Upper East Side, Lauder and her husband/business partner found entrance into a more promising market. Besides supplying the new salon, the tireless Lauder gave demonstrations at resort hotels and at private social gatherings in New York City and Palm Beach, Florida. Determined to move her client base upscale, she set out on a strategy of targeting elite department stores such as Saks Fifth Avenue, I. Magnin, and Neiman Marcus. Some of her main competitors— Max Factor, Helena Rubenstein, and Revlon—often sold through drugstores. By the end of the century Lauder's company had annual revenues of almost $4 billion, and a 45 percent share of the cosmetics market in U.S. department stores. Lauder herself had acquired a reputation as one of the most energetic, ruthless, and resourceful business executives of the century.

Mary Kay Ash started her company in 1963 at the age of 45. After investing her life savings of $5,000, she began to teach hundreds of other women how to sell cosmetics door to door. She imbued these agents with a cheerleading spirit and a reluctance to take any customer's "no" for an answer. She gave her agents a 50 percent commission, and her business prospered almost at once. By the end of the century it had annual sales of about $1 billion. At that time several hundred thousand women worked part-time selling Mary Kay cosmetics. Some 8,000 full-time employees were company "directors" and about 100 were National Sales Directors earning six-figure incomes. "We offer them the opportunity to have it all," Ash said of her policy of encouraging women to combine their careers with a full family life. She liked to wear a bumblebee lapel pin, and to say that bumblebees flew quite well even though the laws of physics seemed to suggest that they could never get off the ground.

Only in the closing decades of the century did it become possible for large numbers of women to seek the kind of entrepreneurial independence pioneered by Walker, Lauder, and Ash. As late as 1972, less than 5 percent of all U.S. companies were owned by women. Just one in seven of these women-owned firms had paid employees, and the aggregate receipts of women-owned firms were a minuscule 0.3 percent of the national total for all companies. Then came dramatic progress. Only ten years later, in 1982, women-owned businesses comprised one-fourth of all companies and generated about 10 percent of total receipts. By 1992 these numbers had risen to more than one-third of all firms, generating nearly 20 percent of total receipts. Minority women had made especially large gains. Between 1987 and 1996, the number of firms owned by Hispanic women rose by about 200 percent, by Asian women 150 percent, and by African-American women 135 percent. At the close of the century businesses owned by women accounted for nearly a quarter of all U.S. sales. In addition, women were starting more than 40 percent of all new firms.

Evolving Attitudes and Arrangements

American opinion toward the issue of women in business and the out-of-home workforce flip-flopped between the 1970s and the end of the century. In a poll taken in 1977, a sample of adults had been asked "Do you agree or disagree that it is much better for everyone involved if the man is the achiever outside the home and the woman takes care of the home and the family?" Sixty-six percent endorsed the statement. The same question asked in 1996 elicited only 38 percent agreement.

By then, about 65 percent of mothers with preschoolers were working outside the home, a figure five times what it had been in 1950. Of married women with children of school age, more than three-fourths had paying jobs or were looking for work. (The phenomenon of mothers working full time and then taking care of children after returning home had long been called "the double day.") By the late 1990s, about 30 percent of children aged five and under were being taken to daycare centers, up from only 6 percent in 1965. The number of these centers increased markedly during the 1990s, as did the number of companies offering onsite child care. In addition, by the end of the century some 25 percent of employed mothers, and more than 60 percent of mothers in poor families, were receiving help from relatives in taking care of preschool children during working hours.

Highly Compensated Women

Opportunities in top management were slow in coming. As late as 1970, a time in which women made up 75 percent of all American clerical workers, they accounted for less than 4 percent of all managers and administrators earning over $15,000 per year. In 1977 the median income of employed women was only 60 percent that of employed men, in part because of the types of jobs to which most women were relegated. Despite passage of the 1964 Civil Rights Act, overall gains in most lines of business remained sluggish until the late 1970s.

It was symptomatic of the problem that for three generations most elite business schools admitted only men. Harvard took no women into its regular MBA program until 1963, and even its class of 1973 was less than 5 percent female. By 1983 this figure had plateaued at about 26 percent, still a minority but a big gain nonetheless. (Nationwide, MBA's awarded to women grew from 4 percent of the total in 1960 to 38 percent in 1996.) In a survey taken 15 years after graduation, members of the Harvard class of 1983 were asked, "How has being a woman affected your career?" In response, more than half said negatively and less than a fourth said positively.

As the century came to an end, highly compensated female executives were earning only 68 percent as much as their male counterparts, a wider gap than for working women in general, who earned 76 percent of the male wage. Part of the reason why higher ranking women suffered a greater gender-based discrepancy in pay was that in large corporations women tended to be relegated to positions in staff departments known as the "three R's": public relations, industrial relations, and human resources. A smaller percentage were assigned to so-called "line" jobs (such as division presidents or vice-presidents, and general managers of sales or production departments), which entailed profit-and-loss responsibilities and carried higher salaries.

In *Fortune* 500 companies toward the close of the century, 11 percent of all corporate directors were women, as were 11 percent of corporate officers. There were, however, only three female Chief Executive Officers (CEOs) in the *Fortune* 500: Carleton Fiorina of Hewlett-Packard, Jill Barad of Mattel, and Marion Sandler of Golden West Financial. On the fringe of the 500 list, the CEO of the large advertising firm Ogilvy & Mather was Shelly Lazarus. The CEO of eBay, the Internet auction firm, was Margaret Whitman. The managing partner of Bain & Co., a leading consulting firm, was Orit Gadiesh. Another major consulting company, McKinsey, had 52 women among its 650 partners.

As the twenty-first century dawned, only a small percentage of women had broken through the "glass ceiling" and attained top management positions in big American businesses. The proportion was even lower in other countries. Whereas 11 percent of the directors of large U.S. companies were women, the corresponding figure in Britain was 5 percent. According to one survey, women held about 40 percent of management positions at all ranks in American firms, but only 20 to 30 percent in European ones, and, by most estimates, less than that in Asian companies.

The ultimate pattern of women's roles in American management was hard to predict. For one thing, there remained a perception that many women wished to follow an uninterrupted career path while others opted for what the writer Felice Schwartz called the "mommy track," a phrase that in itself angered some women. Then, too, a significant number of male executives still seemed threatened by the idea of having a female boss. Many women believed that this attitude had to be met head-on, with forthright assertions of authority. Darla Moore, president of Rainwater, Inc., a financial firm that wielded power as an institutional investor, commented in 1998 that she and other high-ranking women tended to be "outliers, mavericks, misfits"—and that this was a good thing.

She advised other women who aspired to power to ignore such counsel as: "You should be a nice girl," and "You ought to fit in." Moore derided this kind of guidance as leading to "a colossal waste of time."

Between 1920 and 2000 women had made immense progress in business. Not only were more women participating at all levels but their influence had changed some fundamental aspects of business culture. Family-friendly policies such as "flex time" and liberal leave for new parents had emerged from women's insistence that companies take a more realistic attitude toward human needs. In addition to women's direct accomplishments in business, the policy changes they had effected were, in and of themselves, major contributions to the larger society.

CHAPTER FIVE

The New Deal and World War II, 1933–1945: Regulation and Decentralization

Eleanor and Franklin Roosevelt

One of the most prominent women of the twentieth century was Eleanor Roosevelt (1884–1962). Both before and after her years as First Lady (1933–45), she advocated greater rights not only for women but also for African Americans and the poor. She wrote a daily newspaper column ("My Day"), traveled widely, and made frequent public speeches. She served as a delegate to the United Nations from 1945 to 1952, then again in 1961–62.

Both Eleanor Roosevelt and her husband Franklin D. Roosevelt (1882–1945) were strong personalities, and many Americans viewed them as passionately engaged in trying to improve people's lives. For millions of citizens they became symbols of humane understanding—caring friends who happened to live in the White House. Year after year, Eleanor Roosevelt worked as an advocate for groups living on the margins of society. Her husband, who was 51 years old when he became president, had himself become severely disabled at the age of 38, through a polio attack that paralyzed his legs.

No president had ever served more than two terms, but Roosevelt was elected for four. During his years in office he became an inspirational figure, in part because voters sensed that his confidence and good humor were offered up in defiance of his own handicap. Against heavy odds, he had won a spiritual victory in his fight against polio. People felt that he could help the country do the same against the economic catastrophe of the Great Depression and the emergency of World War II. The president never publicly acknowledged his disability until March of 1945, when, exhausted by a long trip to Yalta to confer with Winston Churchill and Joseph Stalin, he remained seated while addressing Congress. A month later he died.

Roosevelt was a career politician who knew much less about business than had his predecessor Herbert Hoover. Nonetheless, he became one of the most important figures in the history of American capitalism. Professing faith in the country's economic system, Roosevelt insisted that important parts of it be changed, and he led a fight that blunted its excesses and thereby strengthened it.

When the 1930s began, the United States differed from many European countries in the small degree of public influence exercised by nonbusiness sectors of society. But this situation changed during the 1930s and early 1940s, for several related reasons: the expansion of the federal government during President Roosevelt's New Deal (1933–38), the rise of organized labor, and the massive mobilization effort for World War II (1939–1945).

The spotlight in this chapter therefore falls on business-government relations, in particular the wartime federal effort called the Controlled Materials Plan. But before we reach the war years, it is important to examine how government became a more prominent player not only in the affairs of business but also in society as a whole. That, in itself, is an absorbing story.

The Roosevelt "revolution" of the 1930s embodied not just an *economic* movement, it also achieved a partial *political* settlement of some long-festering issues. These included the excessive power of business and various kinds of prejudice against women, the elderly, the poor, the disabled, and numerous racial and ethnic minorities. Although the New Deal did not solve any of these problems, it ameliorated all of them.

The gap in income distribution, for example, which had been extreme in the 1920s, narrowed during the New Deal and even more so just afterward, during World War II. From 1941 to 1945, the incomes of the poorest 40 percent of American families increased twice as fast as those of the richest 20 percent. In later periods, especially the 1980s and 1990s, this trend would go the other way. But during the intervening 50 years, U.S. society in general was overwhelmingly middle class.

That situation derived in part from demographic trends and changes in the nature of work. But it also owed much to laws and other government actions instituted during Roosevelt's presidency. The most important of these were Social Security, unemployment compensation, the minimum wage, support of the labor movement, and the management of aggregate demand through deficit spending—all of which, together with the regulatory measures described below, became part of what some historians came to call "the New Deal Order."

The attitude of many American businesspeople toward Roosevelt's policies, after a brief honeymoon during 1933, became one of downright hostility. Bankers, other financiers, and managers of big businesses were especially belligerent. Many of them regarded the New Deal as a grab for power by unscrupulous Democratic party politicians. Even sophisticated executives such as Alfred Sloan and Pierre du Pont exhibited an almost irrational hatred of Roosevelt, and they poured part of their fortunes into campaigns to unseat him. Several anti-Roosevelt groups, such as the American Liberty League, were so transparently dominated by the du Ponts and other moneyed families that their efforts actually enhanced Roosevelt's standing with voters. In a context of economic depression, it was easy for FDR and other savvy politicians to make common cause with the masses and array themselves against what Roosevelt called "economic royalists" and "organized money." The president was a superlative orator, and in a speech at Madison Square Garden just before the 1936 election he said of these wealthy enemies, "They are unanimous in their hate for me, and I welcome their hatred." This was an extraordinary statement, and the crowd's reaction to it approached the point of hysteria. Even some of the president's closest supporters, including Eleanor Roosevelt herself, found both the speech and the crowd's response a little frightening. This was, after all, a period of widespread demagoguery in Europe.

The Regulation of Business

The New Deal did not "revolutionize" the American economy, as both its supporters and enemies liked to claim. The business system retained the same overall structure in 1940 that it had in 1930. Yet government supervision did increase markedly during the thirties, as industries such as trucking, airlines, and interstate gas and electric utilities came under federal regulation. Other industries already regulated, including railroads, banking, telecommunications, and broadcasting, became even more so. Some New Deal measures, passed in an atmosphere of emergency, turned out to be inappropriate in the long run for the industries concerned and finally were repealed during the deregulation movements of the 1970s and 1980s. But as a whole, the regulatory acts pushed through in the 1930s made the economic system more legitimate in the eyes of the American people.

The most significant New Deal business reform was a complex series of laws designed to reshape the nation's capital markets. This legislation affected not only firms in the banking and securities industries, but also the thousands of important companies whose shares were traded on stock exchanges. The Securities Act of 1933 and the Securities Exchange Act of 1934 required that all such companies issue to stockholders and deliver to the government detailed annual reports. These reports contained copious amounts of information, which had to be laid out in prescribed form and certified for accuracy by independent accountants.

A few firms, such as United States Steel, had been voluntarily issuing reports to their stockholders for several decades. In addition, railroads and utilities were required to submit annual reports to regulatory commissions. But for most other firms the 1930s legislation brought a new world of doing business in the sunshine. Companies now had to reveal precise data on their sales, profits, salaries and bonuses paid to officers and directors, and numerous other matters.

The securities laws were drafted with great care. They were fashioned so as to place the burden of enforcement on the private sector, thereby avoiding the need for a large public bureaucracy. Because of their rigorous requirements, which included criminal penalties for violations, the laws provided a lot of new business for attorneys. They brought even more work for professional accountants, whose numbers grew rapidly to meet the need for private enforcement.

The laws had especially beneficial long-term effects on the investment banking industry—that is, Wall Street firms such as Goldman Sachs and Lehman Brothers—which helped businesses raise money through the sale of stocks and bonds. Just how bad the crisis in this industry had been can be seen from a few statistics. For the year 1933, at the nadir of the Great Depression, new corporate issues of securities had totaled only $161 million nationwide, about one-fiftieth the figure for 1929. The number of shares traded on the New York Stock Exchange had languished at under half a billion for the year 1932, one-third the figure for 1929. It did not again reach the 1929 number until 1963, some 34 years after the Crash.

By comparison, more than one billion shares were traded on a single *day* in 1997. That volume would never have been possible without the foundation laid down by the reforms of the New Deal and strengthened in later years. The many elements of this intricate and decentralized regulatory system formed a solid basis for confidence on the part of investors. The new system helped the capital markets not only to recover, but to achieve new levels of prosperity and world leadership.

Commercial banking was another arena of far-reaching New Deal reforms. Legislation of 1933 created the Federal Deposit Insurance Corporation, thereby stopping almost altogether the phenomenon of "runs" on banks and consequent bank failures, which had cost so many Americans their life savings. The same New

Deal measure forced a split between commercial banking and investment banking. This division of functions, Roosevelt said, would make it harder for bankers to speculate using "other people's money." The legislation caused the breakup of banks such as J. P. Morgan & Co. into separate entities. In this particular case those firms came to include Morgan Stanley, Morgan Guaranty, and Bankers Trust, in addition to the original J. P. Morgan bank.

Meanwhile, federal price-support systems reshaped the conduct of commercial agriculture, practically ending the depression that had begun in this sector during the early 1920s. Under the National Industrial Recovery Act of 1933, similar systems were instituted for hundreds of other industries. The early thirties were a time of serious *de*flation (falling prices), and federal price supports were imposed in hopes of stopping the downward spiral. The general plan was to use "codes of fair competition" to maintain standard prices for products made by different companies in the same industry.

These codes seldom worked well, for a variety of reasons: the difficulty of classifying product lines, the disparate cost structures of big firms as opposed to small ones, and the impossibility of setting prices that manufacturers, distributors, and consumers would all judge to be "fair." Even if agreement had been possible, too many opportunities existed for firms to differentiate their products and thereby evade the codes. Nor could even the best cost-accounting systems set "fair" standard prices in advance of some sense of eventual demand for specific items. So the effort to support prices was abandoned for many industries even before 1935, when the Supreme Court declared the National Industrial Recovery Act of 1933 unconstitutional.

As this flurry of activity went on, the New Deal also launched some important antitrust suits, and the rate of prosecution increased as the 1930s wore on. But here the policy was inconsistent and the message to business managers about what they could or could not do a little confusing.

The New Deal began to run out of steam in the late 1930s, and the country's attention shifted to ominous events unfolding in Europe and Asia. As Roosevelt put it, "Dr. New Deal" was now obliged to become "Dr. Win the War." The war began in Europe in September of 1939, and the United States entered it officially after the Japanese attack on Pearl Harbor in Hawaii on December 7, 1941.

The World Conflict, 1939–1945

In its effect on American business, as in many other ways, World War II was the most significant event of the twentieth century. Its ramifications were almost endless. Because of the pressing need to develop high-tech weapons, and also to deal with the heavy toll of casualties and sickness, the war either created or gave new momentum to industries that would become the most important of the late twentieth century. These industries were so different in nature from those of the Second Industrial Revolution (steel, automobiles, electrical equipment) that they formed the core of a Third Industrial Revolution, rooted in scientific research and based more on knowledge work than on machine mass production. The new industries included advanced electronics and telecommunications, aviation and aerospace, atomic energy, synthetic chemicals and pharmaceuticals, and sophisticated medical devices.

The war gave a profound jolt to American society in general, and therefore to business across all industries. Some of the changes were momentous: the movement of masses of women to jobs outside the home; the conditioning of millions of people to life in big business and the military; the creation of large populations on the West Coast and in the Sunbelt; the smoothing out of the business cycle; an enormous jump in spending on research and development; the introduction of mass income taxation and the withholding system; and, perhaps most important of all, the start of a very long stretch of economic prosperity. The period from the early 1940s to the early 1970s became a kind of golden age for American business.

The overall impact of World War II and its aftermath was at least as strong in several places overseas as in the United States. The defeat of Germany, Japan, and Italy set the conditions for eventual democratic government in those countries. In addition, the postwar breakup of colonial empires created dozens of independent new nations in Asia and Africa. The volume of international trade increased throughout much of the world, as an American-led drive to reduce barriers to imports and exports achieved remarkable success.

The Allied victory over Germany, to which the Soviet Union made the single greatest contribution, solidified Soviet dominance of Eastern and Central Europe. This set the stage for a Cold War with the United States, which lasted from 1947 to 1989. During that long period, most of the world was divided into two armed camps: the "communist bloc" versus the "free world." The possibility of a World War III fought with nuclear weapons seemed a constant threat. Because of these developments, the American tradition of isolation from "permanent alliances," against which George Washington had warned in his Farewell Address of 1796, now ended.

In the years just before World War II, the United States had possessed only a tiny army, one insignificant as compared with those of the European powers. (It ranked about number 17 in the world.) But owing to the Cold War, the mighty American military machine built to fight World War II was never fully demobilized. From 1949 onward the alliance called the North Atlantic Treaty Organization (NATO, the original major members of which were the United States, Great Britain, and France, which were united in their determination to prevent further Soviet expansion) became formal and apparently permanent. For decades afterward, what President Dwight Eisenhower called a "military-industrial complex" formed an integral part of American life, with significant implications for the nation's business system. In his own farewell address of 1961, Eisenhower warned that a too-powerful combination of government and business, even for the purpose of defending the country, might threaten its democratic traditions.

The Problem of Wartime Management

A theme of this book is the critical importance in business management of striking a proper balance between centralized control and decentralized decision making. The inauguration of General

Motors' multi-divisional structure in the 1920s and of Procter & Gamble's brand management in the 1930s were examples of administrative pioneering to meet certain kinds of challenges. These same challenges emerged in mobilization management during World War II, and in this case they confronted both business and government. In the effort to mobilize the economy for all-out war, the issue of centralization versus decentralization became *the* crucial management problem.

The heart of the question was, how could a democratic capitalist country mobilize without having the central government dictate all business decisions and thereby wreck the decentralized market mechanism on which the economy was based? At the other theoretical extreme, how could a laissez-faire government completely bereft of economic powers fight the war at all?

Every country involved in World War II confronted the same general problem of mobilization management. But the United States faced special difficulties. Despite the regulatory measures of the New Deal, the American government as of 1941 still had less control over its national economy than did any other major country fighting in the war. The task of mobilization presented the most serious administrative challenge the nation had ever faced. Yet in the end the United States solved this problem extraordinarily well, much better than Germany or Japan, both of which, it is clear in retrospect, gave too much authority to military officers.

In Germany, these officers often sacrificed quantity production in favor of achieving the highest quality. The airplanes and other tools of Germany's war machine were superbly designed, but they were so diversified and nonstandardized that lengthy production runs at factories became impossible. Repair of German equipment on the battlefields turned into a nightmare, and some spare parts remained unavailable because there were too many varieties to keep in stock. By the middle of the war, owing to interference from military people stationed at industrial plants, the German army was using 151 different truck models and 150 different motorcycles. The air force had 425 models or variants of planes in use or under construction. Partly for this reason, the productivity of aircraft workers in Germany was only half that of their

American counterparts. (In the late years of the war, under the rationalization programs led by Albert Speer, German productivity did increase.) Japan's industrial mobilization, in addition to being badly managed, suffered from a shortage of essential materials. The country itself had a paucity of natural resources, and wartime American naval action slowly choked off most of its imports. As for the army and aviation output of Italy, the third major Axis power, it amounted to less than that of the Ford Motor Company, which was the number-three American defense contractor. Ford made all sorts of engines, and in its vast Willow Run plant near Detroit produced thousands of standardized B-24 bombers almost by assembly-line methods.

The U.S. Production Miracle

During the war years the American business system turned out 86,000 tanks, 2 million army trucks, 193,000 artillery pieces, 17 million handguns and rifles, and 41 billion rounds of ammunition. Shipyards on both coasts, led in production technology by the standardized Kaiser works in California, launched 12,000 warships and merchant ships and added almost 65,000 smaller craft for use in coastal patrols and amphibious landings. All of these numbers denote colossal outputs. For just the ships and smaller craft, it is hard for the mind's eye to picture what such a fleet might look like. Placed end to end on land, the line of vessels would stretch approximately from New York to Omaha.

Most remarkably of all, aircraft companies in the United States built almost 300,000 planes during the war years. By comparison, the leading American postwar producer of airliners, Boeing, manufactured about 6,000 passenger jets during the entire 30-year period from 1960 to 1990. These modern jetliners were a lot more complicated and expensive than the warplanes of the 1940s, but the fiftyfold difference in numbers, produced in one-sixth of the time, remains striking.

During World War II the U.S. production of aluminum increased by a factor of four, and of magnesium, also used in aircraft, by a factor of 350. Mobilization also gave birth to the modern synthetic rubber industry. By war's end, U.S. plants were producing 85 percent of the great quantities of tires and other rubber products needed by both the military and civilian economy. Before the war the United States had produced almost no rubber and had been the leading importer of the commodity; after the war it became the largest exporter. All of the imports had been natural rubber, but all of the exports were synthetic.

Nearly every part of the economy changed in some way. Numerous manufacturing plants converted from civilian to military production, and munitions companies grew much bigger. Supplies of highway fuel fell by one-third during the war, as the output of aviation gasoline leaped twentyfold. The production of steel increased from 28 million tons in 1938 to 101 million by 1943, almost all of it now directed to military use. For steel and several other materials, the biggest single shift came from diversions away from the manufacture of automobiles. Carmakers began to build tanks, armored personnel carriers, and other military equipment.

Almost 40 percent of the car companies' output went into aircraft and related items. General Motors, Ford, and other auto firms became heavily involved in producing planes. And of the 813,000 aircraft *engines* built in the United States during World War II, the car companies made 456,000 of them. Most of these engines were complex machines, and it was essential that they be utterly reliable. Their production technology differed from that of automobile engines and the assembly line, and both the physical conversion of the plants as well as the modified managerial operations caused serious problems for every manufacturer.

American industrial mobilization as a whole was brilliantly successful. Without question it was the key to victory over Japan, and it was the most important single element in the triumph on the Western Front in Europe. By 1944 the Americans were outproducing the British, Germans, and Soviets combined. In perhaps the most dramatic way possible, this performance demonstrated once more the strength and resilience of the American business system and the flexibility of the U.S. government.

Almost no part of the colossal effort came easily, however, and the strain on mobilization planners was severe.

The Struggle to Manage Mobilization

Evidence of this strain is clear from the planners' prolonged trial-and-error approach. For many months stretching from 1939 to 1942, they set up one special body after another, but only a few of the many agencies worked well. Most were staffed with business executives called to Washington as "dollar-a-year men" who remained on their firms' payrolls and served without much compensation from the government. In 1939 Roosevelt set up the War Resources Board, headed by Edward Stettinius of United States Steel. In May 1940 came the National Defense Advisory Commission, which included William S. Knudsen, a production genius from General Motors who in 1937 had succeeded Alfred Sloan as the company's president.

Many agencies created during the early years of mobilization had overlapping jurisdictions: the Army and Navy Munitions Board, the Supply Priorities and Allocation Board, and the War Production Board. This last body was headed by Donald Nelson, who had come to Washington from Sears, Roebuck. Nelson was regarded as a peacemaker, someone who could listen to the demands of contending parties from business, government, and the military without losing his temper. The War Production Board took overall charge of industrial mobilization but continued to share its authority with other agencies and with several bureaus of both the Army and the Navy. (At this time there was no independent Air Force. It was formed in 1947 out of what had been the Army Air Corps.)

Given the immense scale of mobilization, there were inevitable foul-ups and disagreements about which kinds of public and private purchasers should have a numbered "priority" to buy vital but scarce raw materials. Business executives protested against impossible targets for production. Military officers threw tantrums when their demands for munitions were unmet. Government planners, tired of refereeing, stalked out of meetings in frustration. The stress was evident to everyone involved, and the memory of it all remained painfully clear after the war's end. In some of the official postwar reports issued by the government itself, a tone of tension creeps into what are usually the driest of bureaucratic documents. Here, for example, is a passage from an authoritative Commerce Department account entitled *The United States at War,* published in 1946:

> Over the war period more than 350,000 contracts were made between the Government and some 40,000 prime contractors. In addition, many times that number of contracts were made between these prime contractors and their suppliers or subcontractors. . . . Over $100 billion of contracts were placed in the first 6 months of 1942. In other words, industry signed up to deliver for war more than the total production of the American economy in the nation's most prosperous and productive prior year. . . . Under this flood of war orders, a number of things were bound to happen, and did happen.
>
> First, it became utterly impossible to produce everything ordered at any time in any near future. It was an industrial impossibility. The total called for was in excess of our industrial capacity.
>
> Second, there was a resulting collision between the various production programs and between the men who were responsible for them. Merchant ships took steel from the Navy, and the landing craft cut into both. The Navy took aluminum from aircraft. Rubber took valves from escort vessels, from petroleum, and from the Navy. The pipe lines took steel from ships, new tools, and the railroads. And at every turn there were foreign demands to be met as well as requirements for new plants.
>
> Third, all semblance of balance in the production program disappeared because of the different rates of contracting and of production that resulted from the scramble to place orders. . . .
>
> Fourth, there was terrific waste in conversion. After a tragically slow start, many a plant was changed over to war production when its normal product was more needed than its new product. Locomotive plants went into tank production, when locomotives were more necessary—but the Tank Division did not know this. Truck plants began to produce airplanes, a change that caused shortages of trucks later on. . . .
>
> Fifth, we built many new factories, and expanded many others, which we could not use and did not need. Many of these factories we could not supply with labor or with raw materials, or if we had, we should not have been able to fly the planes or shoot the ammunition that would have come out of them. . . .
>
> Finally, the priority system broke down because of "priority inflation." People with military contracts had the right to take more scarce materials and components than there were, so that a priority or an allocation became nothing more than a "hunting license."

Early in the war, planners in the mobilization agencies experimented in a hothouse of anger and frustration, trying desperately to figure out some practical way to allocate strategic materials. They began with implementation of the "priority" classification mentioned above. But priority status meant only that certain buyers would get preferences over the normal run of customers. It did not mean they would actually receive supplies in the volumes they requested. Nor could it effectively differentiate between the Army, the Navy, and other authorized purchasers, all of whom might have had an equally weighted "priority" for the same materials. Even within each military service, separate bureaus competed for supplies, and thousands of companies under contract to Army and Navy bureaus ended up with the priorities. The chaos of the priority system continued until November of 1942, three years into the European war and nearly a year after the attack on Pearl Harbor.

Ferdinand Eberstadt
and the Controlled Materials Plan

At that point the Roosevelt Administration announced an imaginative new strategy to which it gave a prosaic name: the Controlled Materials Plan. The Plan was the brainchild of Ferdinand Eberstadt (1890–1969), an investment banker of luminous intelligence who had come to Washington to chair the Army and Navy Munitions Board. He had then become vice-chairman of the powerful War Production Board, within which the new Plan would now be administered.

Eberstadt was the son of a German Jewish father and German-Venezuelan Catholic mother. (He himself became a Presbyterian.) The parents had come to the United States before any of their children were born, settling in New Jersey. There young Ferdinand attended a private prep school before enrolling at Princeton. He made a brilliant college record, despite being temporarily expelled during his freshman year for unruly behavior. After graduation, he went to Europe to continue his studies, then during World War I served in France as a U.S. Army artillery officer. Following the war he received his degree from Columbia Law School and entered a prestigious Wall Street law firm. A bold young man whose personal bearing seemed to alternate randomly between charm and imperiousness, Ferd Eberstadt had little patience with some of the backslapping business types who were coming to prominence during the 1920s. He preferred the rarefied air of innovative corporate finance, where unintelligent people quickly perished. Leaving the practice of law in 1925, he became a partner at Dillon, Read, an elite Wall Street investment bank. There, exploiting his foreign-language skills, he negotiated the firm's most sensitive loans to European clients, particularly German coal and steel firms. Eberstadt pursued his work with single-minded dedication. (Three of his four children were born during his periodic absences in Europe.) He had a vivid sense of his own abilities, and in 1929 he was fired by Dillon, Read after being rebuffed in his bid for a greater share of the firm's profits. In 1931 he established his own firm, F. Eberstadt & Co.

Many investment banks went under during the Great Depression, and almost no new ones attracted much business. The resourceful Eberstadt, however, quickly discovered a niche for his startup firm. Both he and his company flourished to such an extent that in 1939 he was profiled in a *Fortune* article entitled, simply, "Ferdinand Eberstadt." Because big industrial companies were already tied to established investment banks such as Goldman Sachs, Eberstadt sought clients among small to medium-sized companies, most of which were family owned.

Inheritance-tax laws, passed by Congress at the behest of the Roosevelt Administration and replicated in many state legislatures, were forcing numerous families to sell their companies when the founding ancestor died. Eberstadt's solution was for these firms to "go public" during the founder's lifetime. Under his plan, they would sell a large minority of common stock to the public, thereby giving the heirs money to pay inheritance taxes but at the same time making it possible for them to keep voting control of the firm. He called his stable of client companies "little blue chips." Some of them went on to become big businesses: McGraw-Hill, Norwich Pharmacal, Victor Chemical.

Eberstadt's special gift, evident throughout his career, was an uncanny sense of how to design institutional mechanisms to meet novel situations. He proved to be as fearless an entrepreneur in government as he had been in business. Where others tended to waffle, he charged forward. In wartime Washington, as his fellow planner Bernard Gladieux commented, Eberstadt was "a welcome relief" from the many businessmen who arrived "with overrated reputations," then quickly wilted under the intense public glare. Eberstadt, by contrast, "knew how to do things himself, and above all he could make decisions—very tough decisions. Even when they hurt people—influential people—he made them."

In 1942, working as vice-chairman of the War Production Board, Eberstadt was appalled at the disarray he saw. He well understood the nature of the emergency, and he knew that without strong government oversight the existing confusion would degenerate into chaos. As matters stood, the new mobilization agencies were getting in each other's way. As for the military services, they were under such stress that their own discourse seemed to have become a continuous shriek. The most pressing need was for a stern hand to guide the task of industrial mobilization.

At the same time, Eberstadt remained sensitive to the virtues of a market economy. He knew that any plan that did not exploit market forces could not fully tap the potential of American business. The challenge before him was to create a system that would give play to market forces yet steer them to produce the right kind of equipment in the right amounts to arrive at the right places at the right times.

His solution, which took him and his staff several months to work out, was to pull back from all attempts at pervasive centralized direction. Dictatorial management of production was working well in the Soviet Union's mobilization, but it formed a poor fit with the American market economy. Eberstadt's aim was to achieve the maximum effectiveness of production and distribution at all levels, with minimal interference from the top. It was the same kind of goal articulated for peacetime business by Alfred Sloan at General Motors and Neil McElroy at Procter & Gamble. Eberstadt acknowledged Sloan's influence on his own thinking.

With the cold logic that characterized his way of doing things, Eberstadt developed the idea of guiding mobilization by the rationed allocation of only three items: steel, aluminum, and copper.

This technique would be powerful but simple. Now his Controlled Materials Plan moved away from the loose and dysfunctional "priority" regime and toward tight control of these three key metals. Although scores of other materials had also been subjected to "priority" distribution, no important munitions company could operate without its requirements of steel, aluminum, and copper. Therefore, Eberstadt reasoned, it was not necessary for the War Production Board (WPB) to ration additional items. Specialized agencies were already paying attention to the allocation of rubber, petroleum, chemicals, and other materials. Civilian rationing of certain consumer goods was in place as well, and price and wage controls were accomplishing ends that did not have to be addressed directly by the WPB's Controlled Materials Plan.

Eberstadt's animating ideas were to match demand with supply and facilitate quick shifts in allocations of the key metals from one use to another as circumstances changed. The Plan therefore called for a careful sequence of activities. First, forecasters would compute the volume of the three metals, all of which were under high-pressure production schedules, that was expected to be available over the coming months and years. They would then ask "claimant agencies" such as the Army and Navy to submit their "claims," or requests for specific amounts of steel, aluminum, and copper, to the Plan's Requirements Committee. These requests were to be consolidated estimates from prime military contractors such as General Motors and Boeing, which previously would have totaled their own needs and tacked on those of their subcontractors. Significantly, the claimant agencies would deal only with prime contractors, who would negotiate on behalf of themselves and their subcontractors. This policy would reduce the number of transactions in which high-ranking Army and Navy officers had to be involved.

The new system placed a tremendous premium on accuracy. If insufficient estimates crept into the computations at any level, from the bottom of the subcontracting chain all the way up to the claimant agency, then the schedule for manufacturing the affected item would stall for want of necessary materials. On the other hand, if inflated claims were put into the system, then the Requirements Committee, chaired by Eberstadt himself, would impose penalties, including recommendations for criminal indictments. In this way the Plan practically mandated accurate forecasting within individual firms as a matter of self-interest.

The prime contractors, after receiving tickets that entitled them to purchase controlled materials, would next allocate supplies to their own plants, those of their subcontractors, and so on down the line. As a postwar government report put it, "In passing from priorities to allocation, we passed from a queue system, with the military program entitled to go to the head of the line, to a rationing system, under which selected commodities were separately rationed."

At subcontractor levels, managers of small businesses would calculate what they needed to fulfill their obligations, and then submit their estimates to prime contractors. In this way, original requests for materials were made in drafting rooms and on shop floors, where information was most current and engineers and workers best informed. At the prime contractor level, the different needs of various subcontractors would be balanced against the big company's own requirements for the many products it was manufacturing for military use, and the total "claims" for materials adjusted accordingly.

Both the claimant agencies and their prime contractors had the power to shift controlled materials from one use to another at levels up and down within their own bailiwicks. This "vertical" chain of authority, as it came to be called, created a type of internal market within each organizational jurisdiction. It thereby fulfilled one of Eberstadt's overriding aims at WPB, stated even before he developed the Plan, of giving industrial mobilization "greater similarity to the normal commercial practice." If, for example, a prime contractor wanted to switch part of its aluminum allocation from one project to another because of changed circumstances, it could do so without going back to the government for permission. This decentralization of decision rights down the vertical chain made the Controlled Materials Plan a much more flexible instrument than the previous "horizontal" regime. (In that system, nontransferable priorities had been awarded across the board to thousands of contractors and subcontractors, and even to individual factories.)

At the highest levels, only a few strategic decisions would have to be made by top military and civilian planners. The officials in charge of allocating steel might see that over the next few months the Navy and Merchant Marine were going to need steel for a specified number of ships, while the Army needed the same steel for a certain number of big artillery guns. In this scenario, the ships would have to be constructed first, because they had to be afloat and ready to carry those new guns to battlefields overseas. Therefore, competing claims for scarce steel by ship and gun contractors (represented by the Navy and Army in testimony before the WPB's Requirements Committee) must on this occasion be resolved in favor of the Navy. Later on, the situation might be the reverse: guns now, ships later, so the Army gets the steel.

Meanwhile, the Navy itself might have had to choose between using steel for either warships or support ships. And even within those categories, the Navy would have had to establish its own tradeoffs among fighting ships such as aircraft carriers, cruisers, destroyers, and submarines on the one hand, and among supporting cargo ships, troop transports, and fuel tankers on the other.

To such complex problems in mobilization planning, the Controlled Materials Plan brought a stark simplicity. Although only three metals were designated, their rationing had a domino effect on hundreds of other critical materials. Strategic choices, by necessity, still had to be made at the top. But the *production* dynamic now flowed in the opposite direction, from the bottom up. The Plan represented a vast pyramid of decision making in which thousands of individual tradeoffs took place up and down through different layers of operation. Each tradeoff was made at the spot where the information necessary to select the right alternative was most likely to be available. This was administrative elegance at its best.

Eberstadt's Controlled Materials Plan was announced by the WPB in November 1942, implemented during 1943, and kept in operation for the rest of the war. It represented a distinctively American solution to the most challenging of all organizational problems: how to balance centralized control with decentralized execution, and how to fix decision-making authority at the correct spot. In one sense it recalled the old Hamilton-Jefferson debates of the 1790s, which also grappled with striking the right balance be-

tween central authority and individual freedom. And like those debates, the problem of industrial mobilization was resolved by a
long cycle of intense bargaining.

The development of the Controlled Materials Plan brought
some impassioned discord, and Ferdinand Eberstadt was just the
kind of hard-driving executive to see it through. Working 70-hour
weeks over many months, he became obsessed with refining the
Plan's mechanisms—in placing authority at the right levels and
planting incentives that would make the new system as self-en-
forcing as possible. He disdained the social swirl of wartime
Washington. He cared nothing for politics, and he was relatively
uninterested in personal glory.

Eberstadt succeeded beyond his own expectations. But in an
ironic twist, he and several other planners fell victim to one of the
many administrative shakeups deriving from the politics of war
mobilization. In 1943, not long after the Controlled Materials Plan
went into operation, he was relieved of his post as vice-chairman.
By then it didn't matter. His work was done, the Plan was in place,
and for the remaining two and a half years of the war it hummed
along like a well-oiled engine. The Plan alone, of course, cannot
be credited with the American production miracle of World War II.
But a record quite so miraculous could not have occurred without
something very much like it.

In the years after World War II, Ferdinand Eberstadt served on
a small blue-ribbon group as one of the chief behind-the-scenes
architects of what became the Department of Defense, the Central
Intelligence Agency, and the National Security Agency. Back on
Wall Street during the 1950s and 1960s, he pioneered some of the
techniques of the leveraged buyout, a financial device destined to
have major importance in the corporate shakeups of the 1980s.

How the War Was Funded

As part of the War Production Board, the Controlled Materials
Plan guided the expenditure of several hundred billion dollars
(equivalent to several trillion dollars in the early twenty-first century). The money came from the American public through borrowing, taxes, and sales of treasury bonds to the Federal Reserve,

which then authorized the printing of money to pay for the bonds. Planners borrowed in every way they could think of, including sales of high-denomination bonds to institutions and wealthy individuals, and mass sales of "War Bonds" with face values as low as $25. Some campaigns even urged children to buy special 25-cent savings stamps and paste them into a book that when full could be taken to a bank and exchanged for a bond.

Current taxes paid for a little less than half of all military expenditures, and the urgent need for more money gave birth to the modern income-tax system. In 1933, less than 3 percent of the population had been covered by a tax return, either as taxpayers or dependents. By 1943 this figure stood at 69 percent. Even as late as 1940, only about 7 million Americans made enough money to have to pay income tax. By the end of the war that number had multiplied by a factor of six, to 42 million. In 1942, a 5 percent "Victory Tax" was applied to all annual gross incomes exceeding $624, and this new law, almost by itself, quadrupled the number of taxpayers for that year.

During the New Deal, the Roosevelt Administration had argued that wealthy Americans were not contributing enough financial support to the federal government. Consequently, New Deal Congresses sometimes passed "soak the rich" tax bills supported by the President. That pattern changed during the war. In 1943, Congress balked at further taxation targeted mostly at the wealthy, and pushed instead for a broader and flatter tax system. Congress won this battle, overriding a presidential veto in which Roosevelt complained that the House and Senate had passed a bill "providing relief not for the needy but for the greedy." With the tax legislation of 1943 and 1944, the modern income-tax system suddenly matured.

The most important procedural change came in 1943 with the introduction of the withholding tax. Under this system, which is now familiar to almost everyone with a job, employers deducted taxes from workers' wages on a current basis, then forwarded the money to the Internal Revenue Service. Before 1943, taxes had been sent directly to the IRS by individual taxpayers, either quarterly or annually.

Both the income tax and the idea of War Bonds were marketed to the American people through systematic appeals to their patriotism. At the start of each War Bond drive, numerous magazines would do cover stories urging citizens to participate. Well-known entertainers would go on the radio with barrages of announcements endorsing bond drives and the income tax. Irving Berlin, the composer of "White Christmas" and other popular songs, wrote a tune called "I Paid My Income Tax Today." The Disney studios turned out a cartoon film in which Donald Duck computed his tax bill, marking out standard exemptions for his dependent nephews Huey, Louie, and Dewey. The costs of these services were mostly donated—by studios, advertising agencies, publishers, radio networks, and show business personalities.

Throughout the public relations campaign, the new tax system was repeatedly linked to the war effort. Any mention of social programs was omitted. And ever since that time, the American system of taxation has relied on payments of income taxes by millions of individuals, as well as by corporations and other businesses. In most other industrialized countries, a much greater proportion of revenue is collected in the form of indirect value-added taxes computed and paid by firms, and through sales taxes paid by consumers at stores. For the modern American tax system, as in so many other ways, World War II was the salient event of the twentieth century.

Employment and the Growth of the Workforce

For many workers the 1930s and the 1940s were like night and day. The central problem of the Great Depression had been joblessness, but World War II brought unprecedented demands for laborers, both in uniform and out. The number of people in the armed forces increased more than thirtyfold, from 360,000 in 1939 to 11.5 million in 1944. Even though so many workers now wore uniforms, total *civilian* employment jumped at the same time, from 42.7 million in 1939 (the last year of depression-level unemployment), to 50.4 million in 1943. Although the population increased only slightly, the total labor force (employed people in and out of uniform plus those looking for work or in transit between jobs) grew from 51.8 million in 1939 to 62.2 million in 1944.

Unemployment had reached about 25 percent in 1933 and was still at a depression-level 17.2 percent in 1939. But by 1944 it had dropped to just 1.2 percent. Thus, in the narrow space of about one decade, the United States recorded both the worst and best employment numbers in its history. Most people who joined the military services were young men, but the new civilian war workers came from varied demographic groups. The largest single cohort, 3 million, consisted of women aged 21 through 64. An additional 800,000 females aged 14–20 also joined the workforce, together with 2.6 million males aged 21–64, 1.1 million males aged 14–20, and 400,000 males over age 65.

Though these statistics, on paper, may have a cold and lifeless quality, they symbolize staggering increases in both military and civilian employment, and dramatic changes in the lives of masses of people. Overall, 16 million men and women served in uniform during the war, 10 million of whom were drafted. During the four years of fighting, about 405,000 American soldiers and sailors died and 671,000 others were wounded.

The pattern of civilian employment was also transformed. Vast new munitions factories opened their doors, financed mostly with federal funds. The average workweek in manufacturing rose from 38 hours to more than 45. Defense-related employment increased from 9 percent of total employment in 1941 to 40 percent in 1943. It remained at that level through most of 1945, then dropped back to 9 percent in 1946 and continued down to 5 percent by the time the Korean War began in 1950. So World War II dominated employment, just as it did the rest of the nation's economic life.

Population on the Move

Mobilization brought big changes to certain areas of the country. Washington, D.C., had long been a sleepy, medium-sized city, unlike other national capitals such as London, Paris, Moscow, Berlin, Rome, and Tokyo. Throughout the 1930s it remained so despite the excitement of the New Deal. But during the war years Washington's population zoomed by 43 percent, to 1.3 million, and it became the metropolitan core for large numbers of other people living in Maryland and northern Virginia.

Outside Washington, the war stimulated the rise of the Sunbelt (with a major assist afterward from air conditioning, which became widespread beginning in the 1960s). Southern ports that had been quiet since the Civil War emerged to prominence once again. In Charleston, South Carolina, the activities of the U.S. Navy pushed up the population by 47 percent between 1940 and 1944. The number of people in Mobile, Alabama, an old town that happened to contain modern shipyards, increased during the same years by the very high figure of 75 percent.

Port cities on the Pacific coast mushroomed too. San Diego grew by 46 percent, San Francisco by 29 percent. The population of Los Angeles increased by only 15 percent, to 3.3 million, but many LA suburbs such as Long Beach on the coast and Pasadena inland grew by much higher percentages. Workers poured into the area to take jobs in aircraft and other war-related plants. Before the war ended the total number of people living in California had swelled by more than one-third, an immense jump for so large a state. There had been times of rapid urban growth before in the United States, but nothing like gains of this magnitude over a period of only four years.

The incidence of personal travel skyrocketed during the war. Recruits reporting to Army, Navy, and Marine bases logged millions of miles by car, bus, and rail. Sometimes accompanied by their families, they then traveled to duty stations located throughout the country, and many continued on to ports of embarkation for the trip overseas. At the same time, hordes of young civilians relocated to new places that offered war-related jobs. Over a million African Americans moved from southern farms to northern factories. Families of all races moved once, twice, half a dozen times. World War II brought the greatest internal mass migration in American history.

Rationing, the Draft, and Decentralized Administration

Meanwhile, retail business was changing fast, as thousands of small establishments with no connection to war work closed their doors. Among them were service stations, garages, grocery stores, and appliance dealers. There were 3.2 million business firms in the United States in 1939, but only 2.9 million remained by 1943, even though the nation's economy was booming. Because of rationing and the priorities of military production, some stores had little to sell. By order of the War Production Board, practically no radio sets were manufactured for civilian use during the war, and the same was true of electric washing machines, shavers, irons, toasters, stoves, mixers, waffle irons, and heating pads. The manufacture of home refrigerators, the most prized of all household appliances, dropped by 99.7 percent between 1941 and 1943. Most significantly, no civilian cars were produced. The last one rolled off the assembly line in March 1942. Even the production of pianos stopped, as such companies as Steinway, Baldwin, and Kimball began making wooden and aluminum parts for military aircraft.

Many consumer goods were rationed: rubber, gasoline, fuel oil, nylon, work shoes, meat, sugar, coffee, fats, and oils. In an effort to conserve rubber and gasoline further, the government imposed a national speed limit of 35 miles per hour. As a means of saving fabrics for uniforms, tents, and parachutes, clothing companies were forbidden to make trousers with cuffs, suits with vests, or full-cut skirts. The War Production Board issued a pledge to "the women and girls of America that there will be no extremes in dress styles during this war . . . and that their present wardrobes will not be made obsolete by radical fashion changes."

The consumer-goods rationing program was run mostly by the Office of Price Administration (OPA), a new agency created to control what otherwise would have become disorderly inflation. In a capitalist economy, the control of inflation in times of ample money but a shortage of goods is impossible so long as markets are allowed to operate unfettered. But OPA and other agencies, through skillful use of their rationing and price-control powers, did a good job of minimizing price increases. These agencies were staffed with some of the country's ablest young economists.

It was crucial that price control and rationing be decentralized. For the administration of rationing, the government set up about 6,000 community boards across the nation, including at least one for every county in every state. All were staffed with civic leaders, who promoted compliance by appealing to the patriotism of their neighbors. Families were allocated so many gallons of gasoline per month, so many pounds of meat, and so much sugar and coffee, according to how many people lived in the household and the kinds of jobs held by the adults. Almost the entire population became familiar with coupons and rationing books, with their perforated stamps and tickets. Had this system been run entirely from Washington, gridlock would likely have resulted because the government would have been hopelessly ill informed.

The same was true of the conscription system. To manage conscription, the U.S. Selective Service System relied on thousands of local draft boards to classify men as 1-A (ready to be drafted immediately) through 4-F (not physically fit for military service).

Local rationing and draft boards, therefore, represented pragmatic compromises between the conflicting needs for centralized policy making on the one hand and decentralized decision making on the other. In this sense both resembled Alfred Sloan's multidivisional structure at General Motors, Neil McElroy's brand-management system at Procter & Gamble, and Ferdinand Eberstadt's Controlled Materials Plan.

Overall, more than 150 emergency agencies were created during the war, not counting new military departments. Once the war was over, most of them disappeared. It was the genius of the American political system to set up agencies on an ad hoc basis and then quickly dismantle them. Although several New Deal regulatory commissions were destined to have a long life, only a few wartime mobilization agencies survived after 1945. The most important was the Selective Service System, whose local draft boards remained active until the 1970s.

Consumption and Output

Despite all the rationing and the great diversion of resources to the war effort, aggregate consumer spending actually increased during World War II. The United States was the only major combatant for which this was true, partly because no battles were fought on the American mainland and no bombing campaigns disrupted agricultural and industrial production. In Britain, per-capita consumer spending declined in inflation-adjusted terms by 20 percent between 1938 and 1944. In the United States it rose by 22 percent. Consumer spending did not increase uniformly. For rationed goods it shrank, naturally, as people began to change some of their living patterns. When tires and gasoline became scarce, many travelers opted for public transportation. They logged more railway passenger-miles during the war than at any other period in American history before or since. At the same time, people spent relatively more on housing, furniture, clothing, tobacco, and alcoholic drinks, while spending about the same on food, books, magazines, and amusements. But considering the national emergency and the drive to produce military equipment, the general increase in consumption was remarkable.

The industrial output of the American economy grew by much more than the 22 percent figure for consumption. Direct comparisons of wartime and peacetime statistics raise apples-and-oranges issues because of the command-economy nature of much wartime production. But the official numbers indicate that Gross National Product, adjusted for inflation, increased by 93 percent between 1939 and 1944. Considering that the United States had by far the largest economy in the world, an increase of this magnitude over so brief a time was little short of unbelievable.

Big and Small Business

The situation confronting mobilization managers remained urgent throughout the war, and they chose to rely on companies they knew to be capable of producing in volume. Usually this meant big businesses. At one point the army general in charge of buying munitions said bluntly (and inaccurately), "All the small plants of the country could not turn out one day's requirements of ammunition." Although the national culture idealized small entrepreneurial firms, time pressures led planners to award most of the major procurement contracts to large companies. The 55 percent jump in manufacturing employment between 1939 and 1944 took place mainly in big firms. Very large companies employing 10,000 or more workers represented only 13 percent of total manufacturing employment in 1940, but more than 30 percent by 1945. Even big consumer-products firms contributed. Procter & Gamble put 14,000 people to work stuffing powder into artillery shell casings, and filled about a quarter of all the shells made in the United States during the war.

This tilt toward reliance on big business turned out to be a thorny political issue. In 1942, a Senate committee reported with alarm that three-fourths of all military procurement contracts had been awarded to only 56 of the nation's 184,000 manufacturing companies. To help finance the operation of "small businesses" (those employing fewer than 500 people), Congress created the Smaller War Plants Corporation, an agency that evolved after the war into the permanent Small Business Administration.

Despite such efforts, the pattern of relying on big business to propel industrial mobilization held firm. Between June 1940 and September 1944, the government placed prime defense contracts aggregating $175 billion, the equivalent of well over a trillion dollars in the early twenty-first century. About 30 percent of this sum went to only 10 companies:

1. General Motors (8 percent of the total)
2. Curtiss-Wright (aircraft and engines) (4 percent)
3. Ford (3 percent)
4. Consolidated Vultee (aircraft) (3 percent)
5. Douglas Aircraft (2.5 percent)
6. United Aircraft (2 percent)
7. Bethlehem Steel (2 percent)
8. Chrysler (2 percent)
9. General Electric (2 percent)
10. Lockheed (aircraft) (2 percent)

The Production Triumph in Aviation

Five of these top ten contractors were aircraft firms, and, as we have seen, General Motors, Ford, and others also produced planes and aircraft engines. The manufacture of airframes, engines, and propellers had suddenly become America's number-one industry measured by value of output, up from number 44 in 1939. In addition to five of the top ten contractors, other aviation-related companies were ranked number 11 (North American, owned by General Motors), 12 (Boeing), 14 (Glenn Martin), 17 (Bendix), 22 (Grumman), 24 (Republic), 25 (Bell), 32 (Aviation Corp.), and 46 (Norden).

Employment in the manufacture of aircraft and related equipment grew from about 80,000 workers in 1940 to 1.3 million in 1943, and from less than 1 percent of total manufacturing employment to more than 7 percent. The makeup of the workforce changed as well. By 1944, women constituted 40 percent of all workers in airframe plants, and 30 percent in engine and propeller plants. The image of "Rosie the Riveter," an idealized young woman employed in an aircraft factory, was stamped onto the national consciousness through a song, posters, a documentary film, and other propaganda. Women were not as well paid as men to do the same work, and after the war many women were forced to relinquish their jobs or otherwise cede some of their gains. But they made a vital contribution to the mobilization effort, and in so doing broke down some employment barriers of long standing.

American production of aircraft was probably the most significant industrial feat of World War II. It surpassed even the Manhattan Project, which brought forth the atomic bomb. Aircraft production was crucial to the prosecution of the war, not only in light of the bombing campaigns against Germany and Japan but also because of the major amphibious invasions of Europe and the Pacific islands, none of which would have been attempted without supremacy in the air.

The American achievement in aviation was especially noteworthy because the industry was built almost from a standing start. During the 20 years before 1939, a total of only 13,500 military aircraft had been manufactured in the United States. Yet in May of 1940, President Roosevelt called for the production of 50,000 planes *per year*. Critics derided his proposal as irresponsible. Charles Lindbergh called it "hysterical chatter." But against this initial background of pessimism, American companies proceeded to turn out the following totals:

1941: 26,000 aircraft
1942: 48,000
1943: 86,000
1944: 96,000
1945: 50,000

U.S. aircraft production easily overwhelmed the combined output of the Axis powers. In Germany, manufacturing peaked in 1944 at 40,000 planes, despite a ferocious effort employing thousands of workers from the conquered nations of Europe. Japan's highest figure, 28,000, was also reached in 1944, exceeding by 10,000 its output in any other year. But most of these German and Japanese planes were small single-engine defensive fighters, whereas a large percentage of the new American aircraft were large, multi-engine bombers and transports. So the dominance was even greater than would appear from the numbers alone.

Aircraft Companies

In every major country involved in World War II except the Soviet Union, private companies built the airplanes—firms such as Vickers in Britain, Messerschmitt in Germany, and Mitsubishi in Japan. Almost all of the funding came either directly or indirectly from the government of each nation.

In the United States, federal funds accounted for about 90 percent of the money for the 350 new aircraft plants that sprang up across the country. Because the Navy and the Army Air Corps bought the planes, admirals and generals as well as civilian planners had much to say about which designs from which companies would be built in what volume, and by whom. There was intense interfirm rivalry, and the traditional aircraft companies grew especially wary of mighty General Motors. Its new diesel engines had begun to conquer the railway locomotive market in 1938, and now the aircraft companies feared that GM could use the war emergency to build a strong position in their industry as well. Despite all the rivalries, much cooperation went on, some of it forced by government directives. Often planes designed by one firm would be built not only by it but by others as well. And the entire effort of aircraft production benefited directly from the operation of Ferdinand Eberstadt's Controlled Materials Plan. One of the three controlled materials, aluminum, was used in immense volumes by the aircraft companies.

In weight of aircraft produced, the largest single manufacturer was Douglas of California, which employed 17,000 people in 1940 and 154,000 by 1943. A young MIT engineer named Donald Douglas (1892–1981) had founded this company in 1921. Its DC-3 (the DC standing for Douglas Commercial), which was developed during the 1930s, became the most reliable and durable transport plane of the mid-twentieth century. The DC-3 carried about 75 percent of all U.S. domestic passenger traffic in the years just prior to World War II, when commercial air transportation was fairly new. It then became the most important cargo carrier during the war, and as late as the 1960s DC-3s still accounted for about a third of all transport aircraft in use throughout the world.

In Douglas Aircraft's early years, the 1920s and 1930s, its production of planes grew slowly, then began to follow the irregular pattern that has since typified the industry as a whole. Here are some sample figures for Douglas's annual output of aircraft:

1922:	6	1939:	314
1923:	23	1943:	9,017
1931:	245	1944:	11,598
1932:	79	1946:	127

From a business viewpoint, these numbers seem surreal. The task of managing any kind of company with such uneven sales raises almost insuperable problems in finance, personnel, production, and marketing. Donald Douglas was a competent manager, but like most other aviation pioneers he was better at running an entrepreneurial startup than a big business over the long term. In the difficult years after World War II, without the benefit of booming sales to the military, Douglas Aircraft did better than many of its competitors. But despite its good performance in the late 1940s and early 1950s with the DC-6 and DC-7 models, Douglas was surpassed during the 1960s by Boeing, largely because of Donald Douglas's reluctance to develop jet airliners. (Still later, Douglas

Aircraft encountered a financial crisis and was absorbed in the 1967 merger that produced McDonnell-Douglas. This new company became the largest defense contractor in the United States. But in 1997, as the end of the Cold War reduced the demand for its products, McDonnell-Douglas itself was acquired by Boeing.)

Boeing Airplane

The company founded by William Boeing in 1916 was the biggest winner in America's wartime aircraft sweepstakes, and it solidified its top position during the half-century following the war. Bill Boeing was the son of immigrant parents from Germany and Austria. He grew up in Michigan, attended Yale, and first went to the state of Washington in search of additional resources for his father's timber company. During World War I he formed Pacific Aero Products Company, the forerunner of Boeing Airplane.

The Boeing Company specialized in seaplanes and was known in the industry as an engineering-oriented firm adept at constructing large aircraft. It experienced a degree of success during the 1920s, then, in 1929, through a series of mergers, became part of the United Aircraft and Transportation Company. This firm represented an attempt to consolidate many different parts of the industry; but like some other big industrial mergers of the late 1920s it did not hold together for long, and Boeing later reverted to being an independent company. Nonetheless, the merger made Bill Boeing and other entrepreneurs immediate millionaires.

After the onset of the Great Depression, Congress began investigating business frauds in several industries, including securities and aviation. When Bill Boeing was called to testify, he became angry and responded by selling all his holdings in the company and withdrawing from any further role in its management. Thereafter Boeing Airplane was run primarily by two men, Clairmont Egtvedt (1892–1975) and Philip Johnson (1894–1944). Both had been recruited by Bill Boeing long before, when they were engineering students as the University of Washington.

When war began in Europe in 1939, the company stood on the edge of bankruptcy, and its position remained precarious for several months afterward. Of the first 6,000 planes ordered by the American military, Boeing received orders for only 255 tiny trainers plus 38 bombers, with a government option for an additional 42. This was not an auspicious start. But the bomber in question, called the B-17, turned out to be one of the most effective weapons of the war on either side. As soon as military planners realized what a jewel it was, orders poured in. Egtvedt and Johnson began a frantic scramble to build more and more B-17s—first in the hundreds, then the thousands. Employment at Boeing's Seattle factories, only 1,755 in 1938, climbed by 1945 to 44,754, a figure that did not include large numbers of other workers at Boeing's subcontractors.

By that time, the B-17 had become famous all over the world under its nickname, the Flying Fortress. From 1942 to 1945, these planes flew many thousands of bombing missions over Germany. Bristling with guns, they shot down two of every three German fighter aircraft that were lost on the Western Front. B-17s suffered heavy casualties themselves, at a rate exceeded in the U.S. military only by the Navy's submarine service. About a third of all Flying Fortresses in the European war were put out of commission by enemy fire.

At the peak of production in June 1944, Boeing was sending B-17s out of its Seattle factory at the rate of one every 90 minutes. Nearly 13,000 of these planes were produced during the war, 55 percent by Boeing, the rest under contract by Douglas and Vega. This was a huge number for so large an aircraft. (The photograph on the cover of this book is of a Douglas Aircraft plant in Long Beach, California, engaged in the manufacture of B-17s.) After the war, the B-17s and their crews were memorialized in such movies as *Twelve O'Clock High* and *Memphis Belle.*

By 1942, Boeing was well into the development of an even bigger airplane, one that turned out to be the most complicated product ever manufactured by American industry up to that time: the B-29 Superfortress bomber. Boeing-designed bombers delivered nearly half of all the tonnage dropped by the Air Corps in Europe during the war, and more than 99 percent of the payload in Japan. Most of the bombs dropped on Japan were carried by B-

29s, including the firebombs that devastated Tokyo and the atomic bombs that fell on Hiroshima and Nagasaki. By the standards of the day the Superfortress was an enormous aircraft, three times the weight of the B-17. Designed specifically as a long-range bomber, it could fly almost 6,000 miles without refueling. By mid-1945, almost 4,000 B-29s had been built, two-thirds by Boeing, one-sixth each by Glenn Martin and Bell. When the war ended in August 1945, an additional 5,000 B-29s were still on order, because American planners had expected the conflict in the Pacific to continue until 1947. Most of those planes on order were never built.

Canceled government contracts created severe management problems for Boeing, as well as for Douglas and other large defense firms. Phil Johnson, the talented manager who served as Boeing's president, had died suddenly in 1944, and the abilities of his old partner Clair Egtvedt lay primarily in design and not administration. Now the direction of the company devolved on William Allen (1900–1985), who had been Boeing's principal legal counsel.

Allen's most daunting postwar challenge was simply to keep the company going. Many other high-tech firms were sliding downhill—laying off workers, closing plants, and losing design engineers. Boeing's employment numbers also dropped drastically, but Bill Allen was determined not to let his company disintegrate. Gambling that the airline industry was about to enter a period of expansion, he directed that large passenger planes be constructed even though he had no orders from customers in hand. He bet that Boeing's 377 "Stratocruiser," a state-of-the-art airliner adapted from a wartime design, could be sold in enough volume for the company to stay afloat. In the end Boeing lost money on this model, but Allen managed to keep the firm's superb engineering and production team together.

Meanwhile, the demands of the Cold War were causing planners at the Pentagon to rethink the nation's strategy for air warfare. The result, in the late 1940s and early 1950s, was the commissioning of a series of medium-sized to very large jet bombers. Boeing, consistently looking ahead, won the contracting competition for most of these planes and began to produce a series of ultramodern swept-wing bombers.

Beginning in 1947, more than 1,300 of its B-47 Stratojets were built, mostly by Boeing itself. Then, in 1952, came the company's eight-engine B-52 Stratofortress. Like the B-47, it was designed to carry either conventional or nuclear weapons, and it became the backbone of the Strategic Air Command. (The B-52 is the plane featured in *Dr. Strangelove,* a Hollywood spoof of the Cold War, widely regarded as one of the greatest films ever made.) In all, Boeing delivered to the Air Force about 750 B-52s, and they played an important role not only in the Strategic Air Command but also during the Vietnam War, the Gulf War of 1991, and the NATO bombing campaign against Yugoslavia in 1999. Hundreds of B-52s were still flying at the start of the twenty-first century. No new ones had been built for several decades, but many had been modified to minimize their detection by radar, carry cruise missiles, and fly longer distances.

The technological advances that accompanied successive moves in design and production from the B-17 to the B-29 to the B-47 to the B-52—in just over a decade—were quite remarkable. The B-52 weighed 12 times as much as the 40,000-pound B-17. At a top speed of 650 miles per hour, it flew twice as fast, and its range of 10,000 miles was more than three times as long. These increased capabilities required a series of scientific and engineering breakthroughs not only in aviation, but also in metallurgy, electronics, and other fields.

Unlike innovations in some defense-related industries, much of the new aerospace technology was transferable to the civilian market. Boeing adapted well, and it became the largest producer of commercial airliners in the world. It overtook the previous leader, Douglas, partly because its quicker move into passenger jets had been facilitated by its experience in building the B-47 and B-52 bombers.

In 1954 Boeing launched its four-engine 707 passenger jet, which quickly became the workhorse of airlines in many countries. Still newer models rolled out of Seattle in regular succession: in 1963 came the 727; in 1967 the 737; in 1969 the 747 (an immense plane, 50 percent heavier than the B-52); in 1982 the more fuel-efficient 757 and 767; and in 1997 the 777, the most sophisticated civilian aircraft ever built up to that time. These planes sold well domestically and in world markets as well. By the 1980s and 1990s Boeing had taken its place among America's leading exporters. In some years it ranked as the number-one exporter among all companies across all industries.

But Boeing's experience during these years was anything but smooth. The aircraft business has always been cyclical, even without the wild distortions from war to peacetime production. Modern airplanes represent very large capital investments, and because the planes are so durable, airline companies can easily postpone new purchases in the short term. Therefore the history of the industry has been characterized by fluctuating demand, cash-flow crises, and canceled or postponed orders for new planes.

In the late 1960s, toward the end of Bill Allen's presidency, Boeing once again approached financial disaster, because of uneven orders for the 747. Allen's successor, Thornton Wilson, took office in 1970 and slashed the company's workforce from 105,000 to 38,000. Eventually Boeing recovered and went on to great prosperity, acquiring other firms in the process. But it is significant that Douglas, Lockheed, Boeing, and other successful defense-related companies had to be bailed out at various times during the postwar era by emergency federal loans or purchases. For reasons related to the cyclical and capital-intensive nature of the business, Boeing's chief competitor at the close of the century was the formidable Airbus Industrie, a consortium funded in part by the governments of several countries in the European Union.

Business-government cooperation in high-tech industries ebbed and flowed during the years after World War II, but it never disappeared. Some of the most important industries of the Third Industrial Revolution found it hard to prosper without the benefit of either patent protection or government assistance, or both. Aerospace was one of them. Others included electronics and chemicals, which will be discussed in later chapters. The growth of these science-based industries—driven by heavy research and development in companies and universities and funded partly by government—was one of the many legacies of the twentieth century's most important event.

Right: Henry Ford and his first car, the "quadricycle" of 1896. From the collections of Henry Ford Museum & Greenfield Village and Ford Motor Company.

Below: The first Ford "factory," on Mack Avenue in Detroit, 1903. From the collections of Henry Ford Museum & Greenfield Village and Ford Motor Company.

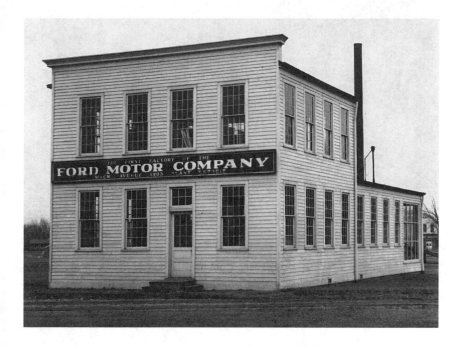

THE FIRST FACTORY OF THE
FORD MOTOR COMPANY
MACK AVENUE 1903 PLANT DETROIT

Opposite top: Henry Ford and his son Edsel with the original quadricycle and the 15 millionth Model T, late 1920s. Baker Library, Harvard Business School and Ford Motor Company.

Opposite bottom: Ford's immense River Rouge industrial complex, whose construction began in the 1920s. Iron ore and hundreds of other raw materials went into "The Rouge," and completed cars came out. From the collections of Henry Ford Museum & Greenfield Village and Ford Motor Company.

Top: Ford assembly line workers polishing freshly painted auto bodies, early 1930s. From the collections of Henry Ford Museum & Greenfield Village and Ford Motor Company.

PONTIAC

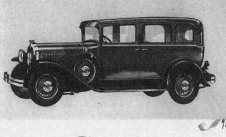

THE New Pontiac Big Six, built by Oakland, exemplifies the value offered in General Motors products—providing a car of exceptional beauty, performance, comfort and size at prices ranging from $745 to $895

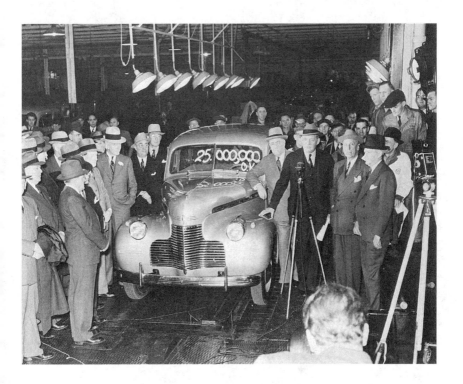

Opposite top: The brilliant Alfred P. Sloan, Jr., of General Motors, still thin as a rail at age 52. This picture was taken in 1927, the year in which competitive pressure from General Motors finally forced Henry Ford to shut down his giant factories and retool for his new Model A. Corbis/ Bettmann-UPI.

Opposite bottom: The 1929 Pontiac, created by Sloan and his team to complete the GM line of nameplates on an ascending scale of price and prestige: first Chevrolet, next Pontiac, then on to Oldsmobile, Buick, and, at the top, Cadillac—"a car for every purse and purpose," as GM's 1929 "Spring Showing" trade catalogue advertised the line. The original Pontiac advertisement was in full color: the car silver with red trim, the flowers pink, yellow, and lavender. GM automobiles were available in many colors and with annual model changes to encourage consumers to trade in as well as upgrade. Sloan's emphasis on this kind of aspirational marketing, in addition to his internal reorganization of the company, led to GM's defeat of Ford in the epic battle for market share. Courtesy of General Motors Corporation and Baker Library, Harvard Business School.

Top: The 25 millionth Chevrolet, which rolled off the line in 1940. Alfred Sloan is in this picture, but, typically, so are many other members of GM's management team, plus a number of workers. Sloan is in the front row, second from right. Corbis/Bettmann.

Red Deupree, the longtime president of Procter & Gamble who cut his own salary in half during the early years of the Great Depression. Courtesy of The Procter & Gamble Company.

The resourceful Doc Smelser, who headed P&G's elite Market Research Department for 34 years. Courtesy of The Procter & Gamble Company.

Top: One of Doc Smelser's 3,000 door-to-door interviewers, calling on a consumer as part of P&G's ceaseless market research, 1940s. Courtesy of The Procter & Gamble Company.

Bottom: A large cast delivering P&G's soap opera "The Guiding Light" over NBC radio, circa 1940. This program began in 1937, moved to television in 1952, and was still on the air at the start of the 21st century. Courtesy of The Procter & Gamble Company.

Opposite top: Neil McElroy, whose now famous memo of 1931 inaugurated Procter & Gamble's strategy of "brand management," a technique later adopted by scores of consumer-products companies throughout the world. Courtesy of The Procter & Gamble Company.

Opposite bottom: During World War II, P&G like many other consumer-products companies produced munitions as well. Here a P&G employee inspects shells that have just been loaded with powder. Courtesy of The Procter & Gamble Company.

Top: Like Ford Motor Co. and nearly all other big businesses, Boeing had modest beginnings. Here is its first home in Seattle, under military guard during World War I. Used with the permission of The Boeing Company.

Overleaf top: Boeing employees stitching fabric onto the wingframe of a biplane for the U.S. Army, 1922. Used with the permission of The Boeing Company.

Overleaf bottom: Boeing's B-17 bomber, the famous Flying Fortress of World War II. Used with the permission of The Boeing Company.

CHAPTER SIX

Overview: African Americans in Business

Still another legacy of World War II was the beginning of a revolution in race relations. Large numbers of African Americans served in all of the armed forces during the war. They were often restricted to segregated units, but their major role in both military action abroad and industrial mobilization at home constituted a milestone in their long quest for equal opportunity. President Harry Truman's executive order to integrate the armed forces, which he issued in 1948, signalled the beginning of the end of legal segregation in the United States. Over the next two decades, a combination of judicial decisions and federal legislation struck down barriers in education, public accommodations, and, finally, employment. Although much remained to be done at the start of the twenty-first century, more progress had been made during the last part of the twentieth than in any other period since the end of legal slavery in 1865.

As businesspeople, African Americans had a long history of entrepreneurship, beginning well before the Civil War. Historically, most black enterprises, like most firms owned by women, had been small, undercapitalized, and in constant danger of insolvency.

Then the early twentieth century brought what some writers have called a "golden age" of black business, as greater numbers of African Americans started companies and a few became millionaires. Between 1900 and 1930 the number of black-owned enterprises increased by 700 percent. Like many women-owned businesses that served women, most black-owned firms targeted African-American consumers. The same was true of other ethnic minorities, whose enterprises often catered to the needs and likes of their own groups.

During the early decades of the century, blacks had achieved notable success in banks and insurance companies that served the black community, and, as the story of Madame C. J. Walker attests, in the hair-care and beauty-aids business. A survey done in 1944 concluded that six types of black-owned firms predominated at that time: beauty parlors, barber shops, restaurants, small grocery stores, shoe-repair shops, and funeral homes.

The question of whether black entrepreneurs should focus on black customers was, and still remains, a controversial issue that cuts across the political spectrum. From the formation of Booker T. Washington's "conservative" National Negro Business League in 1900 to the emergence of the "radical" Nation of Islam 60 years later, such a strategy seemed to be a viable formula for self-help. The African-American intellectual W. E. B. DuBois, who disagreed with Booker T. Washington on many other strategies for black progress, once argued that "Ten million people who join in intelligent self-help can never be long ignored or mistreated." Business was particularly important for advancement because "No race that has anything to contribute to the markets of the world is long in any degree ostracized." DuBois and others acknowledged that for black entrepreneurs to cater only to members of their own race put them at a disadvantage, by targeting a less affluent segment of the population and therefore limiting possibilities for business growth.

During the last decades of the twentieth century, this question acquired an additional dimension. The number of African Americans graduating from college approximately doubled between 1970 and 2000, and a much higher percentage of these graduates entered business than had been the case earlier. (This transformation had many subtexts. Between 1912 and 1938, for example, 73 percent of black college graduates had become either teachers or ministers, because management positions in white-owned businesses were foreclosed to them. Those restrictions did not change very much until the 1970s.) Because of the big increase in college graduates, the black middle class grew very much larger after 1970. At the same time, an economic irony began to appear. Middle-class black consumers became more integrated into the white-dominated mainstream of American business, and therefore less likely to spend their money at traditionally black-owned enterprises. This trend had the unintended consequence of diminishing the relative economic and social status of thousands of local black business leaders. At the start of the twenty-first century, African Americans owned nearly half a million firms. Yet on a per-capita basis, blacks were less than a third as likely to own a business as were whites. The receipts of black-owned firms made up about 1 percent of the national total, even though African Americans comprised 12 percent of the population.

Still, there had been substantial progress in particular sectors. During the twentieth century as a whole, the most important black-owned firms were in the insurance industry. The North Carolina Mutual Life Insurance Company, founded in 1898, attracted first-rate talent and by 1920 already employed 1,100 people. A second major firm, Atlanta Life Insurance, was established in 1905 by Alonzo Herndon, a former slave who had made his seed money in the barber shop business. Other big companies included Supreme Life Insurance (Chicago, 1921), United Mutual Life Insurance (New York, 1933), and Golden State Mutual (Los Angeles, important especially in the 1960s because of its innovations in group sales). By 1960, 46 black-owned insurance companies were in operation, and in 1971 North Carolina Mutual had more than $1 billion of insurance in force. By the 1990s, after a series of mergers, 19 black-owned companies had in force $23 billion of insurance.

During the closing decades of the century, black *incomes* had risen very significantly as a percentage of white incomes. But gains in accumulated *wealth* came more slowly. In 1984, black households had a median net worth only one-twelfth that of white households, and 15 years later this figure had not changed by much. Yet by that time several thousand African Americans had become extraordinarily wealthy through careers in business, entertainment, and professional sports; and this situation was unprecedented in American history.

Entrepreneurs

As late as the mid-1990s only 15 black-owned firms had more than 500 employees. Even so, major black-owned enterprises had succeeded in a wide variety of industries. One of the best-known companies was Motown Records, founded in the 1960s by Berry Gordy, scion of a prominent Detroit family. With sales of $61 million, Motown was America's largest black-owned nonfinancial firm in 1977 and number two in 1985, when its sales reached $149 million. In 1988 the company was sold to MCA Records, and black America suffered a symbolic loss.

Another large firm was Johnson Publishing, which put out *Jet* and *Ebony* magazines and was also involved in radio, real estate, insurance, and beauty products. From the 1970s until the end of the century this company ranked either number one or number two among nonfinancial firms owned by African Americans. The brainchild of John Johnson, perhaps the leading black entrepreneur of his time, Johnson Publishing had sales of $50 million in 1977 and $361 million in 1997.

A third prominent entrepreneur was Reginald Lewis, founder of the TLC Group, a conglomerate that in 1987 engineered a $985 million leveraged buyout of Beatrice International Foods, a company doing most of its business overseas. Lewis thereby created the largest black-owned business in American history; his published autobiography was entitled *Why Should White Guys Have All the Fun?* In 1993 he died of a brain tumor at the age of 50. His wife, Loida Nicolas Lewis, then ran the firm for several years, gradually selling off all of its disparate parts by 1999.

The black-owned H. J. Russell Construction Company of Atlanta built numerous large structures in that city during the closing decades of the twentieth century. These included the Equitable Life Assurance Building, the Carter Presidential Center, the Martin Luther King, Jr. Community Center, the Atlanta City Hall Complex, and, together with another black-owned firm, the principal stadium for the 1996 Olympic Games.

One of the most influential black entrepreneurs was Oprah Winfrey, the actor and TV talk-show host. In addition to her work before the camera, Winfrey founded the Harpo Production Company to create films and television programs, and she sponsored Oprah's Book Club, whose listed titles were almost guaranteed best-seller status. Winfrey's male counterpart in many similar roles was Bill Cosby, the entertainer and philanthropist. Cosby was co-owner of the Philadelphia Coca-Cola Bottling Company, which during the 1990s was the third largest black-owned business after TLC Beatrice and the John Johnson publishing group. The first black-owned cable TV system, Black Entertainment Television (BET) was founded in 1980 by Robert L. Johnson. By 1990 it offered 24-hour programming to 27 million households through 2,200 cable systems in the United States, Puerto Rico, and the Virgin Islands.

In many cities, enterprises of all types owned by African Americans and other minorities benefited from "set-aside" programs begun in 1967 by the U.S. Small Business Administration. These programs specified that a certain percentage of government contracts must be awarded to minority-owned companies. By the 1980s, set-aside contracts were exceeding $2 billion annually. A Supreme Court decision of 1989 cut back on set-aside requirements for projects funded by state and local governments, but the mandates remained a useful promotional device in federal contracts, where they accounted for almost $4 billion in funding by 1990. Federal loans and grants made to businesses owned by African Americans and other minorities grew from $200 million in 1969 to $7 billion in 1991. These firms sold only $83 million in goods and services to the government in 1969, but $17 billion by 1991. (The numbers are in current dollars, not adjusted for inflation.)

Belated Admittance into Big Business

Only in the late twentieth century did predominantly white corporate America begin to give blacks the chance to compete for high-level positions in large firms. One milestone was the appointment in 1957 of the former baseball star Jackie Robinson as vice-president of the food-service company Chock Full O'Nuts. This event is usually regarded as the first occasion of an African American's acceptance into the ranks of top management in a large and predominantly white firm. Yet even during the 1960s and 1970s, when blacks began to be hired as executives in greater numbers, they were often placed in staff departments of human resources, community relations, and public affairs rather than in front-line positions in production and marketing.

In 1987, Clifton R. Wharton, Jr., became the first African-American CEO of a *Fortune* 500 company, TIAA-CREF. In 1995, Noel Hord was named CEO of the Nine West shoe manufacturing company. These examples remained rare, and African Americans' ascent up the hierarchical ladder in big companies was not particularly rapid. Although reliable research on this subject has been sparse, one obvious explanation is that blacks did not gain significant access to the most elite colleges and universities until late in the game.

But even the few blacks who did attend the nation's best schools often found the going rough after graduation. H. Naylor Fitzhugh, for example, who earned degrees at both Harvard College (class of 1931) and the Harvard Business School (1933), was turned away by one prospective employer after another when he entered the job market. Fitzhugh then went into the printing industry, becoming an independent salesman in Washington, D.C. In addition to his own work, he established the New Negro Alliance, through which he persuaded firms operating in mostly African-American neighborhoods to hire local residents. In another initiative, he began what became a 30-year relationship with Howard University, where he was instrumental in establishing a marketing department and organizing the school's Small Business Center. In 1965, some 32 years after receiving his Harvard MBA, Fitzhugh was finally hired by a leading firm, PepsiCo. There he developed an innovative marketing campaign directed specifically at African Americans, who constituted a very significant block of potential consumers. By the time of his death in 1992, Fitzhugh had served as a mentor to scores of other African Americans making their way in the business world.

African Americans' access to the best colleges and universities increased markedly during the last three decades of the twentieth century. While these new opportunities helped some black students a great deal, by no means did graduation from even a prestigious institution assure them of equal treatment in major American firms. African Americans' sometimes slow progress up the corporate ladder was analyzed in an important study by David A. Thomas and John J. Gabarro, published in 1999. They found that because of deep-seated (and often subtle) racism, African-American and other minority recruits in large firms usually had to pay a "tax" in the form of additional time spent proving themselves in entry-level positions as compared to the time spent by white recruits. Once the "tax" was paid—and it frequently had to be paid not only at the entry level but for positions at the next couple of tiers as well—minority executives ascended the corporate ladder at higher levels as rapidly as others. But in the meantime, precious and unrecoverable years had been lost to minority executives' careers.

Outside the culture of big business, African Americans were sometimes less likely to be hindered by the reluctance of supervisors to recommend timely advancement. In a few fields in which comparative ability could be unmistakably identified, such as professional sports and entertainment, blacks were sometimes overrepresented relative to their proportion of the population. African Americans also succeeded in reaching the very highest ranks in the U.S. military, the one large organization that had devoted several decades to systematic efforts toward the achievement of racial equality. By contrast, big businesses in the early twenty-first century still needed to figure out how better to welcome into the high reaches of management not only African Americans, but also other minorities, and women of all races.

CHAPTER SEVEN

Toward a Peak
of Prosperity, 1945–1973:
RCA and Color TV

World War II had provided an initial impetus for the social revolution that began to bring African Americans, other minorities, and women into the mainstream of business. In American life generally, the war was followed by a distinctive 28-year period of rapid social change occurring within a framework of two great constants. First, the era was one of unusual prosperity, punctuated only occasionally by recessions. The second constant was the Cold War, which dominated certain aspects of American culture and directly affected numerous businesses.

From the beginning of World War II until 1973, real per-capita Gross National Product grew at the very healthy compound annual rate of 3 percent. By comparison, the rate from 1890 until World War II had been only 1.2 percent; from 1973 to 2000 it was a little over 2 percent. These apparently small differences in growth rates have big long-run consequences. At a compound rate of 3 percent, per-capita income will double in 24 years, whereas at 2 percent it will double in 36 years, and at 1 percent in 72 years.

A few national economies recorded even faster postwar growth rates, but on the whole the American business system outperformed all others. From the end of the war until the 1960s, output per hour worked in the United States remained more than twice that of most other industrialized nations, and many times that of developing countries. With about one-sixteenth of the world's population, the United States was accounting for two-fifths of its gross production of goods and services.

Nearly every index showed a positive trend. About 40 percent of American families had owned their homes in the decades before World War II, but this number grew to 53 percent in 1950 and to 62 percent by 1970. Thus a key aspect of the "American Dream" had now come true for most of the American people. Several million war veterans and their families received low-cost home loans financed through the Veterans Administration. In education, several million former soldiers and sailors took advantage of the G.I. Bill, which provided funds for college tuition, swelled the ranks of undergraduates, and further democratized higher education.

As mentioned, World War II brought millions of people into what became known as the Sunbelt. After the war, the widespread installation of air conditioning gave the region a second great boost, and the resulting shift in population worked some profound changes in the social and political life of the country. Whereas in 1940 only one American in nine had lived in what are now the three most populous states of the Sunbelt—Texas, Florida, and California (most of which lies in the Sunbelt)—one in four did by 1995.

During the 1960s, after a hundred years of net out-migration, the entire South (defined as the states of the 1861–1865 Confederacy) began to attract new residents, a phenomenon that likely would not have occurred without the development of air conditioning. By the middle 1970s, more than 90 percent of southern high-rise office and apartment buildings were air-conditioned, together with half the school classrooms, and two-thirds of the houses and stores. The population of Florida expanded so fast that by the 1990s the state ranked fourth in the nation, up from twenty-fifth place in 1940. While the population of the country as a whole was doubling between 1940 and the end of the century, Florida's jumped by a factor of eight, from fewer than 2 million to more than 15 million.

The advent of jet airliners facilitated travel to the Sunbelt by great masses of tourists. So did the new Interstate Highway System. This costly project was justified in part by a Cold War rationale. (The initial name, "Interstate and Defense," reflected the idea that another war mobilization would require a better infrastructure.) The 300,000 miles of federal highways in 1945 grew to 640,000 by 1950 and to 895,000 by 1970. Much of the new construction was of four-lane, six-lane, and even eight-lane "freeways" paved in expensive concrete, in all constituting the best highway system in the world.

The robust growth of the American economy was mirrored in almost every aspect of business. The end of the wartime freeze on the production of consumer durables, together with an unprecedented new level of consumer purchasing power, led to the release of what was called "pent-up demand." Shopping centers sprang up across the country, and retail sales multiplied. People bought new cars, TV sets, stereos, and air conditioners by the tens of millions. The aggregate power of consumers took another step forward, and advertisers trumpeted the "American Way of Life" as something akin to an ideal existence.

Social Trends

One of the biggest changes from 1945 to 1973 was a 50 percent rise in the U.S. population. For a large advanced industrialized nation, this increase was nothing short of tremendous, and its principal cause was the postwar "baby boom." Whereas 86 out of every 1,000 women of childbearing age had a baby in 1945, the number jumped to 102 in 1946. This upward trend continued to the very high figure of 123 in 1956, after which it began a decline to about the 1945 level. The baby boom had long-term effects on American education, business, culture, and public policy. The "boomers" born between 1945 and 1960 came to be identified with a certain set of characteristics and values, some of which seemed admirable: sophistication, flexible ideology, and commitment to social justice. Other traits alleged to typify the group were less attractive: narcissism, self-indulgence, and questionable morality. The most prominent individual baby boomer turned out to be President Bill Clinton, who was born in 1946.

The other important social transformations of 1945–1973 were the civil rights crusade, which ended legal segregation on the basis of race, and the feminist movement toward equal status for women. Both required the exertion of herculean energies. And while both achieved breakthrough successes, much still remained to be done as the period ended.

Meanwhile, there were some wrenching challenges to several of the institutions that had long held society together: family, school, business, and government. Beginning in the 1960s, each came under attack in campaigns led mostly by baby boomers. Business and government in particular were portrayed as repositories of wrongdoing and bad faith. Because of their long complicity in suppressing the rights of women, African Americans, and others, the indictment against them had more than a little plausibility.

Domestic life during the late 1940s had been relatively placid, and the "Eisenhower Years" of the 1950s were almost serene, despite the birth and immediate popularity of rock music. But the 1960s brought a wave of violence and political assassinations. Among those killed were the civil rights leaders Medgar Evers (1963), Malcolm X (1965), and Dr. Martin Luther King, Jr. (1968), as well as President John F. Kennedy (1963) and his brother, Senator Robert F. Kennedy (1968). Some of the assassinations set off waves of racially charged arson and looting in American cities.

After these tragic events, and after some U.S. government officials were shown to have lied about casualty rates in the Vietnam War (1963–1975) and about crimes committed at the direction of President Richard M. Nixon during the so-called Watergate crisis (1973–1974), many Americans became disenchanted with politics. Patriotism and national pride began to decline. Most people coming of age during this period found it hard to embrace their parents' notion that the United States was a wondrous and blessed place to live. Instead, an informed cynicism appeared to be the only sensible attitude. Many resolved to look out for themselves and to forget the pursuit of causes however noble.

In the face of these social changes, two conditions of overarching importance to American business stayed constant, as noted: (1) continuing economic prosperity, exemplified by an outpouring of consumer goods and the international primacy of American business; and (2) the Cold War between the United States and the Soviet Union, a conflict that remained potentially catastrophic. During the 1950s and 1960s, both countries amassed nuclear arsenals capable of destroying the world. They approached the brink of nuclear war during the Cuban Missile Crisis of 1962.

Sometimes the Cold War became hot, as in the Soviet suppression of liberation movements in Hungary (1956), and Czechoslovakia (1968), and in the American actions during the Korean War (1950–1953) and the Vietnam conflict (1963–1975). Those last two "limited" wars symbolically pitted the "free world" against communism, and cost the lives of about 3 million Asians and more than 100,000 Americans.

Throughout the Cold War, the perceived necessity that the United States maintain a giant military establishment placed heavy demands on the business system to produce high-quality weapons. The three-way alliance of government, higher education, and business that had emerged during World War II now became entrenched. The alliance changed the internal policies of many universities and high-tech companies, and it reshaped the structure of American science and engineering.

The Cold War and the Importance of R&D

For the period 1945–1973, the most prosperous sectors of the economy besides basic consumer goods and new home construction were high-tech industries—particularly aircraft and guided missiles, chemicals and pharmaceuticals, and electronics. These three industries had obvious relevance to the ongoing Cold War, which itself had begun to seem an essential part of the "American Way of Life."

The Cold War presented hard choices to both public officials and business executives. Federal administrators in charge of science policy had to decide how much expenditure on research and development (R&D) would be necessary for the United States to stay ahead of the Soviet Union militarily. Beyond that, they had to determine whether "fundamental" research—that is, work not directly connected to product development—should be conducted only in universities, or in corporate research labs as well. During most of the postwar era, it seemed essential to do fundamental research in both places. Ample federal funding was possible because of national economic prosperity, and the allocation of those monies to research appeared necessary because of the Cold War. Caught up in the struggle with the Soviet Union, the government channeled stupendous sums to both universities and corporations. During the three postwar decades, federal funds underwrote about 70 percent of all research and development done in the electronics industry. Of federally sponsored industrial research as a whole, about 80 percent concerned military applications. In 1950, when the Korean War broke out, about 15,000 military-related research projects of all kinds were underway. By the early 1960s, this number had grown to 80,000.

It was clear that some of the nation's best research talent was gravitating toward military work and away from commercial projects. Many scientists and engineers preferred to devote their careers to defense-related R&D, and the government furnished the necessary funds for companies and universities to pay them well. For better or worse, in the minds of many scientists and engineers it was more exciting to try to develop a hydrogen bomb or land a person on the moon than to invent or improve some everyday consumer product.

The nation's preoccupation with military-related projects hurt the commercial divisions of some science-based companies slightly, others much more seriously. Into this second category fell much of the American consumer-electronics industry. Over the course of the twentieth century, its story is one of impressive and long-running success, followed by a drift into a series of distractions at the expense of discovering and responding to what consumers wanted.

Television and David Sarnoff

Until the 1970s, U.S. firms led the world in consumer electronics. American companies brought forth a steady output of affordable radios, phonographs, black-and-white television sets, and finally color TVs. Experts everywhere assumed that American companies would remain on top for a long time, perhaps forever. But those firms lost more than just their primacy. After having been almost unchallenged before the 1960s, they fell behind their European and Japanese competitors during the 1970s and 1980s, and succumbed altogether by the 1990s.

Both the rise and fall of the U.S. consumer electronics industry are reflected in the story of the Radio Corporation of America (RCA) and its charismatic leader David Sarnoff (1891–1971). That story also suggests how intimately the American government was involved in science-based industries throughout the century— as customer, protector, promoter, and regulator.

In the spring of 1945, just returned from Army service, David Sarnoff gathered his top managers together and told them that "RCA has one priority: television. Whatever resources are needed will be provided." He intended that RCA be the leader in television sets, tubes, transmitters, components, and research and development. "There's a vast market out there, and we're going to capture it before anyone else."

RCA had begun its TV research in the 1920s. Then, during the depression of the 1930s, when most companies reduced discretionary spending as much as possible, Sarnoff stepped up RCA's efforts. By 1936 the firm had built a series of TV relay stations between a transmitter atop the Empire State Building in New York City and its research labs in Camden, New Jersey. In 1939, Sarnoff decided to showcase RCA's progress in TV at the World's Fair in New York. His demonstration came off well, and an RCA subsidiary began to fill eight to twelve hours of airtime per week with televised baseball games, boxing matches, plays, and variety shows. RCA put its sets on the market at prices ranging from $395 to $675.

These efforts to develop television during the 1930s turned out to be premature. The average annual per-capita income in 1939 was less than $700, and few families could afford to buy a TV set. But the fundamental problem went even deeper. TV was a *systems* innovation. It required a regular schedule of programming, mass sales of sets, industry-wide standards for broadcasting and equipment manufacture, and facilities for repairing and adjusting the many things that could go wrong with sets and with home TV reception. These systems did not yet exist, and the times were not propitious for their quick development. Government regulators, seeing how fast the technology was changing, delayed until mid-1941 the setting of standards for the industry to follow. In December of that year the United States entered World War II, and in April 1942 the federal government banned further commercial development of television. David Sarnoff and RCA would have to wait.

Sarnoff's Talents

In 1975, *Fortune* magazine inaugurated a "Hall of Fame for Business Leadership." The magazine selected 15 charter inductees, including John D. Rockefeller, Andrew Carnegie, J. Pierpont Morgan, Henry Ford, Alfred Sloan, and ten others. One of these ten was Sarnoff, who as head of RCA for nearly forty years did more than any other person to bring radio and television into the American home.

Sarnoff had risen from the deep poverty of a Jewish village in Russia. In 1895, when he was four years old, his father, Abraham, emigrated from Russia to New York, temporarily leaving the family behind. A few years later, once they reassembled in a $10-per-month slum tenement on New York's Lower East Side, young David went to work almost immediately to help support the family. He sold Yiddish newspapers for a penny a copy and earned $1.50 per week singing as a boy soprano at a synagogue. Meanwhile, he received instruction in English, which he learned to speak with grace and without an accent.

David dropped out of school after the eighth grade because of his family's continuing need for money. He found a messenger's job at the American Marconi Company, a subsidiary of the English firm set up by Guglielmo Marconi, the young Italian inventor of wireless telegraphy. Sarnoff soon became one of the firm's quickest "fists" at the telegraph key, and he rose rapidly within the organization. He made it a point to shepherd Marconi around New York during the inventor's frequent visits, and the two became good friends.

At the age of 20, Sarnoff took over the Marconi station at Wanamaker's Department Store in New York, a radiotelegraph facility set up to attract curious shoppers. Not long afterward, on an April night in 1912, the *Titanic* struck an iceberg in the North Atlantic and began to sink. Suddenly the air was filled with signals sent out from the sinking ship, from rescue vessels, and from amateur radio operators up and down the East Coast. The moment Sarnoff heard the news about the *Titanic*, he rushed to Wanamaker's, where he stayed at his radio for 72 hours. He was not able to accomplish much, but a story soon arose portraying a heroic young David picking up the S.O.S., making order out of the cacophony of signals, and passing along critical information about who had died and who had survived.

However misleading the legend, which was concocted by Sarnoff himself and retold in many future magazine profiles, the *Titanic* disaster "brought radio to the front, and incidentally me." After the incident Congress passed a law requiring large passenger ships to install wireless communications. The business of American Marconi grew rapidly, and the company gave its young operator new responsibilities and a raise in pay.

Only a few years later, barely out of his teens, Sarnoff began to transform himself into the business dandy he would remain for the rest of his life. Five feet seven with a round baby face, he affected tailored suits, a Homburg, and a walking stick. By the 1920s, after he had become a power at RCA, he was smoking expensive cigars throughout the day, and by the 1930s he was traveling around New York strictly by limousine. His staff of retainers came to include a masseuse and a barber, who worked on him daily in a private room off his opulent headquarters. Sarnoff possessed a biting wit, and he could lose his temper in a hurry. "I don't get ulcers," he liked to say. "I give them."

His characteristic bravado was backed by a keen appreciation of technology and a sense of its potential in creating new business opportunities. When he became general manager of RCA in 1921, he was only 30, but he had already worked in electronics for 14 years. In a 1928 speech at the Harvard Business School, Sarnoff described the role of a new kind of executive, one able to develop high-tech products and bring them to market. This new-model manager, like Sarnoff himself, would have a personal understanding of technology, a good idea of where both it and market forces were headed, and an ability to meld the two.

Sarnoff entered the Army Signal Corps during World War II and received a colonel's commission. He spent most of his time in London, serving as Dwight Eisenhower's adviser on communications in connection with the invasion of Europe. In December 1944, after relentless lobbying, he got himself promoted to brigadier general. Three weeks later, he went on inactive duty and returned to RCA. Enthralled by honors and titles, he afterward insisted on being called "General."

The Birth of Broadcasting

Sarnoff's life coincided almost exactly with the development of radio and television. He knew every important person in the industry from Marconi onward. He often commented that he was lucky to have been born at just the right time and to have decided in his youth to "hitch my wagon to the electron."

In his early years, radio's primary role was expected to be "point-to-point" transmission, as in ship-to-ship and ship-to-shore telegraph. As the young Sarnoff sent and received these signals on behalf of American Marconi, he began to speculate that the industry's real future might lie in "point-to-mass" communication, or what came to be called "broadcasting" on the electromagnetic spectrum. A memorandum he sent to his Marconi superiors, dated 1915, anticipated modern radio operations:

The idea is to bring music into the house by wireless . . . all the receivers attuned to the transmitting wave length should be capable of receiving such music. The receiver can be designed in the form of a simple "Radio Music Box" and arranged for several different wave lengths, which should be changeable . . . [and] supplied with amplifying tubes and a loudspeaking telephone, all of which can be neatly mounted in one box. The box can be placed on a table in the parlor or living room, the switch set accordingly, and the transmitted music received.

Sarnoff's Radio Music Box memo received little attention, mainly because the Marconi firm was so busy with defense work that it couldn't handle much else. But throughout World War I (1914–1918), the radio industry was propelled forward by the urgent communication needs of armies and navies on both sides of the battle lines. Throughout Europe and in the laboratories of American companies such as American Telephone & Telegraph (AT&T), Westinghouse, and General Electric (GE), radio research was pursued vigorously. Because American Marconi was a foreign-owned corporation, at the end of the war the Navy asked GE, the leading domestic electrical manufacturer, to help set up a U.S. company to take charge of wireless communication for both business and government. That new company became RCA. The Navy contributed its own array of electronics patents to be combined with those of GE and other firms, to create for RCA a workable *pool* of inventions. These in turn would form the basis for future research and development in all areas of electronics.

In 1919, after prolonged negotiations, the Marconi company withdrew from the field, selling its stock for $3.5 million to the consortium of American firms (mostly GE and Westinghouse) that owned the new RCA. David Sarnoff, 28 years old at the time, became one of RCA's key executives as soon as it was formed and shortly thereafter was made its general manager.

During the months of deal making that led to RCA's creation, a Westinghouse engineer operating from his house in Pittsburgh had begun as a hobby to send out radio signals of recorded music. Soon he began receiving letters from enthusiasts who picked up the signals on their home-made "crystal sets," as early radios were called. A Westinghouse executive, sensing the market potential, asked the Department of Commerce for a license to broadcast. Thus in 1920 was born KDKA of Pittsburgh, America's first commercial radio station. Suddenly electronics executives in several companies realized that a rich market might be exploited with a relatively small investment.

Sarnoff viewed the emergence of KDKA with some unease. But he saw that Westinghouse's initiative had not yet foreclosed the opportunity for RCA and its chief parent, General Electric, to dominate the industry. Radio, like television later on, required several elements to make it commercially viable. These included sets to receive signals, a distribution structure to market the sets, stations to broadcast programs, and a reliable source of funds to produce programs. None of the elements was yet in place. So Sarnoff resurrected his 1915 Radio Music Box memo and sent it to the headquarters of GE, where it was taken quite seriously.

Sarnoff also decided to make a personal splash by arranging to broadcast a live account of the biggest sporting event of 1921, the boxing match between heavyweight champion Jack Dempsey and French challenger Georges Carpentier. Acting on behalf of RCA, Sarnoff commandeered a GE transmitter, moved it to the Jersey City site of the match, and hired an announcer. The broadcast went off without serious problems, at least for the brief time it lasted. Dempsey knocked out Carpentier in the fourth round, which was lucky for Sarnoff, because a moment later the GE radio transmitter went up in smoke. But by that time 300,000 Americans had already heard the broadcast, most of them in movie theaters whose owners Sarnoff had persuaded to join the hookup.

In the months after the big fight, Sarnoff began to organize the first radio network, which was to be a subsidiary of RCA. Here he ran into a serious dispute with AT&T, which had started to put together its own system of stations. But AT&T, as the existing telephone monopoly, was in a disadvantageous political position, and in 1926 an arbitrator worked out a resolution of the dispute along lines favorable to RCA. Under his ruling the ownership of a new firm called the National Broadcasting Company (NBC) would be divided among RCA (50 percent), GE (30 percent), and Westinghouse (20 percent). AT&T would exit broadcasting, and its affiliated stations would go to RCA and be networked under the name NBC Red. RCA's existing stations, together with those of Westinghouse and General Electric, would be networked as NBC Blue. All of the new affiliates tapped a central feed in New York, then used telephone lines leased from AT&T to carry signals to distant stations from which they could be broadcast over local airwaves. (In 1941, at the request of the U.S. government, RCA divested NBC Blue, which then became the basis for ABC, the American Broadcasting Company. NBC Red became simply NBC.)

In the mid-1920s a competing network, the Columbia Broadcasting System (CBS), had been organized under the leadership of a young entrepreneur named Bill Paley, and the number of radio stations began to increase rapidly. The country had only one station in 1921, but by 1940 there were 850. As the increase continued, the number of stations reached 2,800 by 1950, then, accelerated by the rapid spread of FM stations, reached 9,400 by 1990. But even as early as the 1930s a majority of American households had a radio set. On December 8, 1941, almost the entire nation tuned in to hear President Roosevelt ask Congress to declare war after the Japanese attack on Pearl Harbor.

The Rise of RCA

David Sarnoff proved especially adept at absorbing insights from wars and other major events. The lesson he took from World War I was that a central authority—in this case the U.S. Navy—could impose order on a chaotic new industry. By asserting its power and helping to get the required legislation, the Navy had been able to allocate radio frequencies, sponsor R&D, and sort out conflicting claims of inventors.

In the early days of radio, the signals that operators transmitted often overlapped each other's frequencies, turning much wireless "communication" into gibberish. Obviously, it was going to be necessary to earmark certain parts of the electromagnetic spectrum for certain purposes, and perhaps to license its overall use. But what principles should guide the allocation? Who should make the decisions? And, in regard to the equally important issue of equipment manufacture, how could the competing claims of rival inventors and operators be reconciled?

Given America's nonstatist traditions, it seemed inappropriate for the government to assume complete charge of radio, as happened in many other countries. Somehow, a nongovernmental organization would have to take over the Navy's role in radio once World War I ended. It was largely for this purpose that the Radio Corporation of America had been organized. The selection of

RCA as inheritor of the Navy's technology typified the flexibility of business-government relations that had been evident throughout American history. The arrangement took what had been a government monopoly and lodged it in the hands of this new company owned by a consortium of private firms that otherwise would have competed with each other.

During the 1920s the potential for great profits attracted hundreds of companies to radio. Sets at first sold for prices ranging from $25 to $500 (the latter figure the equivalent of several thousand dollars in the early twenty-first century). By 1923 more than 200 manufacturers of radio sets and 5,000 makers of components had entered the market. From 1923 to 1934, 1,070 additional companies began to manufacture sets, but 960 of them failed or were absorbed by competitors. For its part, RCA marketed sets, parts, and vacuum tubes, all of which were manufactured by its parent GE. Of these products, tubes were by far the most important. Without them there would have been no home radios except crystal sets, no sound movies, and no broadcasting networks. Much like transistors in the 1950s and 1960s, and microchips in the 1980s and 1990s, vacuum tubes were incorporated into more and more applications as they became progressively smaller and less expensive to produce.

RCA had been created in part to manage communications from ship to shore and from American stations to those overseas. Its other function was to market equipment made by General Electric. But by the mid-1920s it was encountering a whirlwind of other business problems, all of which had to be managed simultaneously. Sarnoff found himself under intense pressure from a variety of sources. Competitors were unhappy with RCA's exclusive pool of electronics patents from its parent companies and the Navy. Federal regulators believed that RCA was trying to monopolize the electronics industry. And certain executives at GE regarded RCA as an uppity child and Sarnoff himself as a brazen young Jew encroaching on what had long been a preserve of white Anglo-Saxon Protestants. Sarnoff's salvation came from his own obvious talents and the patronage of Owen D. Young, the officer of

General Electric who had selected Sarnoff to be RCA's general manager back in 1921. Young was also a nationally prominent lawyer whose name was often mentioned as a potential presidential candidate.

It was testament to Sarnoff's abilities that he managed this situation with such resourcefulness that both he and RCA came out on top. He solved the maelstrom of problems by taking three strategic steps:

1. As noted earlier, he brought order to the broadcasting side of the business by organizing NBC, the first network.

2. On the manufacturing side, he worked out a plan not to fight those who infringed RCA's patents but instead to license these patents to all comers on a nonexclusive basis. This would remove the temptation to infringe in the first place, and at the same time provide RCA with an income stream from royalties. In the beginning, RCA charged 7.5 percent of each company's retail sales of the licensed item, then reduced the figure over the next few decades to 1.5 percent. From the middle 1920s until the patents began to expire (and new ones came along regularly), more than 90 percent of American radios were manufactured under RCA licenses. Sarnoff plowed much of the income back into research and development.

3. The third strategic step was achieving independence from RCA's corporate owners. In 1928, Sarnoff closed an agreement with Joseph P. Kennedy (the millionaire father of the future President) to set up Radio-Keith-Orpheum (RKO) motion pictures, which absorbed the new movie technology into an existing organizational structure from vaudeville days. In 1929, through a merger with the Victor Company, a leading manufacturer of phonograph sets, Sarnoff created RCA Victor, which he then turned into a phonograph record company as well. In January of 1930, still only 39 years of age, he was made president of RCA, again with the support of Owen D. Young.

Throughout the 1920s, Sarnoff became more convinced that RCA must break free of its owners so that it could act faster in the face of changing technology. As he said years later, "We were submerged under too many layers of electrical company management." He could never have detached RCA from its parents by himself, but at just the right moment he received decisive assistance from the government. In 1930, the Antitrust Division of the Justice Department brought a lawsuit against RCA, General Electric, Westinghouse, and AT&T. The suit charged that the original electronics patent pool, plus the cross-licensing agreements, leased telephone lines, and other arrangements that bound the companies together, were illegal under the Sherman Antitrust Act.

This case threatened the existence of RCA, and executives within the defendant companies disagreed vehemently about whether to fight the government's charges or try to work out a settlement. In a series of negotiations guided by Sarnoff himself and lasting almost two years, the companies finally reached a compromise. In November 1932, they submitted a proposal that became the basis for a consent decree granted by the government just one week before the antitrust trial was scheduled to begin.

Under the terms of this decree, RCA would become independent, and could begin to make its own tubes and radios. GE and Westinghouse would pledge not to compete in radio manufacturing for two and a half years, after which they could produce sets under license from RCA. In the meantime, they would distribute their entire holdings of RCA common stock to their own shareholders. They would have no representation on RCA's board, and RCA itself would retain control of the crucial patent pool.

These terms were just what Sarnoff wanted. In this case as in earlier (and later) ones, he showed himself a master at winning from the government conditions favorable to his company. He had long spoken of the need for "unification" of the electronics industry, and now he had the proper instrument—an unfettered RCA. In 1933 he moved the company's New York headquarters to Rockefeller Center, which had just been built in the city block surrounded by 49th and 50th streets and Fifth and Sixth avenues. He then set up a plush office on the 53rd floor of the newly christened RCA Building. The company, after having lost money during the two worst years of the Great Depression, in 1934 earned $4.2 million on sales of $79 million. Sarnoff then began in earnest to promote television research. RCA had reached the verge of success when World War II intervened and forced a temporary moratorium.

Television Flourishes

When the war ended in 1945, the government lifted its restraints on the development of commercial TV, and Sarnoff resumed his all-out campaign for RCA to dominate the new medium. In 1946 the company sold about 10,000 TV sets. The next year it sold 200,000, or four-fifths of all TVs sold in the United States during 1947. Fifteen television stations were operating by this time, some owned by large electronics companies, some independent. Nearly all stations used RCA cameras and other equipment. NBC was telecasting from New York and building new stations in Cleveland, Chicago, and Los Angeles. Most consumers at this time found it necessary to erect outdoor antennas, usually atop roofs, in order to achieve reasonably good reception, and even then their sets could pick up only three or four stations. Further progress seemed slow at the time, but once TV broadcasting gained a foothold, it grew quickly:

Year	Number of TV Stations	Percentage of Households Served
1940	None	None
1950	100	9%
1960	580	83%
1970	680	95%

The three major radio networks—NBC, CBS, and ABC—easily branched into television. From the 1940s until the spread of cable systems in the 1980s, nationally broadcast TV programs of all types were produced by, or under contract to, these three networks. (By 1990 about a thousand regional cable TV systems served more than half of all households, and by the year 2000 the big three networks' prime-time share of viewers had dropped from 80 percent to 30 percent.)

Of the many companies involved in the industry from the 1930s onward, only RCA was fully integrated. It had big operations in radio and TV broadcasting, as well as in the manufacture of sets, industrial electronics, phonographs and records, and, most notably, TV picture tubes, which it sold to other set manufacturers. Below is a summary of the rise of U.S. radio and TV set production.

Radios Produced in the U.S. Per Year, in Millions	Black-and-White TV Sets Produced in the U.S. Per Year, in Millions
1922: 0.1	1948: 1.0
1925: 2	1949: 3.0
1930: 4, including 34,000 car radios	1950: 7.5
1935: 6, including over 1 million car radios	1956: 7.4
1940: 12, including 2 million car radios and over 1 million portables	
1947: 20, the biggest single year of domestic radio production in history	
1955: 14.5, including 7 million car radios, 2 million portables, and over 2 million clock radios	

In 1955, American manufacturers' share of the U.S. radio set market stood at 96 percent. But then came a competitive surge by several companies in Japan, which was experiencing a "miracle" economic recovery after World War II. As inexpensive Japanese imports poured in, the market share of U.S. radio-set producers began a steady decline—to only 30 percent by 1965, and then to almost zero by 1975. This same pattern was duplicated in later years, first with black-and-white TVs, then with color sets.

Until the 1960s, television sets were almost entirely domestic products. Few imports gained substantial market share, nor did American firms export very many sets. TV manufacturing companies were relatively large, because a big investment was required to acquire and maintain the production equipment and to employ a trained workforce to assemble sets and repair them after sale. Even so, the television industry also contained hundreds of small firms that supplied components under contract.

RCA's technological edge in TV sets gave it a powerful advantage that might well have translated into a wide lead in market share. But RCA was never the most vigorous marketer. Emerson, Philco, Zenith, and Admiral all emphasized marketing much more, even though they paid RCA a licensing fee for every set they sold. Most of RCA's manufacturing facilities were located in Indianapolis, far from its New York headquarters and, more significantly, from its New Jersey research labs.

During the late 1940s and early 1950s, the profitability of TV set manufacturers rose quickly once the industry took hold, then declined under sharp price competition—a phenomenon typical of many new industries. Following the earlier experience in radio, numerous manufacturers began to exit the TV-set industry. In 1956 alone, eight major firms, including Raytheon, CBS-Columbia, Crosley, and Hallicrafters, stopped producing sets. In that year the U.S. market shares of American TV-set manufacturers were as follows: RCA 17 percent, GE-Hotpoint 16, Admiral 9, Philco 9, Motorola 9, Zenith 7, Silvertone 6, Emerson 5, Magnavox 4, Westinghouse 3, and all others 15.

Between 1950 and 1970, sales of electronics products grew twice as fast as GNP, but the primary reason was not the emergence of television. Instead it was the intensification of the Cold War. Whereas products developed and produced for military applications accounted for less than 20 percent of electronics-industry revenues in 1950, by 1970 they accounted for almost 50 percent. Military planners were continually pushing the frontiers of electronics R&D in order to maintain a technological edge over the Soviet Union. Many companies vied for well-paying defense contracts, but much of the work was so complex that only leading firms such as GE, RCA, and Raytheon could meet the stringent requirements.

David Sarnoff was himself an ardent cold warrior. He missed few opportunities to excoriate communism, which he associated with pre-industrial life. During the 1950s he proposed that RCA donate millions of tiny phonographs to be parachuted into the Soviet Union, along with recordings in Russian narrating the wonders of capitalism. The proposal was rejected by the government, but it exemplified Sarnoff's identification of RCA and himself with America's Cold War crusade.

Broadcasting and Advertising

In the early days of RCA, Sarnoff had hoped that broadcasting could be financed through payments from stations, usage taxes on radio sets, and percentage-of-sales taxes or contributions by set manufacturers. He did not anticipate the endless commercials that became a hallmark of radio in the 1920s and then, of course, of TV. He abhorred them, and until the end of his life protested bitterly that excessive advertising had "debased" the new media.

NBC broadcast the first TV advertisement on July 1, 1941. This commercial, perhaps the dullest ever made, depicted the face of a Bulova clock ticking off 60 seconds, for which Bulova paid $4 to WNBT, the New York NBC affiliate. World War II interrupted television broadcasting, but in the late 1940s, when TV went back on the air, companies such as Procter & Gamble, Colgate-Palmolive, Gillette, Anheuser-Busch, Ford, and General Motors quickly grasped the potential of TV commercials. They then redirected much of their advertising toward the new medium.

In the seven years from 1949 to 1956, dollars spent on television ads rose from about 10 percent of the amount spent on radio advertising to nearly 250 percent. Meanwhile, the cost of network air time to advertisers grew by about 280 percent, but the size of the audience increased so fast that the advertisers' cost per household reached fell by more than 50 percent.

Soon it became hard to find enough good material to put on the air. In the mid-1950s, a typical TV station had to fill about 5,000 hours per year with programming. (Today the figure is 8,760 hours, in other words, all day every day.) In 1958 the newsman Edward R. Murrow lamented that what should be a great educational medium was instead "being used to distract, delude, amuse and insulate us." The Federal Communications Commission (FCC), created by Congress in 1934 to regulate the telecommunications industry (then consisting primarily of telephones and radio), by this time had supervisory authority over television as well. In 1961, FCC Chairman Newton F. Minow, speaking at the annual convention of the National Association of Broadcasters, told his audience that "When television is bad, nothing is worse." He challenged each member to go home, sit down, and watch a full day of programming on his or her own station. "I can assure you," said Minow, "that you will observe a vast wasteland." For better or worse, however, television had come to stay.

Color TV

Television images originally were produced only in black-and-white tones. But Sarnoff had long known that it was possible to broadcast in color, and his commitment to this goal eventually came to border on monomania. When RCA resumed work on color TV after World War II, it found the technological problems of its all-electronic system daunting. Throughout the 1940s, RCA's rival CBS had been experimenting with a partly electronic technology that filtered transmission signals through a mechanical spinning disk inside the TV set in such a way as to produce a color image. The RCA team regarded this method as archaic, and was stunned when the Federal Communications Commission in 1950 accepted the CBS system as the industry standard.

RCA appealed this decision in federal court, but in the meantime was rescued by external events. As World War II had done in the 1940s, the Korean War focused most of the efforts of the electronics industry on defense needs. The National Production Authority, a mobilization agency, invoked a ban on the manufacture of color TV sets that held until 1953. In that year, after renewed hearings, the FCC approved new standards based on the all-electronic RCA system.

Having won the acrimonious battle of the standards, Sarnoff expected a quick surge in the mass production and marketing of color sets. Wall Street agreed, and the price of RCA common stock climbed from $16 to $23 per share. As it turned out, almost everyone was too optimistic. Like radio and black-and-white TV before it, color television was a systems technology. Getting it into operation was not just a matter of tooling up to manufacture and sell color TV sets. Color broadcasts had to be planned, color cameras installed, transmission facilities upgraded, and legions of repair technicians trained. In the end, it took the industry about 15 years to move from black-and-white to color broadcasting.

RCA began volume production of color sets in 1954, offering a model with a 12¹/₂-inch screen at a price of $1,000 (equivalent to more than $4,000 in the early twenty-first century). In the mid-1950s, 21-inch black-and-white sets were selling for under $300. Meanwhile, production difficulties involving the color picture tube, which was the most complicated consumer good ever manufactured up to that time, were resulting in a rejection rate of about two-thirds during factory inspections. Sarnoff had predicted sales of 75,000 color sets in 1954, 350,000 in 1955, and 5 million in 1958. In fact, few sets were sold at all in 1954 and only 5,000 in 1955.

The price of color TV was simply too high for the quality of the picture that home viewers saw on their screens. Colors bled together, especially for programs not broadcast live. Sets were hard to tune. Despite Sarnoff's claims about the "compatibility" of RCA color receivers, pictures broadcast in black-and-white appeared fuzzy when received on color sets. In 1956, *Time* pronounced color TV the year's "most resounding industrial flop," and quoted RCA's competitors as saying that the whole introduction had been premature. For Zenith, Westinghouse, and other companies, a strategic retreat was the obvious course. But for RCA the road was less clear, and Sarnoff faced what he later called "the toughest battle of my life."

In an unusual step, RCA's board of directors in 1956 gave its 65-year-old chief executive a new ten-year contract, even though the company was losing money and was being forced by market conditions to halve the price of its color TV sets. That reduction triggered a $150 million antitrust suit by Philco, alleging that "unreasonably low" prices signaled a bid by RCA to monopolize the market. Meanwhile, RCA's precious pool of 10,000 TV-related patents was again under assault in antitrust litigation brought by the Justice Department.

Sarnoff was by nature a combative person, and his life-long habit had been to fight any challenge with ruthless tenacity. This time, however, because of intense government pressure, he decided to bow out of the lawsuits. In 1958 RCA paid off Philco, and, in a landmark step, settled with the Justice Department by making most of RCA's patents available to domestic competitors at little or no cost. Then RCA tried to recoup its lost domestic royalties by licensing its patents to European and Japanese companies. Every major Japanese TV-manufacturing firm became a licensee. By the 1970s RCA's annual royalty income from consumer-electronics patents reached $100 million, most of it from color-TV technology.

During the early 1960s, RCA had improved its picture tubes through a crash R&D effort, and TV color images had become sharper in home reception. RCA's subsidiary NBC did everything it could to help, broadcasting more and more programs in color. Because of these efforts, in the 1960s color TV finally began to take off, and all major domestic manufacturers plunged into the market. In 1961 even Zenith, a long-time nemesis of Sarnoff's, ordered 50,000 of RCA's color picture tubes. RCA was equipping many other competitors as well, at a profit of $35 for every picture tube sold. It was also selling production and transmission equipment to TV stations all over the country.

The 5-million-set sales year Sarnoff had predicted for 1958 finally materialized in 1965. "This is the year of fulfillment for our long struggle," the 74-year-old CEO said at RCA's annual stockholders' meeting. The company was earning good profits, and by the mid-1960s its common stock was selling at over $100 per share. The triumph of color TV was the supreme achievement of Sarnoff's career. He received lavish accolades in the United States and Europe, and in Japan he was awarded the Order of the Rising Sun, the highest honor given to foreigners.

Few developments of the twentieth century, if any, had more profound social consequences than television. For good or ill, its importance in everyday life rivaled and perhaps surpassed that of all other innovations, even the automobile and the computer. Sarnoff, whose hunger for publicity and personal honors had by now become insatiable, basked in his success with color TV. He gave more interviews than ever. He trumpeted the glories of science and rashly predicted the imminent development of atomic batteries, electronic air conditioners, and amplifiers of light. "A degree-bearing engineer might have been hooted down," said Elmer Engstrom, the number-two person at RCA and himself a graduate engineer. "But Sarnoff could get away with it."

Progress and Missteps

In addition to its integrated manufacturing businesses in radio, TV, and audio recording, RCA maintained extensive research and development laboratories. The company also produced electronic systems for guided missiles and other military hardware under defense contracts. It was an article of faith with Sarnoff that RCA be involved in all things electronic, and that it remain on the cutting edge of R&D.

Ultimately, Sarnoff's R&D licensing strategy may have worked to RCA's disadvantage, especially in foreign markets. The company did a substantial overseas business in industrial products as well as in licensing, but Sarnoff decided not to aggressively market or manufacture consumer items abroad because he didn't want RCA to compete with its R&D licensees. (In the case of the large Japanese market he had little choice, since local officials had all but closed the country to both imported consumer electronics and to foreign firms' manufacturing plants.) So RCA mostly confined its sales and its factories to North America, unlike dozens of other big American companies that exported their products and built plants overseas.

This practice also differed from the strategies of European and especially Japanese consumer-electronics firms. Companies such as Sony, Matsushita (Panasonic), Hitachi, and Mitsubishi exported their goods from Japan in great volume. Under the umbrella of a protected home market, they constructed world-class facilities, charged high prices within Japan, and sometimes sold at lower prices abroad. They took full advantage of the freer postwar trading system that had evolved under American foreign-policy leadership. To penetrate the rich U.S. market, they exploited the efficient American distribution network, selling through Sears and other mass retailers. Eventually they built manufacturing plants in many countries, including the United States.

In the end, competition from across the Pacific destroyed much of RCA's TV-set business and along with it almost the entire American consumer-electronics industry. Japanese companies won this high-stakes contest on the basis of the superior quality of their products, offered at prices that U.S. companies found impossible to match. Some American firms, notably Zenith, protested vehemently against Japanese trade practices, alleging that their products were being "dumped" into the U.S. market at artificially low prices. Zenith persisted in its fight for two decades, going all the way to the Supreme Court. There, in 1986, it lost its case in a 5 to 4 decision.

The domestic market share in color TVs held by U.S.-owned firms declined from 94 percent in the mid-1960s to 67 percent in the mid-1970s, then to 43 percent in the mid-1980s and to nearly zero by the mid-1990s. During this period, many once-great U.S. brands were acquired by foreign firms: Motorola and its Quasar brand by Matsushita; Magnavox, Philco, and Sylvania by N. V. Philips (Holland); RCA and GE by Thomson (France); Zenith by LG Electronics (Korea).

On the entertainment side of RCA's business, which David Sarnoff detested, he was repeatedly outmaneuvered by Bill Paley of CBS. In the late 1940s, NBC radio lost its crucial ratings lead because Sarnoff refused to match Paley's rich offers to Jack Benny, Red Skelton, and other members of NBC's stable of on-air stars. CBS radio gained the largest audience share in 1949, and CBS television did the same in 1953. Meanwhile, RCA Victor seldom sold as many phonograph records as CBS's Columbia Records. In 1949 Columbia established its 33⅓-rpm "long-playing" record as the new industry standard, winning out over RCA's 45-rpm "extended play," which had less capacity. Later, no American company participated seriously in the compact-disc revolution of the 1980s. By then the U.S. consumer electronics industry had yielded primacy to European and Japanese firms. In 1988 even CBS Records was sold to Sony for $2 billion, which at that time was the largest Japanese acquisition of any U.S. company.

RCA lagged both domestic and foreign competitors in developing several other important products that emerged during the 1950s. For example, although RCA had led the world in vacuum-tube technology, it made no breakthroughs in transistors. These revolutionary devices were invented at AT&T's Bell Labs in 1947 and developed during the 1950s and 1960s by Texas Instruments, Motorola, Sony, and other firms. The transistor could perform the same work as a vacuum tube, using much less energy and a tiny fraction of the space. Transistors also were resistant to shock and could be installed in large numbers on printed circuit boards. First used in hearing aids, transistors were then introduced into car radios during the middle 1950s, and within two years they had become the industry standard.

Without the transistor, a whole series of electronics applications based on printed circuits and microchips would never have been possible. The most conspicuous such use, of course, was in the computer, which as long as it had to rely on vacuum tubes remained the size of a small truck. RCA's sluggishness with transistors derived partly from its huge investment in the manufacture of tubes. It was now in the unenviable position of staying ahead in the wrong technology.

In contrast to RCA and other American firms, Japanese companies such as Sony and Matsushita quickly took advantage of the transistor's possibilities in developing "solid-state" (tubeless) technology. Cognizant of space constraints in many Japanese homes, they began to miniaturize radios and TVs. For the global market, Sony also developed its Trinitron color TV technology and began to sell appealing new items such as the Walkman, which combined a tiny AM-FM radio, a small audio tape player, and a portable headset. As a matter of policy, leading Japanese firms devoted continuous attention to incremental improvements. They tried to avoid American-style obsessions with new blockbuster products, especially in the early years of their TV work. Far more than their U.S. counterparts, they emphasized within their own firms cross-functional teamwork in design, manufacturing, and marketing.

Another 1950s technology developed in the United States but not fully exploited by American companies was video tape recording. Videotape could be used immediately, without the delays needed for processing film. In addition, the quality of the TV image recorded on tape was much superior in rebroadcasts. RCA's engineers calculated that they could tape black-and-white TV shows for about 20 percent of the cost of filming them, and color shows for just 5 percent. But to RCA's embarrassment, videotape was invented not in its own labs but by Ampex, a small California firm.

During the 1960s the American TV industry began to employ videotape in the production of programs, but failed to commercialize it for consumers' use. Thus the field remained open for Sony and Matsushita to develop both videotape and the videocassette recorder, which they did after a long and arduous R&D effort.

Computers and Conglomerates

Sometimes RCA failed because it *did* enter into a new business. The company committed perhaps its gravest blunder when it dived into the computer industry during the 1950s and 1960s. Here RCA possessed the requisite technical skills but fell short in manufacturing and particularly in marketing. Consequently, it suffered a public humiliation at the hands of IBM.

Thomas J. Watson, Sr., who headed IBM for about as long as Sarnoff led RCA, was a skilled marketer who had started his business career in the late nineteenth century peddling goods from the back of a wagon. From that lowly beginning he rose to become one of the eminent business leaders of the twentieth century. In the words of Carl Dreher, who was Sarnoff's engineering assistant at RCA, "Watson was corny as hell, but no one ever denied that he was a first-rate salesman." Dreher went on to say that Watson trained his employees to ask themselves, "What does the buyer expect to get out of this elaborate machine?" "How will it help him reduce costs and increase profits?" "What type of computer will he buy (or lease) and how much will he pay?"

During the 1950s and 1960s, the bold and able Tom Watson, Jr., his father's successor at the helm, steered IBM to unquestioned dominance of the computer industry. All the while, the younger Watson continued to emphasize customer service.

By contrast, RCA's computer efforts flowed in the opposite direction—from the labs to the manufacturers, then to the marketers. The customer came last of all, and for that inverted logic the company paid a grievous price. When RCA finally exited the computer business in 1970, it was forced to write off about a quarter of its net worth.

But the actual penalty went even deeper. Because it had squandered 40 percent of its researchers' total time on computers, the company had neglected its R&D in other areas. As the engineer who headed RCA's labs later said, "We shot a whole generation of research and engineering on computers, and starved the real cow—color television—to do it." RCA had pioneered color TV in the greatest long-term effort in the company's history. Yet at the very moment of its triumph, it not only lost the computer war to IBM but also began to surrender its lead in TV technology to other companies.

The 1960s became the age of the conglomerate in American business, and RCA plunged wholeheartedly into this ill-fated adventure. First it acquired the publisher Random House, rationalizing the move as a natural one into "communications," albeit in nonelectronic form. The next major acquisition came after David Sarnoff had passed the CEO's reins to his son Robert, and in retrospect it seems a bizarre choice: the Hertz rent-a-car company. Robert Sarnoff then caused RCA to purchase Coronet carpets, the Banquet Foods frozen-dinner company, a golfing-attire firm, and many other enterprises with no connection to electronics.

Why did RCA do these things? The basic reason was the same one that lay behind the conglomerate movement as a whole. American companies, not yet disciplined by the sting of foreign competition, were making lots of money but did not wish to pay most of it out to shareholders as dividends. Prevented by antitrust laws from acquiring other firms in the same business, executives became convinced that they could use their cash flows to buy companies in unrelated lines and thereby further improve their own firms' overall profit performance. This logic almost mandated that the purchased firms be located in industries with different kinds of customers and seasonal sales patterns. Thus the diverse companies making up the new "portfolio" might complement each other by leveling out the annual income stream of the conglomerate as a whole. Wall Street at this time took a favorable view of the conglomerate movement, and the financial support of investors was readily forthcoming.

Top executives at many companies further assumed that if a talented manager could run an electronics firm effectively, then he (seldom she at this time) could also oversee a car rental company, a TV dinner firm, a carpet manufacturer, or any other kind of business. That assumption usually proved to be incorrect. Consequently, the acquisition boom of the 1960s was followed by a rash of divestitures during the 1970s, as many conglomerates realized their mistakes and sold off companies they had acquired only a few years earlier. But in its own conglomerate gambits, RCA had taken another step toward its ultimate fall.

The VideoDisc Disaster

Of all RCA's vicissitudes, perhaps the most revealing was its pursuit of a would-be blockbuster product called the VideoDisc. This episode carried with it a larger message about the tension in hightech businesses between the R&D function and commercial success. In RCA's case it helped to kill the firm.

By the late 1960s, the glory of the color-TV triumph was beginning to fade within the company's labs, even though much additional work remained to be done. Because of its blockbuster-obsessed corporate culture, RCA downplayed further R&D efforts in color TV and instead began to look for another new breakthrough product. How else, its R&D leaders reasoned, could the company's 6,200 scientists and engineers be usefully employed? Yet RCA was now in a more vulnerable position than it had been at any time since the 1930s. Not only were other American firms challenging its lead in color TV and defense electronics, but European companies such as France's Thomson and Holland's N. V. Philips had also developed world-class enterprises. And in Japan, firms such as Sony, Matsushita, Hitachi, Toshiba, and Sharp were showing clear signs of being able to compete against anybody.

Paying too little attention to these changing circumstances, RCA became fixated on the VideoDisc, a technology that would make it possible for TV viewers to watch particular programs whenever they wished. Just as phonographs had reproduced recorded music, a VideoDisc system could play back recorded films, concerts, ballets, and other programs, all without commercial interruptions.

If this sounds familiar, it's because the same virtues apply to videotape. RCA had pursued a videotape project, but abandoned it when company executives saw the superior Sony Beta system in 1974. RCA's VideoDisc system was not yet ready to market when videocassette recorders (VCRs) appeared in the mid-1970s, but

RCA believed that when VideoDisc was ready it would sell for much less than a VCR. Even so, videotape had an overriding advantage: it could be used to record programs from commercial broadcasts for later viewing at a time convenient for the consumer.

It is useful to keep in mind how all of this looked in prospect. We know now that videotape won decisively, that Japanese companies dominated the sale of VCRs and videocameras, that a vast tape-rental business arose in the 1980s and 1990s, and that the American consumer-electronics industry collapsed. But developments in high-tech markets are very hard to forecast, and in the 1960s and 1970s some of these outcomes seemed extremely unlikely. For one thing, it was by no means certain at the time that U.S. copyright law would allow consumers to videotape programs off the air. Then, too, VideoDisc was viewed as a technology that was less expensive, more elegant, and less easily copied than videotape. Meanwhile, Japanese, European, and American firms were all making expensive bets on their own versions of an uncertain future, as all high-tech enterprises must do all the time.

It came down to this: RCA executives bet their company that VideoDisc would emerge triumphant. During the 1970s the firm estimated that by about 1990 VideoDisc would generate annual revenues of $7.5 billion. This wishful thinking was based on the assumption that VideoDisc would become the industry standard. That assumption, in turn, derived from RCA's own hubris and its preoccupation with developing blockbuster products.

Nor was this kind of thinking confined to RCA and the electronics industry. In varying degrees it also appeared at Du Pont, Xerox, and other leading-edge technology companies. These firms funded expensive fundamental research laboratories, many of whose projects had only tenuous connections to future commercial products.

RCA's own labs had evolved into what people in other parts of the company began to call "the country club." There, it was believed, scientists and engineers were wasting company money on hare-brained experiments, pursuing projects satisfying only to themselves. Some of this was perhaps inevitable, since today's lunatic idea might well turn into tomorrow's breakthrough product; the distinction between good and bad R&D can never be completely clear. But in the case of RCA, other circumstances made the problem worse than it should have been. For example, there was intense mutual dislike between the researchers in New Jersey and the manufacturing managers in Indianapolis. Their physical separation symbolized a real lack of communication, and in the end that proved very costly.

Country-club labs in many firms often did what the scientists in charge of them wanted to do rather than what the company needed. For RCA there was an additional hitch—the tradition of royalties from other electronics firms. In a peculiar sense RCA's labs in effect had their own source of income, independent of the company's operating divisions. Ideally the management of technology, like any other function, should be closely related to a firm's markets. In most cases labs should not produce research for sale to all comers unless the company is engaged only in the research business. But RCA's way of thinking had been instilled into its culture long before, beginning with the patent pools of the 1920s. Only later did it turn out to be a serious flaw.

RCA's Management Report Card

The endgame of the RCA story—the disastrous strategies of conglomerate diversification, inattention to color TV, and the ill-fated gambles on computers and the VideoDisc—represents an outstanding example of sustained failure to get management relationships right. At no time did RCA develop the techniques of decentralization so conspicuous in the government's Controlled Materials Plan under Ferdinand Eberstadt, Procter & Gamble's brand management under Neil McElroy, and General Motors' multi-divisional structure under Alfred Sloan.

As it happened, five decades earlier Sloan himself had gone through an experience similar to the VideoDisc debacle at RCA. This was General Motors' struggle to develop the "copper-cooled engine," a favorite project of Charles Kettering, the company's resident inventive genius. Kettering's idea had been to eliminate altogether the automobile's water-cooled engine system, with its unwieldy network of radiators and hoses. Instead he would build an engine with copper fins, so as to facilitate cooling by air. GM expended large sums of money on this project, but CEO Sloan soon figured out that "we were in the situation of supporting a research position against the judgment of the division men who would in the end have to produce and sell the new car." Meanwhile, the company's R&D on traditional water-cooled engines had all but ceased, endangering GM's leadership position. So Sloan quietly killed the copper-cooled engine, cut the company's losses, and increased R&D on the water-cooled engine—all without alienating Charles Kettering, who remained one of GM's most valuable assets.

RCA, by contrast, failed partly for the same reason that the Ford Motor Company had faltered during the 1920s. Both companies paid too little heed to what the customer wanted and lodged too much authority in the hands of one person. David Sarnoff was a far more sophisticated businessman than Henry Ford. But like Ford he began to believe reports of his own infallibility, made too many decisions himself, and stayed too long at the helm. More than anyone else, he created a culture that made something like the computer and VideoDisc disasters not just possible but probable.

One important clue to the shortcomings of his management style is that RCA, like the Ford Motor Company, was not as profitable as it should have been. At Sarnoff's direction, his firm again and again sacrificed profits to research and development. By the early 1960s, RCA ranked number 26 on the *Fortune* 500 list of America's largest industrial corporations, right behind Procter & Gamble. But it could hardly have been a more different kind of company. RCA never followed P&G's policies of decentralizing its management structure, finding out what the consumer wanted, and tying all of its R&D efforts to commercial applications.

It might be argued that Sarnoff's emphasis on R&D sometimes paid off for society as a whole at the expense of RCA, and this issue raises the interesting question of what, ultimately, is the purpose of business. (Whatever one's answer to that many-sided question, it does not seem reasonable in cases like RCA's to require suicide by the company.) Certainly the advent of black-and-white television was accelerated by several years because of RCA's generous research expenditures during the 1930s depression. Similarly, the coming of high-quality color TV would have been delayed for at least a decade without RCA's leadership. Through the years, Sarnoff positioned his company as a kind of national electronics utility whose purpose was to move things forward not on behalf of shareholders or employees but rather for the national interest and his own aggrandizement. In this way too, he resembled Henry Ford, another technological prophet, more than Alfred Sloan, the consummate businessman.

Like Ford, Sarnoff groomed no successors, encouraged no management professionals to develop an independent voice, pontificated on matters he knew little about, and disdained formal organization. When he summoned the public relations consultant Edward Bernays to help clarify the confused lines of authority within NBC, Bernays began by asking to see the network's organization chart. "My dear Eddie," Sarnoff told him, "this is a company of men, not of charts." In an excellent biography entitled *The General,* Sarnoff's long-time executive assistant Kenneth Bilby gives a useful account of his boss's approach to the daily routine of management. Sarnoff dismissed visitors and employees at the instant when the point of his meeting with them had been settled. He made so many decisions that his schedule became impossibly compressed. He spurned small talk and cultivated no close relationships with colleagues, who had to address him as "General."

Sarnoff's style did form a good fit with some parts of the company. Year after year, his unfailing enthusiasm for technology continued to inspire the scientists and engineers at RCA's New Jersey research labs, which were moved from Camden to Princeton and renamed the David Sarnoff Laboratories. As Sarnoff said in 1948, "Princeton is the heart of RCA; the other parts of the company are the organs of the body that function only as the heart functions." But in those other parts that interested him less, including NBC's broadcasting and RCA's manufacturing and sales, his dictatorial approach killed initiatives and did serious harm. His overall method, as RCA engineer Carl Dreher put it, "required periodic technological breakthroughs, and the time came when none was in sight." When RCA couldn't make its own markets with new products from the R&D labs, it didn't know how to behave as a company.

In 1966, Sarnoff reached the age of 75. He refused to countenance total retirement but was willing to turn over much of his day-to-day work to the next generation of management. It proved unfortunate that the RCA board chose his son to succeed him. Forty-eight years old in 1966, Robert Sarnoff had risen through the company's ranks, chiefly at NBC. Unlike his father, he enjoyed hobnobbing with entertainers, and he did an acceptable job as head of the TV network. But as CEO of the parent RCA from 1966 until 1974, when the board fired him, his performance approached incompetence. He lacked strategic vision and was given to unpredictable shifts in policy. "Bobby Sarnoff had an attention span that wasn't ninety seconds long," one RCA executive remarked. "When you talked with him, he always communicated somehow that he wished you and he were someplace else." During his tenure, RCA drifted aimlessly into its conglomerate phase while losing its edge in electronics.

David Sarnoff, by now in poor health, watched the company's deterioration without being able to do much about it. He died in 1971, two weeks before his eightieth birthday and five years after his son became CEO. As noted earlier, he was posthumously selected in 1975 as a charter member of *Fortune*'s business Hall of Fame. But only a few years after that, RCA appeared on the same magazine's list of America's least admired companies.

RCA's final crisis came in 1981, a year in which it lost $27 million. Now the board gave the CEO's job to Thornton Bradshaw, a widely admired business statesman who immediately began to sell off unrelated subsidiaries and refocus the company on broadcasting and electronics. NBC jumped from last place to first place in network ratings, and in 1984 RCA turned a profit of $340 million. During Bradshaw's five years as chairman, RCA's common stock tripled in value, buoyed by NBC. But the company never came close to regaining its luster as a leader in technology.

In 1986, Bradshaw surprised the American business community by arranging to sell RCA in its entirety to General Electric, which back in the 1920s had been the firm's chief parent. At a price of $6.3 billion, the acquisition was one of the biggest in history up to that time. General Electric now became the seventh largest American industrial company, ranking just behind IBM. GE's aggressive chief executive officer, Jack Welch, was interested in RCA not for its technological prowess, which had long since faded. Instead he wanted ownership of NBC, which he saw as a major asset for the Information Age. Welch quickly divested most of what had been RCA. He peddled manufacturing plants and the RCA brand name to Thomson and other foreign-owned companies. Without much hesitation, he sold off the David Sarnoff Laboratories.

The Perils of High-Tech Markets

The general collapse of the American consumer-electronics industry is not, of course, a story just of RCA and David Sarnoff. In addition, there is the complex issue of national industry life cycles as they have evolved through each of the three industrial revolutions.

For example, during the late eighteenth century machine-based textile manufacturing began in Britain. Then during the nineteenth century it spread to other industrialized countries, and in the twentieth it gradually migrated to lower-wage countries. The pattern in consumer-electronics manufacturing was similar. What happened in the United States with the rise and decline of RCA, General Electric, Westinghouse, and other TV-set manufacturers later began to happen in Japan as well. High domestic wages prompted Sony, Matsushita, Hitachi, and other firms to move some of their manufacturing offshore to countries such as Mexico and Malaysia. But the difference between these Japanese companies and RCA is that they adapted and survived as ongoing enterprises. In the United States, General Electric and Westinghouse also survived, although both divested their consumer-electronics divisions.

In addition to national industry life cycles, the fate of RCA and the American consumer-electronics industry was also related to geopolitical forces. Within the United States, defense expenditures associated with World War II and the Cold War changed the nature of R&D inside many high-tech companies. AT&T's renowned Bell Labs had devoted only 2.5 percent of its budget to military projects in 1940, but was spending 85 percent of its budget on defense-related projects by 1944. The number never returned to a level even close to 2.5 percent. The federal Office of Scientific Research and Development, set up in 1941 to coordinate federal funding of war-related R&D, was reborn in 1950 as the National Science Foundation (NSF). For decades thereafter, NSF influenced the overall direction of R&D in the United States. The expensive exertions in military R&D by high-tech U.S. companies turned out to be an essential and perhaps decisive factor in winning the Cold War. Then, too, in the case of the computer industry, government outlays for defense-related projects helped give IBM and other firms a commanding lead over foreign competitors, a lead they readily transferred from military to civilian markets. Here the experience of IBM resembled that of Boeing. Both companies' skillful adaptations of military technology facilitated their rise to the top of their industries worldwide.

In numerous other high-tech firms, by contrast, both fundamental research and defense work tended to crowd out commercial R&D. That process likely accelerated the loss of market share to overseas competitors. Although it is hard to make all-purpose generalizations on this subject, the final verdict may be that from the standpoint of their own long-term commercial viability, many American high-tech companies overinvested in defense projects and fundamental research, while underinvesting in R&D that had direct connections to their consumer markets. Certainly that was true of RCA, where the hostile split between the researchers in New Jersey and the manufacturing managers in Indianapolis symbolized deep-seated internal problems.

One lesson of RCA's experience is plain. No matter how big the company, how resplendent its heritage, and how talented its R&D staff, continued success is *never* assured. In the end, all business comes down to a ceaseless struggle to stay ahead or abreast of the competition. That, in turn, requires constant vigilance toward local, national, and international markets, and unremitting attention to consumers' desires. In markets for high-tech goods and services, trends in consumer preferences are notoriously unpredictable. In the 1970s this uncertainty applied to videotape and VideoDisc. Within a few years, it reappeared with hand-held calculators, fax machines, personal computers, video games, spreadsheets, word-processing software, cellular telephones, and the Internet.

In none of these cases was the size and nature of the market forecast very accurately, even by well-informed experts. One never knows exactly where the next hot item is going to emerge, and expensive R&D bets must be placed routinely, on a continuing basis. But in the meantime, the company cannot neglect incremental improvements in its existing products, so long as the products themselves are not about to become obsolete. For all of these reasons, high-tech firms are perhaps the hardest businesses to manage well.

There is also the matter of changes in external conditions. From 1945 to 1965, in a context of continuous domestic prosperity, immense Cold War defense expenditures, and no effective foreign competition, RCA and many other American firms grew powerful, profitable, and smug. But during the last third of the century, consumer markets in many industries suddenly became international and much more competitive. At that point American industrial dominance began to erode in the face of European and Japanese economic recovery—a foreseeable development but one that occurred faster than U.S. business managers had anticipated. As this catch-up process matured, the relatively free ride enjoyed by American companies during the first two postwar decades ended abruptly. Foreign competition then inflicted severe and sometimes fatal damage to U.S. companies in the consumer-electronics, machine-tool, rubber-tire, steel, and automobile industries.

For RCA, the tilt toward globalism brought profound consequences. Once consumers became aware of superior alternative products, the company could find no sanctuary in its glorious history or even its once-revered brand name. In thousands of stores throughout the United States, millions of customers encountered a choice between a good RCA color TV set and a better one made by Sony or Panasonic and offered at a similar price. They made the selection most consumers inevitably make.

This book contains few examples of business failures, and in one sense that is regrettable, because the majority of firms do not survive even over the medium term, let alone the long run. The mortality rate is higher for small companies than for major firms, as one might expect. But RCA's experience underscores the transcendent principle that no company is exempt from the discipline of the market. If it does not pay scrupulous attention to consumer preferences and competitive pressures, it invites extinction.

CHAPTER EIGHT

Overview: Industrial Chemicals and Pharmaceuticals

Industrial Chemicals

Japanese and European consumer-electronics companies defeated their American competitors during the late twentieth century, but the same thing did not happen in chemicals. From 1945 to the end of the century, no industry with the possible exception of computers played a bigger role in U.S. economic growth.

During the period 1945–1973, as the American economy was growing at a healthy rate, the chemical industry grew two-and-a-half times as fast. Then, in the decades of slower growth after 1973, U.S. chemical firms came to understand that they could not afford to keep pouring immense sums into research projects that had little relationship to their commercial markets. Du Pont and other leading firms therefore reduced their emphasis on fundamental research. They also cut down their reliance on defense contracts, identified their own core competencies, addressed more directly the question of what their customers wanted—and returned to prosperity.

Historically, American firms were not the first movers in chemicals, as they had been in several other industries. In the early years of the twentieth century, the world's top three chemical companies were all German: Bayer, Hoechst, and BASF. Heavily staffed with scientists and engineers, these firms pioneered in dyestuffs, ammonia-based fertilizers, and synthetic drugs such as aspirin. Then, during the course of World War I (1914–1918), German firms of all types were barred from the U.S. market. In this newly protected atmosphere, American chemical companies prospered by taking advantage of patented German technology, which was made available by the federal agency set up to manage the U.S.-based assets of enemy countries. (The German firms eventually recovered from the blows they absorbed during both world wars, and in the early twenty-first century the three companies named above remained among the world leaders in chemicals.)

The American chemical industry's evolution over the 80 years following World War I reflected major military and social events. The industry responded especially well to the need for munitions during World War II and the Cold War, and—in its production of fertilizers, pesticides, and synthetic fibers—to increasing demands for food and clothing during the baby boom. It also benefited from the emergence of overseas markets for many kinds of chemical products after the freeing up of international trade. By the start of the twenty-first century, branded products such as Dacron fiber, Lycra elastic fabric, and Tyvek building wrap had become well known throughout the world. All were developed after World War II. The scientific breakthrough that underlay most of these items, plus a vast array of others, came to be known as the "polymer revolution" in organic chemistry.

Polymers and Science

Inorganic chemistry is concerned with elements that form familiar compounds: two atoms of hydrogen plus one of oxygen yield one molecule of water; two of hydrogen, one of sulfur, and four of oxygen form sulfuric acid; and so on. More complex inorganic chemicals are used in the manufacture of optics, superconductors, and silicon-based semiconductors. *Organic* chemicals, on the other hand, contain carbon, most of which has been recycled through once-living organisms. Carbon is unusual in that it can form four symmetric bonds with other elements and therefore serve as the scaffolding for a very diverse range of substances, from DNA to polymer plastics. Carbon's atomic structure lends itself to the creation of endlessly repeating chains of molecules.

A polymer is an organic compound or mixture of compounds, usually of high molecular weight, composed of these repeating structural units. Some polymers occur naturally, but synthetic new ones can be designed to have particular combinations of strength and flexibility. They are first produced in a laboratory, and, if regarded as commercially promising, then scaled up for large-batch or continuous-process manufacturing. Synthetic compounds fit a growing list of applications, and their development by American chemical companies had tremendous importance for the national economy.

During the 1930s, at the dawn of the polymer revolution, petroleum was beginning to replace coal as the industry's chief raw material for organic chemicals. Oil companies therefore joined chemical firms in the pursuit of polymer research. The process to produce synthetic rubber, developed during World War II by Standard Oil of New Jersey (Exxon), led to the transformation of the rubber industry. Exxon and other firms such as Phillips Petroleum and Standard Oil of California (Chevron) set up petrochemical divisions and began to manufacture vast quantities of new synthetic products.

In the laboratories of these companies, and even more so in those of chemical giants such as Du Pont, Monsanto, Dow, and 3M, scientists and engineers began to realize that they were practicing something akin to alchemy. Instead of turning base metals into gold, as medieval alchemists had tried to do, they now seemed capable of turning petroleum into almost anything. By the end of the century they were producing substitutes for natural fabrics (nylon, Orlon, polyesters), wood (plastic paneling, Fiberglas), cloth tape (Scotch), glass (Lucite, Plexiglas), and a multitude of other materials—latex paints and varnishes, insulators, adhesives, and synthetic building materials. Especially strong plastics could even substitute for tiles (Formica) and metals (Kevlar protective vests).

The Companies

The progress of the chemical industry as a whole can be illustrated through glimpses of two important companies, Monsanto and Du Pont. Monsanto, founded in St. Louis in 1901 to produce the artificial sweetener saccharin, by 1915 had grown to a medium-sized firm that manufactured caffeine and vanillin as well. After the outbreak of World War I it began to make aspirin, of which it eventually became the world's largest bulk producer. Throughout the 1920s and 1930s, Monsanto continued to grow and diversify. During World War II it fulfilled large government contracts, and after 1945 it became a major producer of lawn fertilizers, benefiting from the millions of suburban housing starts that took place during the baby boom. In 1955, Monsanto purchased Lion Oil Company to insure its supply of petroleum, and then proceeded to achieve world leadership in agricultural chemicals. One of its products, Roundup, became a best-selling weed killer.

During and after the passage of environmental legislation in the 1960s and 1970s, Monsanto, like other chemical firms, was a frequent target of a hostile press. In response, the company adapted its corporate strategy to the imperatives of pollution control and grew especially strong in research and development. Pioneering in biotechnology, Monsanto's scientists developed a line of seeds that produced insect-resistant crops, thereby reducing the need for insecticides. Monsanto also began to offer a line of "Roundup-Ready" seeds that would produce crops resistant to its own weed-killer. Farmers using these seeds could spray Roundup freely on their fields, killing every plant except the cash crop. In effect, Monsanto was trying to have it both ways, selling not only insect-resistant seeds but also herbicide-resistant ones. Only the first of these two strategies was unambiguously friendly to the environment, and Monsanto continued to attract criticism. The same was true of the industry as a whole.

The second illustrative chemical company, Du Pont, had been founded in Delaware in 1802 as a small manufacturer of gunpowder. Over the next two centuries, Du Pont supplied munitions for every war fought by the United States. By the 1920s, however, its main business was not in munitions but in a variety of chemical products such as paints, varnishes, cellophane (the rights to which it purchased from a French company), and rayon (also of French origin). The most profitable item in Du Pont's long history turned out to be nylon, a polymer synthesized in 1934 in its research labs. All kinds of clothing could be made from nylon, either alone or blended with natural fibers, and the same was true of carpets. As a replacement for silk, nylon made sheer stockings affordable to millions of women for the first time in history. It also became the chief fiber used in parachutes and was adapted for cord material in the manufacture of tires. Its exceptional strength made it ideal also for nautical ropes. Nylon became so popular that Du Pont not only produced it in vast amounts but also licensed the rights to its manufacture to other firms. By the end of the century the company had earned over $20 billion in profits on this one polymer.

The breakthrough in nylon during the 1930s changed Du Pont's corporate culture. As it happened, the discovery of nylon (and of neoprene as well, Du Pont's version of synthetic rubber) had come about through serendipitous events during lab experiments. These occurrences seemed to suggest that if researchers got down to the foundations of chemistry and physics without thinking of immediate commercial applications, then they might come upon a series of products that would make new fortunes for Du Pont. So, during and after World War II, the company invested unprecedented sums in basic research, looking for useful new polymers but willing to spend lavishly on almost any promising project. For a while this approach seemed to pay off. Du Pont's synthetic fibers—nylon, Orlon, and polyesters—practically transformed the carpet, textile, and apparel industries. By the 1980s more than 70 percent of all fibers used in American manufacturing were synthetics.

On the other hand, hundreds of research projects worked on by thousands of Du Pont scientists and engineers yielded no marketable results at all. And some products that did reach the consumer flopped in a big way. The company lost lots of money on Qiana, a luxury artificial silk that impressed few buyers. It lost even more on Corfam, a synthetic leather that Du Pont executives were convinced would revolutionize the world market for shoes and boots. That, of course, did not happen. Corfam was durable enough, but it didn't breathe well and was too stiff to be broken in like shoe leather. In the end, Du Pont's adventures with both Qiana and Corfam proved disastrous. In addition, the company's emphasis on synthetic fibers caused some frustration during the 1970s, when demand dropped in the wake of changing consumer tastes in apparel and the development of "permanent press" 100-percent cotton.

Yet Du Pont, like Monsanto, Dow, and other American chemical firms, maintained its leadership in many markets. Having acquired Conoco, a major oil company, Du Pont assured itself of plentiful feedstocks for its petrochemicals business. Then, too, like several other major U.S. chemical companies, Du Pont restructured itself during the 1970s and 1980s, divesting low-margin commodity chemicals in order to focus on specialty chemicals and other high-tech items.

Pharmaceuticals

The pharmaceutical industry underwent even bigger changes than did industrial chemicals. In 1929, only 32 percent of the medicines sold in the United States (by value) were prescription drugs, but 40 years later, in 1969, this percentage had risen to 83. By that time, in much of the world, antibiotics had all but wiped out numerous diseases that had plagued human beings for hundreds of years. In addition, beginning in the 1950s there had been a series of breakthroughs in psychopharmacology. By the end of the century Prozac and similar drugs were delivering relief to millions of people suffering from clinical depression.

The years between World War II and the end of the century brought spectacular new arrays of pharmaceuticals. Besides antibiotics and antidepressants, there were tranquilizers, contraceptives, antihistamines, and many other "antis," including anticancer, anti-ulcer, anti-cholesterol, anti-high-blood-pressure, anti-baldness, anti-menopausal, and anti-impotence drugs. Only a few years earlier, such products would have seemed figments of some frenzied imagination.

By the close of the century, annual retail expenditures on pharmaceuticals worldwide exceeded $300 billion. Of this sum, a disproportionate one-third was spent in the United States, where consumers had become familiar with such brand names as Ortho-Novum (for contraception), Valium (anxiety), Retin-A (skin care), Minoxidil and Propecia (hair loss), Zantac and Prilosec (excess stomach acid), Ritalin (attention deficit disorder), Viagra (impotence), Crixivan and Virocept (AIDS), Zocor (high cholesterol), Vasotec (high blood pressure), and Estradiol and Evista (estrogen replacement).

American leadership of the pharmaceutical industry had risen in the 1940s and 1950s, then had declined in the 1960s and 1970s. It recovered powerfully during the 1980s and 1990s, riding the momentum of a scientific revolution in biotechnology. At the end of the century, 14 of the world's 20 largest drug firms were head-quartered in the United States. The most science-based companies on this list (Merck, Pfizer, Abbott, Eli Lilly, Warner-Lambert, Schering-Plough, and Pharmacia & Upjohn), along with their British and European competitors Glaxo-Wellcome, Hoechst, Novartis, and Rhone-Poulenc, spent billions of dollars annually on research and development.

The pharmaceutical industry differed from most others in that companies involved in the race to create new drug compounds had little choice but to spend immense sums on R&D with no guarantee of a return. In this industry, only a minuscule number of potential products made it to market—about one in ten thousand compounds, according to some estimates. Those that did could easily cost several hundred million dollars in R&D before a single dose of the new drug was prescribed for a paying patient. In this situation of un-avoidably high capital investments, mergers become common and the most ambitious drug companies grew to giant size.

The tendency toward bigness did not apply to pure biotechnology companies such as Genentech, Biogen, and Genzyme. By the end of the century more than 1,300 biotech companies had been created in the United States, and most were relatively small firms with entrepreneurial cultures. Although few made any profits, several were viewed as having great potential. Many were partly owned by large drug firms or venture capitalists, and some were associated with universities.

Because of the odd economics of the pharmaceutical industry, companies that did develop breakthrough drugs were almost compelled to market them at high prices. They had to do so in order to recover their huge R&D expenditures within 14 years, the limit on a new drug's patent protection. Since many of those years were often taken up in testing for toxicity and securing authorization from the Food and Drug Administration, the window was sometimes only five to seven years. After that, generic drug firms could manufacture and sell cheap knockoffs.

A rapid turnover in new drugs became apparent almost as soon as the biotechnology revolution started. For example, only 4 of the 30 best-selling prescription drug items of 1965 were still in the top 30 in 1980. Thus, companies with heavy R&D investments found themselves in a perpetual race against the clock.

This situation led to several new strategies on the part of leading pharmaceutical firms. First, during their brief time as monopolies on the market, patented "miracle" drugs sometimes sold for several dollars per pill. In addition, firms' incentives for worldwide distribution were much stronger than for products in most other industries. Still a third new strategy was the onset in 1997 of direct advertising of new prescription drugs to consumers, through magazine ads and TV commercials. This practice broke a long-held taboo and was vehemently opposed by most doctors and managed-care companies. But in this case, as in so many others throughout the twentieth century, decision rights were gravitating toward the ultimate consumer. Though the consumer might know little about pharmacology, he or she often did best sense when medical attention was necessary and naturally had a much stronger incentive than anyone else to initiate treatment.

However one might view the recent history of the American pharmaceutical industry from a business perspective, a more important story was that the new drugs brought incalculable benefits to millions of people. For patients who could afford to buy them, or whose insurers would pay for them, these drugs prolonged life or improved its quality in ways difficult to quantify by a monetary index.

Nor had the underlying scientific revolution peaked by the year 2000. In the pharmaceutical industry, as in the related field of genetic engineering, many scientists were confident that the twenty-first century would bring even greater miracles. Chemical and pharmaceutical firms responded to the exciting new opportunities in a variety of ways. Monsanto divided itself into separate companies in 1997, splitting off its chemical operations and focusing its attention on biotechnology-based "life sciences." The biggest chemical company, Du Pont, undertook a similar reevaluation of its fundamental corporate strategy. Betting heavily on its own Life Sciences division, Du Pont divested itself of the Conoco oil subsidiary in 1998, intending to spend about $20 billion of the sale price of the oil company on agricultural biotechnology R&D and $5 billion on pharmaceuticals.

These risky corporate reorientations were based on the premise that a convergence of research in genetics, information technology, and other fields had created a situation in which pharmaceuticals, agribusiness, and polymer materials all shared a common R&D platform. This platform, called genomics, offered almost unlimited potential for the engineering of new products ranging across the spectrum of organic chemicals from hydrocarbons to carbohydrates. The new situation posed severe challenges to Monsanto, Du Pont, and other firms—but also unusual opportunities.

CHAPTER NINE

1973–2000: Slower Economic Growth, Franchising, and the Case of McDonald's

The Oil Shocks and Macroeconomic Performance

Monsanto had acquired Lion Oil Company in 1955 to ensure against any sharp price rise or interruption of supply in this key feedstock for petrochemicals. Monsanto's fears, and those of many other companies, were borne out in the "oil shock" of 1973, when the Organization of Petroleum Exporting Countries (OPEC), led by Venezuela and Saudi Arabia, quadrupled the price of crude oil. OPEC inflicted a second shock in 1979, and by 1980 the real price of oil on world markets was more than 12 times what it had been in 1970.

Oil is such a vital resource, and is consumed in such immense volume, that these price rises affected the entire world economy. In many countries, including the United States, the oil shock started a long period of chronic inflation. From 1973 to 1983, the average annual rise in the U.S. consumer price index zoomed to 8.2 percent, the highest rate of inflation for any ten-year period in American history. (It dropped to 3.8 percent from 1983 to 1993, then to less than 2 percent for the remainder of the century.)

The simultaneous onset of inflation and economic stagnation during the 1970s led to the coining of a new term: "stagflation." America's industrial self-confidence plummeted, particularly since the period of stagflation coincided with the loss of U.S. leadership in several important industries. Firms in steel, heavy machinery, automobiles, tires, and machine tools lost substantial market share to overseas producers. There occurred a general hollowing out of the midwestern "Rust Belt," stretching from western Pennsylvania across Ohio, Indiana, Illinois, and up into Michigan and Wisconsin.

The change was especially traumatic in automobiles, where American producers had been dominant for so long. In 1950, as Europe and Japan were still recovering from the damage of World War II, 85 percent of all cars produced in the world had been made in the United States. As late as 1955 the Big Three (General Motors, Ford, and Chrysler) had enjoyed a combined share of 96 percent of the huge American market. Imports into the United States from all countries accounted for less than 1 percent. But these numbers changed rapidly during the 1960s and 1970s, and in 1980 Japan overtook the U.S. as the world's leading producer of cars. In that same year Chrysler posted a loss of $1.7 billion and had to be bailed out by a loan guarantee from the federal government. For a time it seemed that Ford might be next in line. The small Japanese cars were much more fuel-efficient than the traditionally large products of Detroit, so the oil crisis worked to the Japanese carmakers' advantage. But even beyond this, Japanese cars were so superior to American cars of the same price that U.S. automakers seemed about to follow the nation's consumer-electronics industry into oblivion.

After the middle 1980s, the American Big Three began to recover. They did this by getting tough with unions and by partially adopting Japanese management techniques such as the Toyota

Production System, which emphasized lean staffing and just-in-time inventory control. As anti-Japanese protectionism arose in the United States, in the form of tariffs and quotas, and as the yen appreciated against the dollar (making cars produced in Japan more expensive in the United States), Japanese firms began to build "transplant" factories overseas. Honda opened such a facility in Ohio, as did Nissan in Tennessee, Toyota in Kentucky, and Mazda in Michigan. In 1994, with the help of these transplants, the U.S. regained the top position in number of cars produced, though Japan remained the world champion in production technology.

As for the price of oil, the OPEC cartel proved to be unstable over the long run. Unlike oil-rich but sparsely populated countries such as Saudi Arabia and Kuwait, populous member nations such as Iran, Iraq, and Mexico could not easily afford to reduce their production levels for the purpose of propping up the world market price. Eventually the populous countries started to deviate from the cartel agreements, and during the 1980s oil prices began what would become a long decline.

These price movements up and down caused major shake-outs within the oil industry, including numerous acquisitions, divestitures, and mergers. Large companies such as Gulf and Conoco were acquired by direct competitors or by chemical firms, often to be divested later by these same firms. Other leading companies such as Exxon, Mobil, Chevron, and Texaco remained relatively strong, exploiting their overseas sources of crude oil but still potentially at the mercy of OPEC. In 1999 Exxon and Mobil themselves merged into one gigantic firm, a reflection of the lowered price of crude oil and reduced opportunities for competitive profits.

Deficits

As rising imports of oil, cars, and consumer electronics outstripped exports of other products, the United States drifted into a chronic trade deficit. At the same time, a second type of deficit developed, this one in the federal budget. Each year from 1975 until the early 1990s, the government spent, on average, about $200 billion more than it took in. These budget deficits ranged from about 3 to 6 percent of GNP, and by this measure were not especially high compared to those of other advanced industrial countries. But as a long-term phenomenon they were unprecedented in peacetime America. Some analysts interpreted the new situation as an attempt by the government to meet two goals simultaneously, stimulating prosperity by cutting taxes while at the same time spending so much on weaponry that the Soviet Union would be forced into a dilemma: either concede victory in the Cold War or try to match American defense spending.

As it turned out, the Soviets could not afford to compete. The bankruptcy of their own economic system compelled them to give up the long contest, and the U.S.S.R. disintegrated into 15 separate countries beginning in 1991. The Russian Federation remained a major nuclear power, but the Cold War seemed to be over at last. Partly because of the reduced need for military expenditures, the American fiscal deficit then began to shrink, and in 1998 it became a surplus for the first time in a generation. But the end of the annual *deficit* could not quickly reduce the immense accumulated national *debt,* which at the start of the new century still exceeded $5 trillion.

Throughout the 1973–2000 period, the United States maintained the lowest gross domestic savings rate of all leading industrial nations—about two-thirds that of Germany and half that of Japan. By the 1990s American consumers were in possession of more than a billion credit cards, and the average household was spending one-sixth of its annual disposable income on interest payments of various kinds, including home mortgages. In 1984 the ratio of overall household debt to after-tax income had been just under 60 percent, but by 1998 it had grown to 83 percent. Personal bankruptcies became common even in times of national prosperity—partly because of credit-card abuse, partly because of changes in the bankruptcy law, and partly because of the spread of legalized gambling. From the early 1970s to the late 1990s, the rate of personal bankruptcies increased by a factor of five, reaching an all-time high of almost 1.5 million in 1998.

Apparently Slower Economic Growth

From the start of World War II until 1973, real GNP in the United States had grown by an average annual per-capita rate of 3 percent—a very robust figure. In subsequent years it weakened to about half that rate before recovering in the late 1990s. The reasons for this significant slowdown are not well understood, but the principal cause seems to have been a drop in annual productivity gains—that is, in growth of output per hour worked. From 1900 to 1960 this figure had held steady at a rate of about 2 percent per year for the nonfarm business sector. After rising to 3 percent from 1960 to 1973, it dropped to about 1 percent from 1973 through the mid-1990s, after which it turned upward once more.

Part of the reason for this decline was the nation's broad shift toward a service economy and the difficulty in measuring productivity gains in services. Between 1960 and 1993, hours worked in manufacturing as a percentage of all employment fell from 29 percent to 18 percent, but manufacturing output remained stable as a percentage of real GNP: 19 percent in 1960, 19 percent in 1993. Obviously, these numbers denoted large gains in manufacturing productivity.

Service productivity, on the other hand, was much harder to measure because of improvements in the quality of some kinds of services and the related rise of computerization. An hour's work by a health-care professional with access to sophisticated technology was obviously more productive in the year 2000 than it had been in 1970, but this difference was not satisfactorily captured by official statistics. The same was true in other service-sector work such as education and law enforcement. Many firms and government agencies continued trying to develop more accurate figures, and what came to be called the "productivity paradox" in services remains a puzzlement.

The Globalization of Business

During the postwar years, the United States led a prolonged movement for freer trade worldwide. Tariff barriers dropped, cross-border trade increased, and the global economy became much more integrated. The sum of American imports and exports rose from less than 9 percent of GNP in 1960 to more than 25 percent by the end of the century, a very significant change. Meanwhile, money and other forms of capital began to move more rapidly from one country to another, as the opportunity for high returns appeared now here, now there, and forever in motion. There was also a big increase in the establishment of factories and sales offices in other countries. Multinational corporations based in the United States, Europe, and Japan led the globalization movement, in both production and marketing. Companies set up manufacturing facilities wherever the cost of production or of marketing was most favorable. For production, this often meant the place where sufficiently skilled labor was least expensive. For marketing, it often meant the place with the best combination of low internal trade barriers and large numbers of potential customers. The United States served as host for a large number of incoming transplant factories, and outward-looking firms such as IBM, Ford, General Motors, and scores of others built numerous factories in other countries.

The expanded activity in global financial markets was even more striking. It was driven both by investment and by "arbitrage" in the trading of national currencies. By 1997, the *daily* turnover in international currency markets had reached about $1.3 trillion. Financial firms specializing in currency arbitrage, as well as individual speculators seeking quick profits, fueled some of this volatility. The treasurers of multinational corporations were compelled to participate too, so as to minimize their companies' exposure in weakening currencies. The crash of Asian financial markets that began in 1997 and rippled through the world economy over the next two years was related to this rapid and largely unregulated movement into and out of foreign currencies.

The Growing Gap between Rich and Poor

The disparity in shares of wealth and income among Americans had narrowed substantially between 1933 and 1973. The 1960s, one of the most prosperous decades in American history measured by rate of economic growth, was also the time of the most nearly equal distribution of the fruits of capitalism. After that, trends in the apportionment of wealth and income began to diverge, for reasons that are still not entirely clear.

One factor was a greater spread in the wage premium for education. In 1979, on average, college graduates had earned almost 40 percent more than high-school graduates, but the gap had widened to almost 70 percent twenty years later. This very large change derived from movements at both ends of the spectrum. High-school graduates who did not attend college earned 20 percent less in 1997 than in 1979, and even those with one to three years of college made 13 percent less. At the same time, most people with MBAs, JDs, and MDs enjoyed larger wage premiums than they had in earlier periods.

The 1980s became known as the "Greed Decade," a time when financial innovators such as Michael Milken could receive $550 million as a single year's "earnings." (As mentioned earlier in the chapter on the financial system, Milken pioneered in the development of high-yield "junk" bonds.) Milken's employer, the investment banking house Drexel Burnham Lambert, sponsored an annual "Predators' Ball." Here the display of wealth reached heights that might have surprised even Thorstein Veblen, the economist who coined the term "conspicuous consumption." The popular movie *Wall Street* (1987) depicted rapacious financiers blithely breaking up companies after pocketing one-time gains in the sale of their securities. The best-selling novel by Tom Wolfe, *Bonfire of the Vanities* (1987), portrayed a financial community deranged with pointless avarice.

And in real life, some speculators such as Ivan Boesky, who made hundreds of millions of dollars in partly illegal stock manipulations, were indicted and sentenced to jail terms. Michael Milken himself, prosecuted by federal authorities on more than 90 counts, pled guilty to several felonies. He was sentenced to ten years' imprisonment, of which he served almost two years before being paroled.

But the expanding gulf between rich and poor was far more important than individual wrongdoing on Wall Street. Between

1962 and 1990, the net worth of the poorest 20 percent of Americans shrank, while that of the top 20 percent increased by almost 90 percent, and that of the richest 0.5 percent grew by nearly 120 percent. These numbers signified an emphatic reversal of prior trends. In 1929, the richest 1 percent of American households had owned 44 percent of the national net worth. But then, during the 1930s and 1940s, wealth distribution became much more balanced, so that by 1949 the richest 1 percent owned 27 percent of the nation's wealth, and by 1976 only 20 percent.

After that the number began to rise, the richest 1 percent of households owning 30 percent of the nation's wealth by 1980 and, by 1995, almost 40 percent. In that year the average net worth of this richest 1 percent was almost $8 million, while that of the bottom 40 percent averaged less than $1,000. By the end of the century, the wealth of the country's richest individual, Bill Gates of Microsoft, exceeded the combined total of the 60 million poorest American households.

The changing technology of work in the information-based Third Industrial Revolution appeared to be the main cause of the growing spread between rich and poor. But public policies played a role too. Laws passed during the first year of the Reagan Administration in 1981 served to increase the gap by partly flattening the graduated income tax.

Real wages for production and nonsupervisory workers, which had risen at a steady annual rate of about 2 percent for most of the twentieth century, stopped growing altogether in 1973. By the mid-1990s, this large category of employees was taking home about 10 percent less in inflation-adjusted dollars than it had in 1973. Throughout the prosperous 1990s, employers often needed more workers, but wages did not rise in the pattern customarily associated with tight labor markets. New jobs were plentiful, and a few were available at the high end of the pay scale. Most, however, were at the low end, leaving an unusually small percentage in the middle.

Phrases never before heard in the United States, such as "gated communities" and "permanent underclass," now became commonplace. American society seemed be drifting into an income-based class structure of the type associated with certain countries abroad but seldom with the "Land of the Free." By the

1990s, more security personnel worked for private employers—corporations, shopping malls, gated communities—than the total number of police at all levels of government. The construction of new prisons became a premier growth business. By the end of the century close to two million Americans were incarcerated (400,000 of them for drug violations), a number reported to be larger than that for any other country.

The nation's tradition of equitably apportioned increases in income seemed somehow to have gone awry. No longer symbolized by a single model of a rising tide of prosperity lifting all economic boats—a metaphor employed by President Kennedy during the prosperous 1960s—the pattern had splintered into three distinct segments: first, a big increase in wealth and income for "knowledge workers" such as corporate executives, investment bankers, consultants, software engineers, accountants, and lawyers; second, relative stagnation for the bulk of the American middle class; and third, an actual decline in wealth and income for the poorest workers. Measured by aggregate shares in the national income, the bottom 40 percent lost ground during the last quarter of the century. By the late 1990s, the best-paid 10 percent of Americans had an average income 11 times that of the bottom 10 percent—more than twice the ratio for the 15 nations in the European Union and a figure probably without parallel in the history of the United States.

The Money Gap in Business

In the early twenty-first century, CEOs of large U.S. companies were being paid, on average, nearly 400 times as much as the lowest-paid workers in their own firms. That number was far higher than the corresponding ratios in Europe and Japan, and close to ten times the multiple in the United States itself as recently as 1975, when it had been about 40. This new disparity broke a tradition that had held for most of the twentieth century. During the Great Depression of the 1930s, CEO Red Deupree of Procter & Gamble had cut his own salary in half and stopped his annual bonus. Other CEOs, such as Thomas J. Watson, Sr., of IBM, also took voluntary cuts. Even during boom periods such as World War II and the 1960s, most top managers showed a sense of stewardship and moderation about their pay. But from the late 1970s onward into the twenty-first century, many American executives seemed to become obsessed with high pay, much like professional athletes.

A large part of the steep rise in executive pay derived from compensation through stock options during the bull market of the 1990s. Some of it was also related to plausible new theories about rewarding executives for superior achievements by the firms they headed. But in most cases executive compensation seemed to go up regardless of how well a company performed. A study done by the *New York Times* found that for 383 large firms in which the same CEO remained in office from 1993 to 1997, the average price of company shares doubled during those years, but CEO compensation almost quadrupled, from under $2.8 million annually to over $10 million. Company lawyers, behaving like agents for athletes, drafted stock-option and other "incentive" plans that often ensured that executives would come out ahead no matter what happened to the firm. The magazine *Business Week,* which during the 1990s consistently argued that CEO compensation had become excessive, noted in 1999 that "the link between pay and any objective standard of performance has been all but severed."

Much of the sharp increase in top managers' pay occurred during a time of corporate "downsizing" and "re-engineering." From 1973 to 1993, the combined employment of the 500 largest U.S. firms (measured by sales) shrank from 15 million to 11.5 million. Yet the total production of these companies rose, along with the relocation of manufacturing activities to overseas plants employing low-wage labor. Within the domestic workforce, big firms pursued policies of systematic "outsourcing." They laid off employees and arranged for lower-paid, non-union, and part-time workers from small companies to perform functions the core firm had once done for itself.

Downsizing and outsourcing automatically reduced the costs for health insurance, retirement plans, and other benefits available only to full-time employees of the core firm. In many ways this trend represented a logical outcome of what economists call greater perfection of labor markets. But for the laid-off former employees of big firms it seemed a brutal process. For thousands of downsized middle managers, who suddenly found themselves unemployed or working at jobs elsewhere for much less than their former pay—sometimes with no health insurance for themselves and their families—it seemed incredible.

New Patterns of Work and New Needs of Households

The total number of hours a full-time American employee worked per year, after having declined from an average of 2,600 in 1913 to 1,600 in 1990, began to turn upward again. Toward the end of the century it reached 1,950, the highest number for any industrialized nation. This change reflected a broad societal shift in the United States, toward life on the run and frequent "moonlighting" (working at more than one job). Largely because of growing opportunities for (and demands on) female employees, these same societal changes promoted the rise of numerous small service companies and a big increase in franchised businesses. These new companies and franchised outlets supplied a wide range of services once done in the home, such as cooking, housecleaning, laundry, and child care.

Simultaneously, there also emerged a few giant cut-rate retailers such as Wal★Mart, plus several "category-killer" firms such as Toys 'R' Us, Circuit City, Home Depot, Staples, and Office Depot, which threatened small stores in whatever category of goods the big stores chose to sell. Through discount buying, computerized inventory management, and low prices to consumers, the new giants proceeded to annihilate thousands of small retailers throughout the nation. By the close of the century, Wal★Mart alone had come to employ nearly 700,000 workers. For most big manufacturing companies the trend went in the opposite direction, toward downsizing, layoffs, and outsourcing. But the retailing part of the service economy was different.

Some middle- and lower-income families, pressed by declining wages and disappearing benefits, found that one job per household no longer sufficed. From the 1960s to the 1990s, the makeup of households themselves underwent one of the biggest shifts in American history, and in particular the lifestyles of many women changed radically:

	1960	**1995**
Total households, including single persons living alone	53 million	99 million
Married couples, as a percentage of all households	75%	54%
Percentage of couples with children under age 18	48%	26%
Percentage of families headed by single mothers	10%	24%
Percentage of women ages 25–34 not presently married	11.5%	41%

Sources: *U.S. Bureau of the Census* and Andrew Hacker, "The War Over the Family," *New York Review of Books,* 44 (Dec. 4, 1997).

These numbers pointed to rising needs for services provided outside the home, most notably the preparation of food. By the mid-1990s, about 9 million people were working in the food-service industry, making it the nation's largest source of jobs. In a telling change from earlier periods, about half of all money spent by consumers on food now went for restaurant or take-out meals. Fast-food franchises became the major suppliers. They spread so quickly that by the 1980s they not only prepared billions of meals each year but also accounted for 5 of the top 10 brands of all products advertised in prime-time network TV.

Franchising: An Overview

Franchising had originated long before, in the middle decades of the nineteenth century. At that time, companies such as Mc-Cormick Reaper and Singer Sewing Machine set up an early form of franchised outlets to sell their products and show buyers how to use them. These outlets also helped buyers finance their purchases and offered after-sale repair services. Similar reasons prompted the rise of automobile franchising in the early 1900s. Locally owned dealers, not Detroit-based Ford and General Motors, negotiated with customers about repairs, trade-ins, and the sale of new and used cars. Other early franchises included gasoline stations and soft-drink bottlers. In all of these systems, each franchisee was an independent business person operating under a contract to sell at retail the branded products of the parent company, usually at an agreed-upon markup over the wholesale price paid to the parent.

In the years after World War II, a different kind of franchising arose, one organized around service industries rather than sales of products manufactured by the parent company. This new "business-format" franchising offered a wholly standardized system of commerce. Using identical formats nationwide, traditionally small service establishments such as restaurants and dry cleaners could now realize advantages previously available only to big businesses. These included quantity discounts in supplies, access to proven business methods, and—most important—a nationally recognized brand. By the 1960s, franchised outlets had popped up in all kinds of service businesses: convenience stores, motels, dry cleaners, and especially fast-food restaurants.

As American society became more mobile during the postwar decades, franchising grew more rapidly than other kinds of business. Travelers, college students, and people moving to new areas benefited from knowing what to expect from branded service operations such as McDonald's restaurants, 7-Eleven convenience stores, and Kinko's copy shops. As a Holiday Inn television commercial of the 1980s put it, "The best surprise is no surprise." The number of Holiday Inns themselves increased from 162 in 1960 to over 1,200 in 1970, then to over 1,700 in 1980.

By the 1990s, according to the U.S. Census, at least 2,000 different franchisors in many service industries were supervising over half a million retail units, and a new franchised store was opening somewhere in the country every eight minutes. The success rate for franchised outlets was higher than that for independent businesses, although how much so remained a matter of controversy. For one thing, it was hard to get accurate information from such diverse operations. For another, there was the ambiguous definition of "success." (It usually meant simple survival over a certain number of years.) A 1990s study by the U.S. House Committee on Small Business put the success rate for all franchised outlets at between 65 and 75 percent, and for those in highly ranked ones at between 90 and

95 percent. By comparison, only 30 to 40 percent of nonfranchised U.S. retail businesses opening during the latter part of the century survived for five years.

The Champion Franchisor

McDonald's, the top performer of all, claimed a success rate of 98 percent. This company was founded in 1955, and by the 1980s more than 19 out of 20 American consumers between the ages of 7 and 65 were eating at a McDonald's at least once a year. The McDonald's system had become the nation's largest purchaser of beef and was using nearly 8 percent of its food-potato crop. After McDonald's introduced Chicken McNuggets in 1982, it became the nation's second largest seller of chicken, surpassed only by Kentucky Fried Chicken (KFC).

By that time McDonald's share of the U.S. fast-food market was about equal to the combined share of the three next-largest chains. The clown mascot Ronald McDonald ranked second only to Santa Claus as the "person" most familiar to American children. By the year 2000, more than 25,000 McDonald's stores worldwide were grossing close to $40 billion annually, about half of which was coming from non-U.S. operations.

The McDonald Brothers

During the 1930s, in San Bernardino, California, Dick and Maurice "Mac" McDonald had opened their first restaurant, a drive-in with "carhop" waitresses delivering food to customers sitting in automobiles. A few years later, the brothers knocked down the outside walls of their building, installed plate-glass windows, and opened their kitchen to full public view. In 1948 they took an even more radical step. They closed their restaurant for three months, then reopened with a new building and a new service concept described by Mac McDonald as "based on speed, lower prices, and . . . big, big volumes."

They reduced their menu from 25 items to just nine: hamburgers (which they cut in price from 30 to 15 cents), cheeseburgers, potato chips, pie, milk, coffee, and three kinds of soft drinks. Everything customers received from McDonald's now became disposable. The food was to be consumed, and the paper cups and wrappers were thrown away. Inside the restaurant, there would be no more washing of dishes, glasses, or silverware. McDonald's would cease to be a teenagers' hangout and instead become a family restaurant. Its meals were so cheap and of such reliable quality that middle- and low-income parents in San Bernadino could at last feel justified in taking the whole family out to eat.

The McDonald brothers' plan of menu standardization plus high volume meant that staff roles had to be broken down in assembly-line fashion. Like Henry Ford forty years earlier, Dick and Mac now proceeded to define a series of specific jobs: grill man, fry man, counter man, and so on. They let all the carhops go and hired no more female workers, for the brothers were determined to discourage young men from hanging around the restaurant. They invented high-speed custom equipment to do such mundane things as deposit the prescribed amount of both ketchup (one tablespoon) and mustard (one teaspoon) onto a bun with one squeeze of the handle of the same dispenser. Above all, they built such a continuous customer stream that they could cook the food beforehand and deliver it, still fresh, almost at the moment it was ordered.

Dick and Mac continued to prosper, and their new format began to attract nationwide attention. Beginning in 1952, they started licensing their "Speedy Service System," plus the name McDonald's, for a one-time fee of $1,000. Beyond this they provided no guidance and charged their licensees no royalties.

Ray Kroc (1902–1984)

Much as the brothers' system resembled Henry Ford's assembly line, the Alfred Sloan of the fast-food industry turned out to be Ray Kroc, a 52-year-old Chicago-based salesman. Kroc had nationwide marketing rights to the Multimixer, a machine that could make five milkshakes at once. When Dick and Mac McDonald ordered the unlikely total of ten Multimixers, Kroc went to the West

Coast to see for himself how they could possibly sell in such volume out of a single small restaurant. At ten o'clock one morning in 1954, he parked his car in front of the brothers' restaurant and watched as long lines began to form far in advance of lunchtime. Kroc was amazed. "That night in my motel room," he later wrote, "visions of McDonald's restaurants dotting crossroads all over the country paraded through my brain."

In his outstanding history of McDonald's, *Behind the Arches* (1995), the journalist John Love draws a vivid portrait of Ray Kroc. As a youth in Chicago, Kroc had dropped out of high school. A snappy dresser, talented musician, and likeable though sometimes hotheaded young man, he had then combined his daytime sales job with nighttime gigs playing piano in jazz clubs of uneven reputation. During the 1920s he sold real estate in the Florida land boom, then returned to Chicago. Over the next three decades he traveled widely, selling first Lily cups, then Multimixers. In this way he became familiar with soda-fountain and take-out food businesses throughout the country.

By 1954, after so many years on the road, the affable Kroc had become a persuasive salesman of almost anything. Following his first visit to San Bernardino, he introduced himself to the McDonald brothers and quickly talked his way into their confidence. At his suggestion, he became their general franchise agent under a contract stipulating that every person he signed up would pay an initial fee of $950, then a continuing royalty of 1.9 percent of gross sales. Of this, 1.4 percent would go to a new company formed by Kroc (it became McDonald's Corporation), the other 0.5 percent straight into the pockets of Dick and Mac. Kroc was to pay all costs of supervising and servicing the franchisees. The brothers would have no expenses at all. The deal was lopsided in their favor, and it would take Kroc six years to work his way out of it.

The Crusader

Before the Kroc era, the essence of fast-food franchising was simply the sale of franchises. The largest chains, Dairy Queen and Tastee-Freez, sold territorial rights to franchisees who then sublicensed them to store operators. Territorial owners had the responsibility for overseeing local stores, but they seldom discharged it with much energy. Because most entrepreneurs setting up new systems envisioned one-time windfalls more than ongoing business operations, the world of franchising tended to attract people out for a quick score. The big money was to be made in selling the concept, the territory, and often the equipment and supplies—not in operating or supervising stores.

Ray Kroc took precisely the opposite approach, and in the short run he made little money. He supported his family with his ongoing Multimixer business and through a McDonald's restaurant he set up in Des Plaines, Illinois, near Chicago. As an associate of the McDonald brothers put it, Kroc "thought that if franchisors made their franchisees successful, they [the franchisors] would automatically be successful. His new idea was to provide the franchisees with enough services to be successful." As Kroc himself later said, "Our slogan for McDonald's operators is 'In business for yourself, but not by yourself.'" Convinced that the McDonald's format was foolproof, he showed prospective franchisees figures from his Des Plaines store, and even his personal finances. The cornerstone of his system became "sweat equity." Kroc worked brutally long hours and became a personal role model for his franchisees.

Meanwhile, he continued to refine the brothers' original rules. He banned jukeboxes, pay telephones, and vending machines, including coin-operated newspaper boxes and cigarette machines. These items were commonly found in other restaurants because they brought in additional income at little cost to the proprietor. But Kroc wanted no clutter at McDonald's and no hanging out by customers. In the late 1960s, he and his staff converted the restaurants to eat-in as well as take-out establishments. Even then they continued to discourage loiterers by installing seats made of hard plastic, comfortable only for short periods.

From the outset Kroc resolved not to sell supplies and kitchen appliances to captive franchisees. He would specify what equipment they should buy, but would not involve McDonald's Corporation directly in its manufacture and sale. For supplies of beef, cheese, condiments, buns, cups, and napkins, Kroc chose contractors who were themselves small entrepreneurs. He mostly stayed away from major companies catering to the restaurant trade, with the sole exception of Coca-Cola. He courted small firms, imbued them with his vision of a great future, and won price concessions. Some of the suppliers had no other customers, and they later developed an important voice within Kroc's system. Many of them formed associations and contributed advice that affected McDonald's policies. But none of them had a written contract, which meant that Kroc could cut them off at any time. He took pride in his "handshake" agreements, and some of this tradition endured at McDonald's for the rest of the century.

Recruiting Franchisees

At first Kroc limited each operator to one store. Later he based the award of additional units on the performance of the franchisee's existing store. If a franchisee fell short of the company's high standards, Kroc's answer to a request for another unit was always no. "When you sell a big franchise territory, you give up the business to the man who owns the area. He replaces your organization, and you don't have control." Kroc's early experience in selling franchises to his golfing buddies around Chicago turned out badly. They had other jobs and tended to regard themselves not as entrepreneurs but as silent investors.

Instead, Kroc came to look for franchisees like Betty and Sandy Agate, a middle-aged Chicago couple who had little money but an exceptional work ethic. One day in 1955, as Betty Agate was selling Catholic Bibles door to door, she walked into the small office in Chicago's Loop that housed Kroc's Multimixer headquarters. June Martino, Kroc's secretary, bluntly asked Agate, "What the hell is a Jew doing selling Catholic Bibles?" Betty replied that she was just trying to make a living. To that, Martino suggested, "Why don't you get a McDonald's instead?" Soon Betty Agate and her husband Sandy were operating a new McDonald's in a Chicago suburb, and before long their annual income was four times that of Kroc himself.

Kroc used the Agates' story to sell other franchisees on McDonald's potential, saying to prospects that Betty and Sandy were getting rich through sweat equity. Eventually Kroc's re-tellings of their experience spawned more than 200 McDonald's restaurants throughout the country. Nearly all were managed by owner-operators like Betty and Sandy, who meanwhile had opened additional units themselves.

In the end, Sandy Agate turned out to be too autonomous for his own good. After running his restaurants for a few years, he became convinced that Pepsi-Cola would be a better choice for the local market than Coke, Kroc's standard. So in 1975, when the Agates' 20-year franchise was about to expire, they were told it would not be renewed. For years thereafter, Sandy Agate was known throughout the McDonald's system as the man who crossed Ray Kroc and paid the price.

June and Lou Martino

The handshake tradition and the fall of the Agates did not mean that Kroc liked to surround himself with yes people. June Martino, who became secretary, treasurer, and a board member of McDonald's Corporation, was about as independent-minded as a person could be. She had worked for Kroc since 1948, seven years before he set up McDonald's. Offbeat and sometimes eccentric, she nevertheless had topflight skills in persuading hostile factions to get along with each other. She was forever having to reverse the impulsive Kroc's peremptory firings of almost everybody. By force of will, she held together the hodgepodge of personalities that comprised the original McDonald's team. She became known, Kroc later wrote, as "Vice-President of Equilibrium."

June Martino was also a key recruiter. In the early days, she signed up the Agates and dozens of other franchisees. Sometimes prospects would stay at her house while they looked over local stores. She also hired numerous corporate employees, one of whom, a college friend of her son, started in the mail room and went on to become one of Kroc's successors as head of the company. Another recruit was her husband Lou, who quit his job as a Motorola engineer to open a McDonald's in partnership with June.

Lou Martino was the person most responsible for the quality of McDonald's french fries, which became legendary in the fast-food industry. Kroc and his colleagues, despite continual efforts, had been unable to produce fries of dependably uniform quality. They would buy the best Idaho russets, cut them to precise specifications ($9/32$ of an inch), then cook them under controlled conditions. But some batches of the fries would come out limp, and others would look dark brown on the outside while remaining raw in the middle. Working at a lab he persuaded Kroc to set up, Lou Martino discovered that the chemical makeup of potatoes changed after they were dug out of the ground. Accordingly, McDonald's ordered that all potatoes be cured for three weeks before cooking, the interval necessary for their high sugar content to convert to starch, and in turn prevent premature browning. Next the researchers found that when dumped cold into the frying vat, different batches of potatoes caused the temperature of the shortening to drop by varying amounts, making it impossible to establish uniform cooking times. Finally, after months of frustrating work, Lou and his researchers made their big discovery: regardless of how many degrees the temperature of the shortening fell after the introduction of the cut potatoes, the fries were cooked just right at the moment the temperature had regained precisely three degrees. Lou and his ecstatic colleagues now created a "potato computer" that buzzed signals to the fry cook. Later McDonald's adapted the same principle for some of its other products.

The Financial Wizard

One of Kroc's best qualities as a businessman was his recognition of the need for complementary talents. As he once said to some MBA students at a prominent business school, "If a corporation has two executives who think alike, one of them is unnecessary."

Harry Sonneborn, who in the mid-1950s became the third important member of the original team (after Kroc and June Martino), had learned about franchises working at Tastee-Freez. "Harry didn't know or care a damn thing about hamburgers and french fries," said Kroc. "He was a cold, calculating money man, but I needed a guy like that."

Only a few months after Kroc hired him, the youthful Sonneborn developed a way for McDonald's to make a little more money immediately and a great deal more over the long term. He did this by putting the firm into the real estate business, first through leasing, then through land ownership. By the 1980s McDonald's was the largest owner of retail real estate in the world. That position, together with a record of financial success unmatched in the industry, derived mostly from Harry Sonneborn's early strategic moves.

McDonald's Corporation itself usually selected the sites for new stores. Kroc liked to fly over suburban areas in small planes or helicopters, looking for neighborhoods with "schools, church steeples, and new houses." He thought that families who lived in these new neighborhoods would be natural customers. Then, too, nearby commercial land was usually cheap. In the early days, McDonald's franchisees had to come up with the money to buy or lease a property, then build and equip their stores.

Harry Sonneborn now proposed that McDonald's Corporation get into real estate itself by becoming the middle element in what is known as a sandwich lease. The company would take out long-term leases, then sublease the properties to franchisees at a fixed dollar markup. This leasing charge would be in addition to the 1.9-percent-of-gross-sales annual franchise fee, which Kroc later raised to 3 percent. Sonneborn created a subsidiary called Franchise Realty Corporation and gave it the task of locating sites and taking out 20-year leases at a fixed rate. He then persuaded landowners to put up the leased land as collateral for a building loan. This loan, made to a McDonald's franchisee, would finance the construction of a store.

In the sandwich leases, Franchise Realty's markup to subleasing franchisees was first 20 percent of the original lease fee, then 40 percent. In the early days, this markup brought in between $250 and $500 per store per month, and it greatly augmented the cash flow of McDonald's Corporation. Franchisees had to pay all taxes and property insurance costs, which tended to increase with each passing year along with the value of the land. Meanwhile, Franchise Realty's only serious expenses were its fixed-rate lease payments to landowners.

As sales at most stores began to grow, Sonneborn had another flash of inspiration. Once a unit's monthly receipts exceeded a certain threshold, its sublease payments to McDonald's should shift from a percentage of the lease fee to a percentage of the unit's gross sales, which came to be set at 8.5 percent. It was this 8.5 percent, in addition to McDonald's 3-percent-of-gross-sales annual franchise fee, that made the company so profitable over the long run.

In the early 1960s, six or seven years after its founding in 1955, McDonald's had a reliable income stream but little capital of its own. Sonneborn now moved to alleviate a portion of that problem. As part of its deal with new operators, Franchise Realty began to require a "security deposit" of $7,500. Half was to be returned after 15 years, the other half when the 20-year franchise expired.

As security deposits accumulated, Sonneborn used the money to buy land for new stores. Later on, when the original 20-year leases began to expire, McDonald's often bought existing sites as well. Most of the early purchases turned out to be bargains, because they were made at a moment when suburban land prices stood on the verge of a big jump. Eventually about two-thirds of all restaurants in the McDonald's system sat on land owned by the Corporation. Together with the 8.5 percent subleasing system, the whole arrangement constituted a money-making machine for the company. As Kroc said years later, "Harry alone put in the policy that salvaged this company and made it a big-leaguer. His idea is what really made McDonald's rich."

As McDonald's outlets rapidly multiplied during the period from the late 1960s to the early 1980s, a general price inflation was running high throughout the country. But McDonald's fixed-rate lease payments to landowners remained flat. Meanwhile, its income from franchised stores surged because of rising overall prices. By itself, inflation pushed nearly all franchisees past the threshold at which they would start paying the 8.5 percent rental. Even a McDonald's hamburger, which had sold for 15 cents in 1967, was costing customers 50 cents in the early 1980s. By that time the company was earning about 90 percent of the profits it received from franchised stores through real estate payments.

Sonneborn's subleasing fee of 8.5 percent on gross sales also aligned the interests of most concerned parties. It gave Mc-

Donald's Corporation a tremendous incentive to maximize system-wide sales through the development of new products, national advertising, and the enforcement of uniform standards. It slightly diminished the upside profit potential for franchisees, but without in any sense putting a ceiling on it. And still another aspect of the leasing plan practically forced franchisees to keep faith with Kroc's rigorous "QSC" formula (quality, service, cleanliness). As Sonneborn put it, "We connected the lease to the franchise so that any violation of the franchise [that is, any deviation from Kroc's operating procedures] could create termination of the lease." This strategy stretched lease law to its limits, but it held up in court against repeated legal challenges.

The Big Leagues

As late as 1960, five years after setting up McDonald's Corporation, Ray Kroc was still making no money from the company except what his Des Plaines restaurant brought in. Sonneborn as president was being paid only $27,500 annually. In lieu of higher salaries, Kroc had given June Martino 10 percent of the company's stock and Sonneborn 20 percent. All three could now visualize McDonald's as a really large chain, but where were they going to get the capital required for national expansion? Almost no fast-food firms were considered sound long-term bets by investment banks and insurance companies. McDonald's was doing well enough, but its balance sheet looked little better than average for the industry.

To remedy this situation, Sonneborn began to tinker with his company's accounting system, as entrepreneurs often do. In particular, he decided to capitalize McDonald's future lease income. That is, he calculated the amount of money that the company would have to invest currently in order to generate the stream of expected future lease payments by franchisees. Then he boldly placed this number on the company's balance sheet as an asset. "It was the greatest accounting gimmick ever devised," Sonneborn said later. "The bankers were bemused and befuddled by it because they had never seen it before, but it surely helped us get some loans." As is always the case under accounting regulations, explanations of what McDonald's had done were recorded in the footnotes of the accountants' report. But the apparent increase in the company's net worth had the desired effect.

Sonneborn now decided he was ready to approach a major lender and ask for a very large loan. If necessary he would also offer part ownership of McDonald's as an "equity sweetener." After several deals fell through, he finally hit his target with two insurance companies, State Mutual Life and Paul Revere. Each one agreed to lend $750,000 in return for 10 percent of McDonald's stock. Sonneborn saw that the deal was a good one, but "Ray was madder than hell." Kroc also objected when other parties took a finder's fee of 2.5%. He caved in when Sonneborn reminded him "that seventy-eight percent of something is a lot better than one hundred percent of nothing, and nothing is what we've got now."

This was the real beginning of the company's worldwide empire. Among other things, the new financial credibility permitted Kroc to borrow even more money and eventually to buy out the McDonald brothers for $2.7 million in cash.

In 1965, Sonneborn fulfilled his ambition of taking the company public. Its initial offering was quickly subscribed at the opening share price of $22.50. By the end of the first trading day the price had risen to $30, a week later to $36, and a few weeks after that to $49. Sonneborn and June Martino suddenly found themselves wealthy. Kroc, who had earned no money at all from McDonald's Corporation until 1961, was now in possession of stock worth $32 million, which in 1965 was a big fortune. McDonald's was listed on the New York Stock Exchange in 1968, and in 1985 it became the first food-service company included among the 30 premium stocks that make up the Dow-Jones Industrial Average. By that time, Harry Sonneborn had retired from the company after a dispute with Kroc. His name remains obscure in the annals of business history, but he was of almost equal importance with Kroc as the architect of McDonald's success.

Operational Training

In the early days of franchising, as noted earlier, entrepreneurs tried to become rich through one-time sales of their brands and business plans, with little follow-up supervision. Then Kroc engineered a shift by forgoing the quick bonanza and concentrating on long-term quality, service, and cleanliness—QSC. These he enforced without mercy. He installed a rigorous inspection system developed by his protégé Fred Turner, and soon the initials QSC were famous throughout the fast-food industry. Turner later succeeded Kroc as head of the corporation.

When Kroc hired Turner in 1957, his instructions to the new recruit were simple. "Visit the stores" and see what was going on. Turner proceeded to develop a report card, on which each store received a grade of A, B, C, D, or F on quality, service, cleanliness, and overall performance. McDonald's came to employ hundreds of "field service consultants" to make surprise visits once every three months. Twice a year all stores underwent "full field" inspections lasting three days.

Turner's first codification of Kroc's QSC system was laid out in a 15-page mimeographed pamphlet that began with an emphatic statement: "Herein outlined is the successful method." By 1985 the instruction manual, known within the company as "the Bible," had grown to 600 pages. It had color photos demonstrating where the pickles, mustard, ketchup, and onions should go on burgers of various sizes. It gave precise instructions about everything: 32 slices of cheese per pound, one-fourth ounce of onions per hamburger, and so on. McDonald's also made instructional films, which evolved into videotapes sent out several times a year to each store.

In 1961 Kroc opened "Hamburger University" in the basement of a McDonald's near Chicago and required all new franchisees to attend its two-week training course. By 1968, the "campus" included two large classrooms in addition to a restaurant. In 1983, after a big expansion in the number of outlets, McDonald's opened a new $40 million training facility with seven classrooms, 28 faculty members, and a 154-room dormitory. This expanded

Hamburger University received accreditation from the American Council on Education for 36 semester-hours of college credit. After the company went international, students who did not speak English were equipped with earphones delivering the teacher's message in their own languages through simultaneous translation. By the 1990s more than 4,000 people were graduating from Hamburger U. each year, and advanced students were taking follow-up courses.

Fred Turner maintained tight central control of standards. But beyond that both he and Kroc insisted on decentralization in much the same way that Alfred Sloan, Neil McElroy, and Ferdinand Eberstadt had done in other settings. In each case, decentralization increased the flow of information up and down within the company. As one McDonald's franchisee put it, "I am an independent owner, but the company is only a phone call away. They provide staff services, but operations is the lifeblood of the business and that is what I have control over." By this the franchisee meant decisions about whom to hire and fire, how much to pay employees, and how to price items on the menu. The CEO of another major chain, Pizza Hut, emphasized that "In most businesses, there is a risk to complaining. People tell their bosses what they think the boss wants to hear. The franchisee, though, does not work for you and has no hesitation to call you directly and let you know what he thinks. The franchisees make us better."

Most of McDonald's best-known products, such as the Big Mac, Egg McMuffin, and Filet-O-Fish, were first suggested by franchisees. (By contrast, most menu items developed by Kroc himself proved to be losers, such as his beloved Hula Burger, a sandwich containing a slice of fresh pineapple topped with melted cheese.) In addition, the company's independent suppliers proposed numerous procedural innovations. Kroc regarded these bottom-up ideas not as challenges to his authority but as evidence of the virtues of franchising done McDonald's style. The whole system, he said, was "the perfect example of capitalism in action."

During the 1960s McDonald's set up regional networks to coordinate dealings with its local stores. By 1990 the company's operations were divided into 35 areas, each overseen by a Regional

Operators Advisory Board run jointly by managers from Mc-Donald's Corporation and representatives elected by franchisees from their own number. The boards suggested guidelines for wages, made recommendations about menus, and worked with regional advertising cooperatives.

Franchisees exerted considerable power over advertising expenditures through an organization developed during the late 1960s and early 1970s. As Kroc described it, the Operators' National Advertising Fund (OPNAD) "is supported by a voluntary contribution of one percent of gross sales by licensees and company stores that belong to the program. . . . What small businessman wouldn't cheerfully give up one percent of his gross to get our kind of commercials . . . on network television to promote his store? He'd have to be crazy not to."

Here, as in so many other areas, McDonald's developed a way to benefit from centralized management while still drawing on the expertise of local operators. By the 1980s, a 60-member committee divided between elected franchisees and McDonald's regional ad executives was setting OPNAD's policies. Each franchisee on the committee wielded one vote, each ad manager half a vote, so the franchisees had formal control. The 60 OPNAD members held quarterly meetings to oversee McDonald's national advertising budget, which had grown to more than $1 billion annually.

The Importance of Choosing Good Franchisees

Kroc had established the McDonald's system in 1955 on the basis of 20-year renewable franchises. So during the early and middle 1970s, the issue arose of what to do about renewals. Kroc and Fred Turner decided that any store failing to score a consistent average of C or better should be disqualified automatically.

In the broad world of franchising, the termination of a franchisee remained rare, because most companies made their money through licensing of brands and direct sales of equipment and supplies. Kroc and Turner, by contrast, saw the renewal issue as an invaluable tool for disciplining lax operators and improving system performance. They terminated about one of every 14 franchisees who applied for renewal. Though an apparently small percentage, it was much larger than comparable figures by other companies, and it had a powerful incentive effect throughout the McDonald's system. The policy triggered numerous lawsuits by terminated franchisees, but the company won almost all such disputes. Because of its unexcelled record in court, McDonald's terms of franchising became the model for the industry.

By the 1990s the company was receiving over 20,000 inquiries per year from prospective franchisees. About one in ten was granted an interview, and one in ten interviewees wound up with a franchise. At the end of the century McDonald's had a franchisee waiting list of more than 24 months.

As a matter of policy, the company had long turned its back on the credentialism that came to characterize jobs in big business and other areas such as law, accounting, consulting, and academia. None of the three original corporate employees—Kroc, June Martino, and Harry Sonneborn—had completed a formal education, and this pattern was typical of early fast-food entrepreneurs. "Colonel" Harland Sanders of KFC, Dave Thomas of Wendy's, and Kroc himself were all high-school dropouts. As late as the 1980s, after McDonald's had become a big business with more than $10 billion in annual sales, only 14 of its top 26 executives had college degrees. Chairman Fred Turner, who did not, said "For those people who have the ability but who have not been in situations where they could demonstrate it, McDonald's became a place of opportunity with a capital O."

By the 1980s the average McDonald's franchisee was operating 3.1 stores, and some had many more than that. As both the corporation and the number of stores grew, managers working in the headquarters at Oak Brook, Illinois, often took higher-paying jobs offered by "master franchisees" who owned many stores. In this kind of job shift, big-business talents gravitated to medium-sized businesses charged with supervising numerous small-business operations.

The emergence of master franchisees became a salient pattern in the growth of both domestic and international franchising, and not just at McDonald's. A single operator could turn a small firm (one franchise) into a medium-sized business (10 units each grossing $1 million annually) or a large one (200 units, which, if each grossed $1 million, comprised a $200 million company). Multiunit franchising became the dominant mode of growth at McDonald's, Wendy's, and other leading chains. It afforded major entrepreneurial opportunities for successful franchisees, and from the viewpoint of corporate headquarters was often the most efficient way to expand. As a Pizza Hut executive said, "It is much easier to have 140 franchisees add 1 unit per year than to have the company add 140 units per year."

Kroc and Turner reserved many new stores for franchisees with outstanding records. This policy had a snowball effect, and only those snowballs that were doing well were permitted to roll down the hill and grow larger. The development of master franchisees, much like the movement of salaried executives out of McDonald's corporate offices into the field, became a way to test and cultivate managerial ability.

Into the Mouths of Babes

Back in 1948, the first purchase at Dick and Mac McDonald's newly designed San Bernardino store had been made by a nine-year-old girl. She bought a bag of 15-cent hamburgers to take home for the family's dinner. "The kids loved coming to the counter," said Art Bender, the original counterman and later Kroc's first franchisee. "They would come with two bits in their fists and order a hamburger and a Coke. They could still see Mama in the car, but they also could feel independent. Pretty soon, it sinks in that this is great for the business; this is important."

The company began to direct much of its television advertising toward children. In the early days of TV, ad rates for Saturday morning shows were only about one-fourth those for prime time. McDonald's franchisees in many cities recognized the bargain and started sponsoring programs for kids. In and around Washington, D.C., franchisees developed a show featuring a Bozo clown who soon became identified with McDonald's. When it was decided that he should have a new name, the clown himself, a local actor named Willard Scott, invented Ronald McDonald. When the name and the clown went national, Scott did not get the job, but he later achieved fame in his own right as the affable weatherman on NBC's *Today* show. By the 1980s, McDonald's was far and away the leader in fast food, but more so with youngsters than adults. It accounted for better than 40 percent of the market for children under the age of seven, ten percentage points above its overall market share. When Ray Kroc became wealthy, one of his favorite philanthropies was the chain of Ronald McDonald Houses, located near hospitals and offering relatives of seriously ill children an inexpensive place to stay. The concept was conceived by a Philadelphia ad agency.

The children's market was one reason why Kroc's personal fanaticism about cleanliness fit so well with the rest of the company's strategy. Kroc wanted every store to be a place where adults would not feel uncomfortable when their children visited the rest rooms. McDonald's giveaways of toys based on Disney characters and its TV ads for "Happy Meals" for kids further reinforced the message that everything at McDonald's would be wholesome and predictable. As Kroc himself put it, "A child who loves our TV commercials and brings her grandparents to a McDonald's gives us two more customers."

In almost every country where McDonald's came to operate, it had the effect of empowering children—or, in another view, exploiting them. The format encouraged children to choose what they wanted and assured them that they would get it quickly. Ronald McDonald began to appear on TV all over the world. In China he became "Uncle McDonald," in Japan, "Donald Makadonaldo," to accommodate local difficulties in pronouncing the letter "R" in Ronald and in juxtaposing two hard consonants. A group of academic anthropologists studied the company's experiences in East Asia and published their findings in an excellent book called *Golden Arches East* (1997). They discovered that McDonald's not only appealed to children but also became something of a refuge for women in the often male-dominated cultures of East Asia.

The U.S. Workforce

Another academic study, done during the 1970s, found that the average age of fast-food employees was just over 20, number of years of education just under 12, and proportion working part-time 64 percent. The number of employees per store averaged about 40, of whom 64 percent were female, 52 percent students, and 13 percent African American. These figures were for the industry as a whole, not just McDonald's.

By the 1980s, each McDonald's restaurant, on the average, was employing about 65 workers and five salaried managers. More people in the U.S. workforce were getting their first job at McDonald's than at any other employer, including the Army. By the end of the century, according to the company, close to 9 million Americans had worked at McDonald's. The employee turnover rate, like that of other fast-food franchises, sometimes reached 200 percent per year. Many employees were teenagers and senior citizens working part-time, or recent high-school graduates just entering the workforce.

Until 1966, the company continued the McDonald brothers' policy of hiring no women. Nor did it have a good reputation as a place of management opportunity for minorities. But by the 1980s, 57 percent of McDonald's workers were women, and by the 1990s women comprised about 40 percent of its franchisees, either individually or as part of a husband-wife team. There developed a Women Operators' Network, one of many ancillary organizations within the system.

In the 1990s, about 12 percent of McDonald's U.S. franchisees were African Americans, and the company went to special lengths to help black-owned startups, often requiring less than the usual initial investment from their prospective owner-operators. In 1995, a black franchisee in Houston told a reporter from the *Wall Street Journal* that in his view McDonald's was America's "best company for African-American entrepreneurs."

In the food-service business, the key cost is labor, and one important element of McDonald's success was its ruthless policy of shifting most of the risk of uneven customer flow onto employees. When traffic was low, they were told to punch out and go home.

When it was high, they were asked to stay beyond their scheduled working hours. In temporarily slack periods, they were urged to straighten up the store: "If there's time to lean, there's time to clean." Sometimes employees were asked to work split shifts based on customer flows at mealtimes throughout the day. About 90 percent of franchisees and 60 percent of company-owned stores started their part-time employees off at the minimum wage.

Internationalization

By the 1980s, the American market was almost saturated with fast-food outlets, and if McDonald's wished to keep growing, the logical next step was expansion abroad. The same was true for other chains. In the 1980s, about 400 American firms established nearly 40,000 stores outside the United States, an increase of over 70 percent in foreign outlets during this one decade. By the end of the century, almost half of the 25,000 restaurants in the McDonald's system were located outside the United States, scattered in more than 100 countries. A new store was opening somewhere every three hours.

McDonald's followed the lead of IBM and other pioneering multinationals in tailoring its operations to local cultures. In Japan it offered teriyaki burgers, in the Philippines McSpaghetti, in India a beefless hamburger. Customers could get McRibs with beer in Germany, McLaks (grilled salmon) in Norway, and McHuevos (hamburgers topped with poached eggs) in Uruguay. In Saudi Arabia McDonald's had separate seating sections for men and women, and each store closed four times a day for prayers.

The company tried to downplay its American origins. Its Canadian operation, started in 1968, was run by a Canadian. Its large Japanese system began in 1971 as a 50-50 joint venture between McDonald's on the one hand and the young entrepreneur Den Fujita and the Daiichiya Baking Company on the other. Fujita bought out the interest of Daiichiya Baking, ran the operation himself, and became almost as famous in Japan as Ray Kroc was in America. By 1983, the gross sales of McDonald's Japan had surpassed those of the largest indigenous Japanese fast-food chain, Sushi Company, which operated over 2,000 stores.

Eventually McDonald's reached into so many countries that the magazine *The Economist* began to measure relative costs of living by comparing the prices of Big Macs throughout the world. In 1996, for example, the average was $2.36 in the United States, $3.41 in France, and $2.98 in Brazil. *The Economist* drew conclusions from these numbers about the degree to which local currencies were overvalued or undervalued by the standard of the American dollar. The magazine's annual "Big Mac Index" proved remarkably reliable, tracking more complicated statistical methods.

In addition to expansion overseas, franchising continued to spread in other ways. Important adaptations during the closing years of the century included the appearance of McDonald's, Burger Kings, and other franchised restaurants in airports, subway and train stations, and "food courts" located inside shopping malls. Food courts were customarily set up in U-shaped forms around large central dining areas, offering places where several hundred people could choose from a variety of menus.

Pluralism

Toward the close of the twentieth century, the top 50 franchised restaurant systems oversaw more than 100,000 outlets within the United States. Of these, 76 percent were owned by local franchisees, the remaining 24 percent by the franchisor. A Harvard Business School professor, Jeffrey Bradach, called this a "plural system," and in a book on the subject found that the two parts reinforced each other. As one CEO put it, "The chain units give you a system perspective, while the franchisees give you a local perspective. We are constantly working to balance both of these perspectives." Another CEO added, "We are in essence managing six thousand identical factories spread around the world." This, wrote Bradach, represented "the mass production of organization itself," and it was a milestone in the growth of American business.

Then, too, some large corporations began to purchase entire systems. PepsiCo, for example, acquired KFC, Taco Bell, and Pizza Hut, all of which furnished captive markets for Pepsi Cola while retaining their basic organizational structure as franchised operations.

As the following table shows, the pattern of franchisee versus company ownership differed substantially from one system to the next.

The 15 Largest U.S. Franchised Restaurant Systems, 1995			
	Total Number of Stores in U.S. (thousands)	Percentages of Franchisee-Owned Units vs. Company-Owned Units	Average Gross Annual Sales per Store ($ million)
1. McDonald's	12.0	85% vs. 15%	$1.7
2. Subway Sandwiches	10.8	100% vs. 0%	0.3
3. Pizza Hut	8.7	46% vs. 54%	0.6
4. Burger King	7.1	93% vs. 7%	1.1
5. Taco Bell	6.6	60% vs. 40%	0.9
6. KFC	5.1	62% vs. 38%	0.8
7. Dairy Queen	5.0	99% vs. 1%	0.5
8. Wendy's	4.4	73% vs. 27%	1.0
9. Domino's Pizza	4.3	84% vs. 16%	0.5
10. Hardee's	3.2	75% vs. 25%	0.9
11. Dunkin' Donuts	3.2	100% vs. 0%	0.5
12. Arby's Restaurants	2.9	88% vs. 12%	0.7
13. Baskin-Robbins	2.6	100% vs. 0%	0.3
14. TCBY Treats	2.5	100% vs. 0%	0.2
15. Sonic Drive-Ins	1.6	86% vs. 14%	0.7

Source: Techonomic, reported in and adapted here from *Restaurant Business,* November 1, 1997. Numbers in second column are rounded to nearest whole percentage point.

Why Franchising Grew: Capital Scarcity and Principal-Agent Relationships

The explosion of franchising during and after the 1950s was largely unforeseen, much like earlier retail innovations such as department stores, mail-order houses, nonfranchised chain stores, and shopping malls. In retrospect, it is clear that each of these formats filled a new societal need. Researchers have offered two explanations of how franchising filled such a need and grew so rapidly.

One is that it provided a way to spread financial risk and raise money, by tapping local sources of capital in order to fund national operations. Individual franchisees could draw on their personal savings, take out small bank loans, and persuade friends and relatives to invest some of their own money. In this way, even a franchising company that could not attract major bank loans or venture capital *could* still pyramid the savings of thousands of small investors.

A second explanation, grounded in what economists and lawyers call "agency theory," focuses on the nature of relationships among participants in franchised systems. As agency theory is generally understood, "principals" enter into contracts with "agents" to perform tasks that the principals lack the time, expertise, or inclination to do themselves.

Relationships between principals and agents are not confined to franchising, of course. Suburban homeowners (principals) hire teenagers (agents) to mow lawns. Large manufacturing companies (principals) sometimes contract with investment banks (agents) to find suitable complementary firms that the large company might wish to acquire. The "monitoring costs" necessary to ensure that the job gets done well are factored into the principals' business expenses. If monitoring costs are to be minimized, then principals and agents must be striving toward the same end, which in business usually means the maximization of either revenues or profits. The best franchising coalitions align the interests of the parent company, individual franchisees, and other parties such as suppliers and landlords.

Although it is not covered by the data in the table above listing 15 companies, a revealing aspect of the mixed-ownership situation is that franchisee-owned outlets were consistently more profitable than company-owned ones. This was true even though the management staffs in company-owned outlets were typically younger and better educated than those in franchisee-owned ones. Owner-operators (franchisees), whose livelihoods and personal assets were tied up in the business, seemed to pay closer attention to employee performance, local consumer trends, and good prices from suppliers.

It would be hard to imagine a more apt illustration of the explanatory power of agency theory. As principals in the running of their own stores, owner-operators in McDonald's and other franchised systems had stronger incentives to manage well than did the agents of the corporation, however energetic and well-trained they might be.

McDonald's Past and Future

At the start of the twenty-first century, it was becoming increasingly difficult for McDonald's central office to keep all of its franchisees in line. The larger the system grew, the more difficult it was to standardize operations everywhere. Then, too, McDonald's Corporation found it hard to accept consumers' own impatience with menus that were perhaps too standardized. This kind of tension had been present from the start, but consumers' tastes broadened as society became more diverse, and with each passing year the company confronted tougher competition from other franchised systems. In response to these pressures, the company's share price occasionally dipped during the 1990s, and at one point McDonald's corporate board forced the resignation of the CEO. Yet McDonald's continued to record by far the highest sales-per-store figures in the industry, and it was a strong testament to Ray Kroc's original vision that his company remained the leader in fast food two generations after its founding.

Kroc's style of franchising represented another benchmark in the persistent effort by American managers to balance centralization with decentralization through organizational design. Franchising at McDonald's and other companies proved extraordinarily flexible: an individual franchisee with a single store, master franchisees with multiple stores, and plural arrangements in which many outlets were corporate-owned and numerous others franchisee-owned. Then, too, networks of McDonald's suppliers sprang up everywhere, often sponsored by the central corporation but always kept independent of it. In each of these arrangements, the management talent and financial clout of big business complemented the local knowledge, entrepreneurial drive, and sweat equity of small business.

At the beginning, in the 1950s, the McDonald's system had been put together by entrepreneurial visionaries with little schooling but lots of energy and common sense. The special contribution of Kroc, June Martino, and Harry Sonneborn was their ingenious combination of methods for aligning principal and agent relationships so as to make the whole of the McDonald's system exceed the sum of its parts. John Love, whose book *Behind the Arches* remains the best single source on McDonald's, writes that the key to the company's success "is the way it achieves uniformity and allegiance to an operating regimen without sacrificing the strengths of American individualism and diversity."

As Ray Kroc himself liked to put it, "Franchising has become an updated version of the American Dream," because it offered rewards commensurate with individual effort. But he also said, "None of us is as good as all of us." Kroc and his associates perfected an organizational formula used successfully by thousands of McDonald's franchisees in over a hundred countries. Few other companies in any industry have ever matched that kind of achievement, and McDonald's rapid growth continued into the twenty-first century.

"I've found the job where I fit best!"

FIND YOUR WAR JOB
In Industry – Agriculture – Business

Top: In the early 1940s the U.S. Office of War Information distributed posters such as this one urging women to "find your war job." Corbis and Minnesota Historical Society.

Bottom: Individual companies reinforced the idea of women's contributions to the war effort, as in this poster from Westinghouse. Corbis.

Top: The investment banker and War Production Board vice-chairman Ferdinand Eberstadt, whose ingenious Controlled Materials Plan thrust industrial mobilization forward during World War II. Corbis/Bettmann-UPI.

Bottom: The hard-driving Eberstadt, by now back on Wall Street, testifying in 1954 before the Senate Banking Committee. Corbis/Bettmann-UPI.

Opposite top: David Sarnoff of RCA and Guglielmo Marconi, inventor of wireless radiotelegraphy, at the RCA transmitting center on Long Island, New York, 1933. Corbis/Bettmann-UPI.

Opposite bottom: Experimental broadcasting by RCA's subsidiary NBC in 1936, the earliest days of television. Courtesy of Baker Library, Harvard Business School.

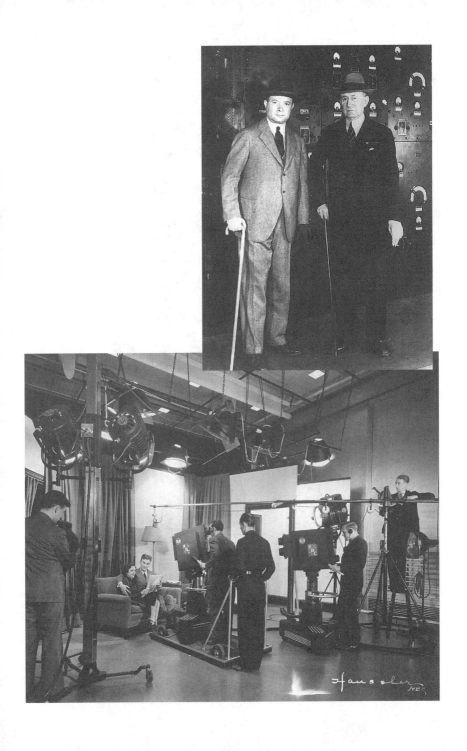

Opposite top: Watching an early model TV set, late 1930s. Corbis/ Schenectady Museum, Hall of Electrical History Foundation.

Opposite bottom: David Sarnoff at the 1939 New York World's Fair, broadcasting announcements about the progress of television. Corbis/ Bettmann-UPI.

Top: Sarnoff after the triumph of color TV in the 1960s: the business dandy at the height of his fame. Courtesy of Baker Library, Harvard Business School.

Bottom: John Johnson, the Chicago businessman whose company published Ebony *and* Jet *and later branched into real estate, beauty products, and other fields. This picture appeared in* Black Enterprise *in 1987, announcing Johnson's selection as Entrepreneur of the Decade.* Courtesy of Johnson Publishing Company, Inc.

Top: Mary Kay Ash in 1978. Ash founded Mary Kay Cosmetics in 1963 and quickly built it into a thriving business based on energetic marketing by thousands of part-time sales agents working on commission. Corbis/Bettmann-UPI.

Bottom: Oprah Winfrey—TV talk-show host, actor, entertainment entrepreneur, and one of the most famous Americans at the start of the twenty-first century. Mitchell Gerber/Corbis.

Opposite top: Ray Kroc's first McDonald's restaurant in Des Plaines, Illinois, built in 1955 and now a museum. Corbis/Bettmann.

Opposite bottom: Ray Kroc in 1963, age 61. McDonald's Corporation had opened 315 restaurants in 37 states, but had not yet gone public. Bettmann/Corbis.

Top: A proud Kroc in the late 1960s, when McDonald's became an eat-in as well as a takeout restaurant. Corbis/Bettmann.

Opposite top: The IBM System/360 mainframe computer, brought out in 1964 and one of the most important industrial products of the twentieth century. Courtesy of IBM Archives.

Opposite bottom: Left to right: Steve Jobs, John Sculley, and Steve Wozniak, unveiling the Apple IIc "briefcase-sized" personal computer in 1984. Jobs and Wozniak founded the company in the 1970s and later brought in the professional manager Sculley from PepsiCo to help run it. Corbis/Bettmann-UPI.

Bill Gates of Microsoft in 1992, on the eve of the Internet revolution.
Corbis/Reuters.

CHAPTER TEN

Overview: Computers, Silicon Valley, and the Internet

Two of the most significant trends in American business during the twentieth century were the decentralization of decision rights within management and the rise of consumers' power in the marketplace. Both of these trends were conspicuous elements in the story of Ray Kroc and McDonald's. Both also received a big boost from the rise of information technology in the Third Industrial Revolution.

Computers

The first modern electronic computer used in business was the Univac, introduced by Remington Rand in 1950. But another company, IBM, quickly emerged as the dominant player. Under IBM's leadership, information technology became the most dynamic industry of the late twentieth century, and perhaps the most important as well.

From the time of its founding in the 1880s, through a series of mergers and name changes later on, IBM's predecessor had been the leader in punch-card calculating machines. In 1924, CEO Thomas J. Watson, Sr., changed the firm's name again, to International Business Machines, even though it was not yet very international. Then, during the 1930s, IBM became a bigger company by fulfilling much of the data-processing demands of the government's new Social Security system. In the 1940s IBM grew still larger because of major defense contracts. All the while, the company maintained its focus on selling to the private sector, where it had a well-earned reputation for superb service to customers.

During the 1950s IBM achieved supremacy in electronic computers by leveraging its skills in marketing and customer relations, even though it sometimes lagged in technology. In the 1960s, after conducting the most expensive privately financed R&D effort in American business history, IBM introduced its revolutionary System/360 series. Just as a full circle has 360 degrees, the new computers would serve all purposes, from scientific to defense to business uses of every kind. System/360's spectacular triumph in the marketplace made IBM so strong that for three decades the company's name was almost synonymous with the information-technology industry around the globe.

At first, computers had not been designed to communicate with each other. With System/360, however, IBM achieved "compatibility" by having a common operating system for all the computers it now began to make, of whatever size or for whatever purpose. Pressure from antitrust authorities then forced IBM to allow its customers to accept "plug compatible" products made by other companies for use with IBM computers. In this way, IBM's immense R&D expenditures indirectly supported many of its competitors in the development and sales of IBM-compatible machines as well as their own peripherals and other products. The result, from the 1960s onward, was a burst of creative energy by scores of hardware and software firms of all kinds and sizes. In the early years, these companies included Control Data, which made peripherals and supercomputers; Amdahl, with its core memories and disk drives; Memorex, a manufacturer of tape drives and other items; and Electronic Data Systems, a service firm whose success made a billionaire of its founder, former IBM salesman H. Ross Perot.

After System/360, the next step in the industry's evolution was the development during the 1960s and 70s of "mini-computers" (many of which weighed over 200 pounds) by Digital and other companies. Then, most important, came the personal computer (PC) in the 1970s and 80s. The first primitive PC appeared in 1974, marketed by a tiny calculator company in Albuquerque, New Mexico. This machine, called the Altair, lacked even fundamental features such as a keyboard and a monitor. It was of interest primarily to electronics hobbyists.

One such hobbyist was Bill Gates, a 19-year-old Harvard undergraduate who quickly became enthralled with the new machine's potential. Gates and his friend Paul Allen wrote a version of the existing BASIC programming language for the Altair and set up the company that later became Microsoft. Convinced that he would have to move quickly, Gates dropped out of Harvard and moved with Allen to Albuquerque, where they marketed their company's programming language to the firm making the Altair. The two men worked furiously to build Microsoft into a viable business, eventually moving it to their hometown of Seattle. The firm that manufactured the Altair failed to prosper, but Microsoft was now positioned to exploit a fabulous opportunity inadvertently handed to it by IBM.

Meanwhile, in 1977, a small California company led by the young entrepreneurs Steve Jobs and Steve Wozniak introduced the Apple II personal computer. This was a modern, user-friendly, and relatively expensive machine that came with a keyboard and external disk drive, and could easily be connected to a monitor and other peripherals. By 1981 the Apple II had been purchased by more than 120,000 customers, most of them business firms using early forms of spreadsheet software.

Because of its technological sophistication and ease of use, the Apple II inspired fierce brand loyalty among its original buyers, many of whom stuck with the company through its later ups and downs. Apple Computer might conceivably have become the dominant player in PCs over the long term. But Apple refused to license its operating system and thereby foreclosed the compatibility with other companies' machines and software so appealing to many purchasers.

With the introduction of IBM's own PC in 1981, overall sales proceeded to take off. IBM shot into the lead, as the industry shipped 800,000 PCs in 1981, 2.5 million in 1982, and more than 6 million in 1985. Most machines were still sold to business customers, who were attracted by the power of IBM's brand, its unmatched reputation for customer service, and its "open architecture," which could accommodate other firms' applications software. IBM's PC itself was not appreciably superior to units offered by other companies, and it was distinctly inferior to the more expensive Macintosh, made by Apple. But the mere fact that such a prestigious firm as IBM had entered the personal computer sweepstakes gave an immense boost to the machine as a legitimate product in both the business and consumer markets.

IBM earned a lot of money from PC sales during the early 1980s, but in so doing planted the seeds of its fall as undisputed ruler of the industry. Determined to cash in on the PC boom as quickly as possible, the company had made two momentous decisions. Pressed for time, IBM had chosen to outsource both its disk operating system and its microprocessor, which is the intricate chip that forms the principal "brain" of all personal computers.

IBM's outsourcing contracts delivered bonanzas to a pair of young firms that soon took their places among the most successful companies in the history of business anywhere. One was Microsoft, founded in 1975 and one of the world's leading software firms by the late 1980s. The other was Intel, founded in 1968 and the world's chief provider of high-end microprocessors by the 1980s. Because of IBM's prior move to an open architecture, Microsoft and Intel were able to supply software and microprocessors not only to IBM but also to the makers of IBM "clones"— PCs produced by dozens of other companies, including foreign ones. Many of these firms offered their PCs on quicker delivery schedules and for lower prices than those of IBM. As a company, IBM now seemed to have become relatively inflexible, burdened by layers of corporate bureaucracy. Not only did it begin to falter in PC deliveries, it also failed to grasp the new importance of the development of software as opposed to hardware.

From 1981 onward, by supplying IBM and other manufacturers as the PC market skyrocketed, Intel and Microsoft grew very fast and earned enormous profits. Their CEOs became international celebrities. In 1997, *Time* selected Andrew Grove of Intel as its "Man of the Year." By that time, Bill Gates had become the wealthiest and best-known businessman on Earth. His company, Microsoft, had grown so powerful through its stranglehold on the standards for operating systems that it began to encounter serious challenges from antitrust authorities, much as had happened earlier to IBM.

At the start of the twenty-first century, the worldwide information-technology industry was divided approximately into 80 percent industrial sales—that is, business-to-business marketing, much of it workstations, PCs, software, and services—and 20 percent sales directly to consumers, mostly of PCs and related software. Americans had purchased more than twice as many personal computers, per capita, as had Europeans or Japanese, and U.S.-based companies led in most other aspects of information technology. IBM was still the world's largest computer firm, and one of the best. After a decade of decline beginning in the 1980s, it had recovered some of its old luster by transforming itself into a services firm with an emphasis on consulting and electronic commerce. But it had not regained its former position of unchallenged primacy in the information-technology industry.

The Changing Role of Government

During and just after World War II, the U.S. government underwrote most R&D expenditures in electronics, including computers. A second pillar of public support came from federal purchases of equipment from IBM and other firms. In addition, the government designed and paid for the complex interconnections that evolved into the Internet. Most of these efforts were made as part of the Cold War struggle to stay ahead of the Soviet Union.

Once the computer industry began to mature in the 1960s and 1970s, and once software became as important as hardware, business replaced government in the leadership role. Government remained a big presence in the industry, but it was no longer the key participant. After IBM's slippage in the 1980s, there was no single chief player in the computer industry, although Microsoft became far and away the leader in software. The most significant *cluster* of information-technology companies was located in and around "Silicon Valley," a small region of California south of San Francisco that included the cities of Palo Alto, Santa Clara, and San Jose. IBM in New York and New Jersey, and other firms clustered around Boston, Minneapolis, and Austin, Texas, were major players as well.

No European company mounted a serious challenge to the American firms' supremacy in either industrial or consumer markets. For a brief period during the 1980s it appeared that powerful Japanese firms such as Fujitsu, NEC, Hitachi, and Toshiba might do to one or both of these markets what Sony and Matsushita had done to the American consumer-electronics industry. But this threat had apparently passed by the early 1990s.

At that time more than 6,000 high-tech firms were operating in Silicon Valley alone. Most were relatively small, many were startups, and almost all were characterized by a porous, informal, and decentralized corporate culture. Even the largest and best-known of the Valley's high-tech companies—Sun Microsystems, Intel, Hewlett-Packard, Apple, Oracle, Cisco Systems—tended to do business in a way different from that of firms in most other industries. These big companies often lived up to their own informal slogans: "Kick Butt and Have Fun" (Sun); "Only the Paranoid Survive" (Intel); and "The H-P Way," a cooperative approach to innovation pioneered by Hewlett-Packard, the oldest of all Silicon Valley firms.

How the Valley Developed

During the 1930s, William Hewlett and David Packard had been students of Frederick Terman (1900–1982), a professor of engineering at Stanford University. Terman, who eventually became known as the "father of Silicon Valley," in 1938 lent Hewlett and Packard $538 to set up an enterprise in Packard's garage in Palo Alto. The new firm, Hewlett-Packard, grew steadily and rose to national prominence when it entered the computer business in the 1960s.

For the rest of the century H-P pioneered in the development of one electronics device after another, some of which it sold directly to consumers rather than to other businesses. The company came to employ more than 100,000 people but retained its ability to reinvent itself and move quickly into the next generation of high-tech equipment. H-P became successively the world leader in hand-held calculators, electronic medical diagnostic instruments, and laser printers. It was especially good at devising custom electronics devices for particular industries. "The H-P Way" of systematic innovation was widely copied. Numerous H-P alumni went on to form their own firms, such as Steve Wozniak, co-founder of Apple Computer.

During the early 1950s, Professor (and by then Dean) Terman persuaded Stanford University officials to set aside 1,000 acres of property adjoining the campus and invite high-tech firms to move in as tenants: thus was born Stanford Industrial Park (later called Stanford Research Park). Over the next 30 years more than a thousand companies spun out of Stanford, and several dozen located their operations in the Park. William Shockley, who won the Nobel Prize as co-inventor of the transistor, moved Shockley Semiconductor Laboratories into the Park in 1955.

Two years later, eight of Shockley's best employees seceded and set up their own firm, Fairchild Semiconductor. Shockley and others referred to the defectors as the "Traitorous Eight." But secession and job-hopping eventually came to be seen as a conventional way of doing business in Silicon Valley, and the Traitorous Eight became simply the "Fairchild Eight." Fairchild itself began to spin off companies, and these firms in turn spawned still newer ones.

In the larger American economy as well, job-hopping was becoming much more common than it was in either Europe or Japan, where both law and custom were more solidly on the side of business stability. In Japan, recruits to major firms tended to assume that they had signed on for their entire careers, an assumption shared by their new employers. And in several European countries, the law required as much as six months' notice before an important person could leave an established firm.

In almost all industrialized countries, including the United States, employees of high-tech companies could be compelled to sign "non-compete" contracts in which they pledged to forgo work on competitive products for a specified period of time after their departure. Courts in some American states, as it turned out, enforced these contracts more stringently than courts in others. California's notably lax approach to enforcement was one reason why entrepreneurs found Silicon Valley such a hospitable environment—more so, for example, than the Route 128 region near Boston, where another cluster of information-technology companies had arisen. The laws of Massachusetts took a sterner position on non-compete violations than did those of California.

But the most important reason for the secession of employees and the creation of new companies in Silicon Valley was neither law nor custom. Instead, it was the extraordinary speed at which electronics technology was hurtling forward. In 1959, one of the Fairchild Eight, Robert Noyce, had invented the integrated circuit, which combined in one small silicon chip numerous functions that earlier had been performed by many discrete transistors and other components wired together on a circuit board. The integrated circuit was invented simultaneously at another company, Texas Instruments, and it soon became for the Third Industrial Revolution what the steam engine had been for the First, and electricity and the internal-combustion engine for the Second.

In 1968, Robert Noyce and another member of the Fairchild Eight, Gordon Moore, co-founded Intel. Moore's name soon became famous because of his prediction that the number of transistors that could be put onto a microchip would double every year. (In 1975 Moore extended the period to 18 months.) Geometric progressions of this sort usually drop off after a short time, but "Moore's Law" held firm for the rest of the century, reflecting the highest sustained rate of efficiency gains in the history of any industry. In 1960, transistors cost about a dollar apiece. This was the equivalent of more than three dollars at the end of the century, but by that time 10 million transistors could be produced for less than a dollar, and the almost unimaginable total of one quadrillion transistors were being turned out each month.

In practical terms, the operation of Moore's Law meant that the cost of any task a microchip could perform was declining so fast that a myriad of applications arose that earlier would have been uneconomical. In the twenty-first century, new cars contain dozens of chips that do everything from monitoring engine operations and scanning radio frequencies to switching off interior lights at precise intervals after passengers leave the car. It would have been possible for computers to perform these operations as early as the 1950s, but a car accommodating the necessary equipment would have had to be the size of a small freight train.

Still another of the Fairchild Eight was Eugene Kleiner, who made his mark primarily as a venture capitalist. The firm Kleiner cofounded in 1972 became a model for similar companies, and together these venture-capital firms took prominent roles in the spinoff-startup-shakeup process that became the essence of doing business in Silicon Valley.

In 1985, a California photographer named Carolyn Caddes put together a book of images and text entitled *Portraits of Success: Impressions of Silicon Valley Pioneers*. She managed to reunite the Fairchild Eight and to array them in the same pose they had taken for a similar portrait made 26 years earlier. At the end of the 1985 session, it struck her that "in spite of graying hair, a few bald spots, and several paunches, these eight men looked like a group of overgrown boys." They still dressed as they wished, worked odd hours, and in general came across as adolescents determined to have fun. The gee-whiz, "geeky" quality retained by the aging Fairchild Eight was also evident in the personalities of Bill Gates and other leaders of the industry. It inspired the writer Robert X. Cringely to entitle his 1992 book on the subject *Accidental Empires: How the Boys of Silicon Valley Make Their Millions, Battle Foreign Competition, and Still Can't Get a Date*.

Organizational Innovation

In a long survey published in 1997, the magazine *The Economist* did a careful analysis of Silicon Valley's success. Many factors identified as central to the region's culture resonate with the themes of this book. They include the creative destruction of old firms and products by new ones, the release of economic energy by resourceful individuals, and the balancing of centralized and decentralized management within organizations. The author of the survey argued that over the long run Silicon Valley's "most important contribution may well be organizational, not technological." He went on to enumerate the essential components of this new kind of business success: a high propensity to take risks, patience with temporary failure, tolerance of job-hopping, rigorous meritocracy, cooperation across firms, and flexibile organizational structures.

Several analysts of Silicon Valley have commented on its similarity to other industry clusters. When the New York Stock Exchange was in its youth, numerous investment banks and brokerage houses sprang up in the environs of Wall Street. Other industries evolved through the same kind of pattern: automobiles around Detroit, motion pictures in southern California, amusement parks in central Florida, and so on. Wherever these kinds of industry clusters arise, it becomes easier for denizens to share ideas, make deals, and accelerate the progress of firms within the cluster—versus their competitors located elsewhere.

Of course, many clusters ultimately fail. In the nineteenth century the British cotton textile industry grew up around Manchester and prospered for several decades. In the twentieth century it lost its lead to overseas competitors who were quicker to modernize, and eventually it collapsed. Something similar happened to Detroit and the American automobile industry, though without such dire results.

One threat to Silicon Valley's continued dominance was a penchant by entrepreneurs to create new firms for the primary purpose of selling them to big companies inside or outside the Valley, such as Cisco Systems and Microsoft. Then there was the Internet, which made innovations immediately available throughout the world, thereby reducing some of the need for physical clustering. A final threat lay in what *The Economist* had identified as the remarkable insensitivity of "Silicon Valley's nerds" to the problems of government and the broader needs of society. Their lack of concern for subjects other than money and the next "cool idea" might itself represent a threat from within. But not even the harshest critics could deny the powerful role of Valley firms in the rise of information technology.

The Internet

Like the computer hardware industry, the Internet was a child of the Cold War. It began life in the 1960s within the Defense Department's Advanced Research Project Agency (ARPA), which set up a series of computer networks for cooperative R&D. The Defense Department endeavored through ARPANET to facilitate "internetworking" among scientists at universities and government agencies across the nation who were working on common problems. Planners decentralized the Internet (as it came to be called) through backup routes involving satellite communications, telephone wires, and other links.

The Internet grew more complex as it expanded from four host computers in the late 1960s to about 2,000 by the mid-1980s. For several years, the Net's heavy users remained scientists and engineers working on advanced R&D projects. But without anyone's having planned it that way, many of those widely dispersed users in universities and research firms began to enter the system in order to "chat" (exchange ideas) and to organize "bulletin boards."

During the 1980s the National Science Foundation (NSF), the government agency most directly concerned with funding R&D of all kinds, took over administration of the Internet. NSF forbade any commercial use of the system, formalizing what had long been an implicit policy. But the Internet's business potential became so attractive to so many users that the NSF prohibition lasted for only a few years. The first providers of commercial services began to use the system in 1989, and a year later the rules were changed. For all practical purposes the Internet was privatized in 1990, and officially so in 1995 when NSF withdrew altogether in favor of privately owned "backbones." By that time the number of linked networks had mushroomed, from about 25 in the early 1980s to 44,000 in 1995.

Over the next several years, growth on all fronts proceeded so fast that statistics about "cyberspace" and the Internet became obsolete almost as soon as they were calculated. The Internet Council, an organization formed in 1995 and funded by telecommunications firms and Silicon Valley businesses, distributed information and predictions such as the following:

In 1993, about 90,000 Americans had regular access to the Internet. Seven years later, at the close of the century, that number had grown by a factor of one thousand, to 90 million.

In 1997, 19 million Americans regularly used the Internet from their homes, and about the same number from computers at work. In 1998, both of these numbers approximately doubled, and they continued to increase rapidly into the twenty-first century.

In 1998, about 830 million pages were available on the Internet. By the end of 1999, the number stood at about 1.5 billion, and was predicted to quintuple to beyond 7.5 billion within three years.

The total number of e-mail messages sent worldwide in 1998 was about 618 billion and was predicted to reach into the low trillions early in the twenty-first century. Much of this would be unwanted advertising ("spam"). By comparison, the U.S. Postal Service delivered about 100 billion pieces of mail annually, and much of this, too, was unwanted advertising ("junk mail").

According to the *Internet Industry Almanac,* about 100 million people around the globe used the Internet in 1997, and over 327 million in 2000. Of these 327 million, about 40 percent were Americans.

The big stimulus to this mushroom growth was the World Wide Web, so named by the English physicist Tim Berners-Lee, one of its developers. During the late 1980s and early 1990s, he and a team of scientists working at a physics research lab in Switzerland had envisioned what Berners-Lee called "a pool of human knowledge" that would be stored on the Internet. It would be made accessible through a system of "hypertext markup language" (html) that could transcend different data formats on various types of computers. Such a system, through a "hypertext transfer protocol" (http), would also manage the movement of data between Web servers (information storage centers) and Web browsers.

A rudimentary version of this system proved immediately popular not only at the Swiss lab but also at similar sites in the United States. One of these U.S. sites was a federally sponsored center at the University of Illinois that had been set up for the further development of supercomputers. When the boom in interconnected PC-based workstations made that mission less urgent, the center shifted its attention to networking technology. A team that included the undergraduate student Marc Andreessen quickly developed an enhanced Web browser ("Mosaic") that could run on most PCs and accommodate color images as well as text. In late 1993 the federal government released Mosaic over the Internet to the general public, free of charge. Within a few months, more than a million copies of the browser had been downloaded. In 1994 the 22-year-old Andreessen and other members of the team left Illinois to go into private business, and soon they were distributing a much improved version of Mosaic, which they called "Netscape Navigator." Their company quickly became one of the hottest properties in American business, and in 1999 it merged with America Online, the leading service provider.

The development of the World Wide Web—plus Mosaic, Netscape Navigator, and other browsers—made the Internet accessible to masses of ordinary people as well as to the engineers and scientists who had been using it for years. All over the world, millions of people began to use the Internet not only to *obtain* information but also to *contribute* new data to the system through their own individual or commercial Web sites. The number of commercial servers (".com" addresses) grew from less than 2 percent of all Web servers in 1993 to over 90 percent of the much larger number in existence by 1996—and the race was on.

As the new century began, it remained difficult for even the best-informed analysts to predict the degree to which cyberspace might replace stores, banks, and other commercial establishments as the preferred place to do business. Most of the profits rung up by Internet businesses up to that time had gone to America Online and other service providers. In 1998, about $27 billion of business-to-business "e-commerce" was transacted, a figure that was predicted by some industry analysts to rise to a trillion dollars within five or six years.

By 1998 the Web navigation company Yahoo!, with 637 employees, had about the same market capitalization as the aerospace giant Boeing, which employed 230,000 people. The stocks of numerous other Internet companies sold at high prices even though the firms themselves lost large sums of money year after year. For consumer purchases, about 13 million U.S. households did at least some shopping on the Internet in 1999, a number projected to triple within five years. Internet companies such as amazon.com (books, CDs, and other items) and eBay (goods listed by individuals for sale to other individuals) became well known throughout the country.

In September of 1999 Jack Welch, CEO of General Electric, was quoted in *Fortune* as saying that electronic commerce "is clearly the biggest revolution in business in our lifetimes." Welch, who was probably the most respected professional manager of his generation, asserted that it would affect every aspect of business: "It will change relationships with employees. We will never again have discussions where knowledge is hidden in somebody's pocket. . . . It will change relationships with customers. Customers will see everything. Nothing will be hidden in paperwork. . . . It will change relationships with suppliers. Within 18 months, all our suppliers will supply us over the Internet or they won't do business with us."

Overall, the proliferation of Internet-related commerce was the most newsworthy trend in American business at the close of the twentieth century. Thousands of entrepreneurs rushed to establish a presence in what they hoped would be the most rewarding marketplace of the twenty-first century.

Themes of an Era, 1920–2000

The Effects of Increased Communication

The outburst of information technology capped an 80-year trend in which decision rights moved mostly downward within business hierarchies. At many companies, the availability of computers and electronic databases gave employees ready access to an ocean of information. The advent of e-mail made communication instantaneous, interactive, and inexpensive, even over long distances. With a few strokes of the keyboard, supervisors could deliver fresh news to particular individuals, to selected subgroups, to large divisions, or to everyone in the company.

Enhanced communication through information technology could, of course, facilitate *either* more centralized management from above *or* more decentralized decision making from below. Adjustments varied according to the needs of the company and the philosophies of its top executives. On balance, however, the clear trend at the start of the new century was toward decentralization. With e-mail, even employees at low levels became more likely to express themselves within the firm. They sent more messages laterally and upward than they had even a short time before using telephones, voice-mail, printers, and copying machines. Something about e-mail seemed to affect the psychology of hierarchies—to instill an egalitarian spirit that encouraged frequent (and, in the view of critics, excessive) communication.

With so much communication going on, it often became possible to eliminate layers of management within hierarchies themselves. Although an irreducible minimum of bureaucratic procedures remained essential for the orderly conduct of business, layers of authority began to diminish in number. Rather than eight or nine levels, many firms ratcheted down to three or four. At the same time, each manager's supervisory reach ("span of control") began to broaden. With a far greater amount of data at a manager's fingertips, he or she could keep track of what was happening in more and more departments. This, too, could result in either more centralization or less, depending on the circumstances and the aims of top management.

As a second-order effect, the gains in information technology began to whittle down the number of essential middle managers— the first time in the twentieth century that this had occurred on a broad scale. The extension of spans of control and the flattening of hierarchies made it possible to "re-engineer" or "downsize" the staffs of numerous companies. At the executive level, these words meant the reassignment or dismissal of middle managers whose roles were no longer necessary.

Decision rights, which had been moving downward for several decades, *could* now become more localized than ever. "Employee empowerment," a phrase that became clichéd toward the end of the century, expressed this phenomenon. However trite the phrase, the new situation itself was no illusion.

Information technology, therefore, enabled many firms to aspire to something like what Ray Kroc's style of franchising had accomplished at McDonald's. Kroc had deliberately divided authority and pushed certain kinds of decision rights downward.

Even at corporate headquarters, where an enormous amount of centralized control over the far-flung McDonald's system remained, Kroc had recognized that for the good of the company he should share control with June Martino, Harry Sonneborn, and Fred Turner. In the field, Kroc put power into the hands of suppliers, master franchisees, regional managers, and individual franchisees. Each McDonald's outlet benefited from the reputational forces of Quality, Service, and Cleanliness built up at every other outlet, and from the constant flow of information up and down the system.

The Persistent Tension between Centralization and Decentralization

The stories of Ray Kroc, Alfred Sloan, Neil McElroy, Ferdinand Eberstadt, and others provide examples of innovative responses by high-ranking executives who faced continual tradeoffs between centralized and decentralized decision making. These managers constantly had to adjust the ways in which people at different levels of the organizations related to each other.

Without continual adjustments, disaster could come at any time, as we saw in the case of Henry Ford. During the 1920s and 1930s, Ford's solo rule had made it much easier for General Motors to defeat the Ford Motor Company in the epic contest for market share. While Henry Ford was gathering complete control over his company into his own hands, Alfred Sloan was systematically delegating authority at GM. Sloan created a new corporate structure in which dozens of product-division heads wielded great power within their own bailiwicks. In formulating the multi-divisional structure, Sloan had worked out a way in which General Motors could benefit from the best of both worlds—"coordinated decentralization," as he liked to call it.

At Procter & Gamble during the 1930s, Neil McElroy's system of brand management accomplished a similar decentralization of authority. Brand managers were responsible to P&G's top executives, but they themselves had a lot of power over those working under their direction. Others in the Procter & Gamble organization, such as Doc Smelser and his market researchers, performed some very important staff functions; but they stood outside the line hierarchy of people with profit-and-loss responsibility for particular brands, divisions, or the company as a whole.

During World War II, Ferdinand Eberstadt created yet another system of decentralized decision rights. The Controlled Materials Plan allocated steel, copper, and aluminum to the Army, Navy, and other claimant agencies on the basis of their own estimates of what they and their primary contractors needed. Where necessary, the claimants could then divert materials from one use to another. They had the authority to do this because Eberstadt, through his "vertical" design of the Plan, had pushed downward the power to make these transfers. The Plan constituted an almost flawless example of systematically placing decision rights in the hands of the person with the best information.

It was hardly coincidental that Eberstadt devised this system during a full-fledged national emergency. The unprecedented scale of war-related activities made it more important than ever that decision rights be thrust downward along numerous fronts at once: the Controlled Materials Plan, the localized conscription system for drafting people into the armed forces, and the community-level rationing boards overseeing the distribution of scarce consumer goods. In all three cases, urgent necessity gave birth to organizational invention.

The story of David Sarnoff and RCA illustrates both the good and bad results that can come from a deliberately *centralized* organizational design. In the early years of radio it made sense for one executive to supervise the development of broadcasting, research, and the manufacture and marketing of equipment. Radio was a systems innovation, and having a person of Sarnoff's great abilities in charge helped to move these many elements forward simultaneously.

When RCA grew much larger, however, and powerful competitors entered the game, it was no longer appropriate to have so much power concentrated in the hands of one person, no matter how talented. But Sarnoff, like Henry Ford before him, refused to change the structure of his company. He would not delegate decision rights, and he neglected the issue of management succession. Sarnoff assumed much too heavy a burden, and the quality of his decisions began to deteriorate. Even before he passed the CEO's job to his son, RCA had entered a downward spiral.

Other Themes of 1920–2000

In addition to the growing need to decentralize management decisions, several other changes stand out over the 80-year period. So do some continuities.

First, consumers gained power, often at the expense of producers and retailers. They enjoyed a lot more discretionary income in the year 2000 than was available to them in 1920, and they came to demand a much broader choice of goods and services. Consumers acquired this new strength despite ceaseless attempts to manipulate them through advertising; indeed the rapid progress of information technology itself had helped to empower them. By the end of the century consumers knew much more about the relative merits of particular products than ever before, and many were buying online at the times of day most convenient for them. Their power also grew because of rising competitive pressures on producers. If producers did not cater to consumers' preferences, then other companies would drive them from the market, as had happened with RCA.

Second, intensified competition made the task of management more difficult. Between 1920 and 2000, the number of American companies grew much faster than the population as a whole. In 1920 about 346,000 U.S. corporations were doing business, but by the close of the century this number had reached 4.5 million, some 13 times the 1920 total. Meanwhile, the population had increased by a factor of 2.6, from 105 million to 270 million.

Not only were far more competitors in the game, but in the case of publicly traded companies an additional force had emerged in the form of mutual funds and pension funds. These institutional investors now exerted constant pressure on managers to increase profits and thereby raise the share prices of their companies' stock.

Still another force was the globalization of business. Beginning in the 1960s, this phenomenon brought acute new competition to several industries in which American managers had assumed that U.S. firms would be permanent world champions. In machine tools, rubber tires, consumer electronics, and automobiles, leadership passed to companies headquartered in Europe or Japan. In other areas, including franchised systems, computer hardware and software, aircraft, and many branded and packaged consumer products, American-based firms entered the twenty-first century still on top.

Third, many U.S. firms were able to stay ahead in part because of their good fortune in having the world's best support system. This multilayered infrastructure encompassed physical facilities such as highways, railroads, airports, electric utilities, and telecommunications. It also included an advanced legal system with sophisticated laws pertaining to contracts, corporations, and torts.

Broadly conceived, the business infrastructure embraced a complex network of companies and other institutions providing financial and informational services to the core systems of production and distribution. On the financial side, these supporting institutions included securities exchanges, commercial banks, insurance companies, investment banks, venture-capital firms, and mutual funds. On the information side, they included law firms, consulting companies, accounting firms, and a broad array of enterprises engaged in the processing and storage of data.

Fourth, at the start of the twenty-first century, infrastructural enterprises were themselves operating under far greater competitive pressures than those faced by their counterparts in 1920. Here one of the strongest forces was not globalization but deregulation. Companies in domestic airlines, railroads, trucking, electric utilities, and some types of telecommunications were largely immune to threats from overseas competitors. So too, though a little less so, were most law, accounting, and consulting firms, both big and small.

But nearly all kinds of firms in this broad variety of industries felt the hot breath of new competition. One by one, industries were deregulated and exposed to the discipline of the marketplace. Air carriers became much more competitive with each other after passage of the Airline Deregulation Act of 1978. The same thing happened to railroads starting in the 1970s, and to firms in trucking, telecommunications, and financial services beginning in the

1980s. The tremendous growth of information technology during the 1980s and 1990s would not have been nearly so strong without the concurrent deregulation of telecommunications. Milestones in this process included the breakup of AT&T's monopolistic Bell System in 1984, the proliferation of new telephone and TV cable companies during the 1980s and 1990s, and the formal privatization of the Internet in 1995.

Even the "self-regulating" professions of law, accounting, engineering, and medicine grew more competitive during the closing years of the century. A wide array of organizations, from law firms to medical clinics, mostly abandoned their traditional forbearance toward unproductive colleagues and slow-moving procedures. Instead these enterprises became more like conventional businesses: profit-oriented, hard-driving, and alert for any edge that would take market share from rivals.

Fifth, the new competitive pressures, while reinvigorating American business, often took a heavy human toll. During the 1980s and especially the 1990s, intensified competition led many companies to "cut the fat" from their employment rolls, in wave after wave of "re-engineering" and "downsizing." All of these words were euphemisms not only for the elimination of middle-management positions, but also for mass layoffs of lower-level workers. A few firms went too far, cutting not only fat but corporate muscle.

Inevitably, institutional loyalty began to decline. From top to bottom within company hierarchies, employees began to recognize that a different kind of working environment had now evolved. Even the most efficient firms, though taking steps to empower employees in day-to-day operations, could not assure that these same people would have long-term employment at the firm, let alone steady increases in pay and fringe benefits. In earlier years, it had been easy for everyone to forget that in the actual experience of Schumpeterian "creative destruction," the destruction is just as real as the creation. In the 1980s and 1990s, that lesson became palpable.

Sixth, despite its painful side, creative destruction did make the American business system more productive. In so doing, it improved material standards of living. From 1920 to the start of the twenty-first century, the amount of time most people were compelled to spend working for pay shrank drastically. Many still put in long hours and worked hard, of course, and at the very end of the century the American workweek again began to lengthen. But large numbers of people could now afford to spend as much time in leisure activities as in the combined tasks of running a household and working outside the home. In the United States, one hour's work at the end of the century would buy, on average, four or five times the goods and services it bought in 1920. In this situation some people even had trouble finding meaningful activity to fill their free hours.

Seventh, in part because so much leisure time was devoted to watching television, Americans were exposed to an astronomical number of commercial advertisements. At the start of the twenty-first century, nearly all households had at least one TV set, and three-fourths had two or more. In the average home a set was on for 7 hours each day, delivering endless commercials designed to increase viewers' feelings of need for "new and improved" products.

This situation in itself carried a profound message about capitalism. As the sociologist Emile Durkheim had written early in the twentieth century, "Our needs are unlimited. The more one has the more one wants." He was right. The ultimate basis of capitalism has been, and still is, the insatiability of human wants.

Eighth, between the years 1920 and 2000 Americans *in general* embraced the capitalist system more wholeheartedly than did people in most other countries. They were decidedly more entrepreneurial, as reflected both in their business behavior and in the enabling laws enacted by their national and state legislatures. They took collective action against the capitalist system less often than was the norm elsewhere, either through their votes or through radical political movements. They had a smaller rate of worker unionization. They showed little tendency to become socialists. They were openly competitive with each other and far more willing to run their rivals out of business.

But Americans were also more forgiving of failure. They had little fear of going into debt, and they were remarkably tolerant of bankruptcy, by both businesses and individuals. In much of the world bankruptcy represented a permanent stigma, but in America it was often regarded as a phase through which entrepreneurs routinely passed on their way to eventual riches. Over most of the nation's history, and again in comparison to other countries, the dominant assumption seemed to be that prosperity at one extreme and destitution at the other were matters of individual responsibility, even personal choice. They were not determined chiefly by luck or social context—or so most citizens apparently believed.

Americans endured economic turmoil more readily than did other people, again speaking generally. Over a national history of more than two centuries, as the business cycle moved up and down, the United States economy, like capitalist economies everywhere, went through frequent recessions. The United States also suffered a few deep depressions—during the 1780s, early 1800s, 1830s, 1850s, 1870s, 1890s, and early 1920s. The worst downturn of all, the Great Depression of the 1930s, was a good deal more severe in the U.S. than it was elsewhere. Yet it provoked less political radicalism in America than it did in France, Germany, Italy, Japan, and several other countries.

By the year 2000, the United States, like all leading industrial nations, had a thoroughly "mixed" economy with very substantial government expenditures: about one-third of GNP, up from one-ninth in 1920. These outlays included large transfer payments in the form of Social Security, Medicare, and unemployment benefits. Among their many results, such measures—along with sophisticated monetary and fiscal policies—tended to flatten the business cycle. They made swings of prosperity and recession a lot less violent than had been the case before World War II.

But in comparison with Europeans, Americans had been noticeably late to develop most of these systems of social welfare. Nor did they enact unemployment, health, and welfare laws of such extensive reach, or spend such a high proportion of public revenue on them. In the early twenty-first century, the total tax burden in the United States, as a percentage of income, was less than that in almost all other industrialized countries. The individualistic, tax-averse, "free-market" ideology of the United States had proved to be invaluable for promoting entrepreneurship and unleashing economic energy.

But there was a downside. As viewed by numerous analysts abroad, and also by many critics at home, American-style capitalism carried unacceptably high social costs. The U.S. business system tolerated wholesale layoffs of employees by large companies and frequent failures by small ones. It offered relatively little succor to those who found it hard to compete. The gap between rich and poor stretched wider than it did in comparable countries.

The question of whether the economic gains were worth the social costs does not have a self-evident answer. Nor does the precise mechanism by which these gains and costs were connected. This book has not addressed those issues directly, because its central focus has been on something else: the internal workings of the business system. But it does take note that the relative speed at which creative destruction is permitted to go forward within any country is in large part a political choice by those who control national priorities, and that the remarkable economic success of American business was not, by itself, cause for unconditional celebration by everyone involved.

BIBLIOGRAPHICAL ESSAY

The Literature of the Field

A formidable array of information is available on twentieth-century American business. In addition to the selected books and articles listed in this essay, other primary and secondary sources covering both historical and contemporary business affairs may be accessed through libraries and online databases. Researchers can save themselves a lot of time by consulting a reference librarian for guidance across what has become a vast sea of data.

Individual companies maintain Web sites and corporate archives, the latter often closed to independent researchers. Publicly owned companies also issue "10-K's" and similar reports to the Securities and Exchange Commission and other government authorities, annual reports to stockholders, and a variety of additional publications. Almost every industry has its trade papers and magazines, which are often useful sources. General business publications such as *The Economist, Fortune, Business Week, Forbes, The Wall Street Journal,* and *The Harvard Business Review* provide valuable information for historical research as well as current coverage.

For part of the period covered by this book, particularly the 1930s through the 1960s, the most readable single source is the magazine *Fortune.* During most of those four decades, *Fortune* was a monthly filled with long, in-depth articles, usually unsigned, by a stable of important writers such as James Agee, Daniel Bell, John Kenneth Galbraith, Archibald MacLeish, and Dwight Macdonald. *Fortune*'s articles for those years represent, in aggregate, perhaps the most distinguished sustained body of writing on business ever produced in any country. Unhappily, during the 1960s *Fortune* went the way of many other business periodicals into a world of sidebars and superficiality.

Scholarly coverage of the field is best represented by the *Business History Review,* published quarterly by the Harvard Business School; *Business and Economic History,* issued once per year by the Business History Conference (in the year 2000 this publication became *Enterprise and Society* and began to be issued quarterly); and *Essays in Economic and Business History,* published annually by the Economic and Business Historical Society. All three of these periodicals cover other countries in addition to the United States. A fourth journal, the British quarterly *Business History,* often contains articles on American business.

Statistical References

All major industries keep detailed statistical series containing a welter of data on companies' performance and the condition of product markets. Most of these reports are published through industry trade associations, of which there are too many to name here but which can be traced through libraries.

For more general statistical references, four publications are indispensable for twentieth-century business, economic, and social history. They are: U.S. Bureau of the Census, *Historical Statistics of the United States: Colonial Times to 1970,* 2 vols. (Washington, DC: Government Printing Office, 1975); *Statistical Abstract of the United States* (Washington, DC: Government

Printing Office, annual editions); Angus Maddison, *Phases of Capitalist Development: A Long-Run Comparative View* (Oxford: Oxford University Press, 1991), a vital source for placing the American experience in cross-national perspective, updated by the same author's *Monitoring the World Economy* (Paris: OECD, 1995); and Stanley Lebergott, *Pursuing Happiness: American Consumers in the Twentieth Century* (Princeton, NJ: Princeton University Press, 1993), a brief and charming treasury of information, of which I have made liberal use in this book. An interesting statistical evaluation of one dimension of American economic growth, emphasizing the processing of raw materials as opposed to their mere harvesting, is Gavin Wright, "The Origins of American Industrial Success, 1879–1940," *American Economic Review,* 80 (September 1990).

Syntheses and Bibliographies

Several specialized encyclopedias, textbooks, and other references are helpful not only for their content but for their extensive bibliographies. The most important include Stanley I. Kutler, ed., *Encyclopedia of the United States in the Twentieth Century* (New York: Simon & Schuster, 1996). Volume III of this work, which I had the good fortune to edit, is devoted entirely to economics and business. It contains 18 long articles on broad topics, written by leading historians. All of those articles were useful in the writing of this book, particularly those on Consumption (Susan Strasser), Marketing (Richard S. Tedlow), Industrial Production (Alfred D. Chandler, Jr.), Economic Performance (Richard H. K. Vietor), Infrastructure (William R. Childs), The Professions (Kenneth Lipartito and Paul Miranti), and Capital Markets (George David Smith and Richard Sylla). In addition to Volume III, portions of Volume II, which includes Science and Technology, have also been useful, particularly the essays on Industrial Research and Manufacturing Technology (David A. Hounshell), Computer and Communications Technology (Steven W. Usselman), and Aerospace Technology (Roger E. Bilstein). Another sweeping and very helpful source, which covers not just the twentieth century but the whole of the nation's economic history, is Glenn Porter, ed., *Encyclopedia of American Economic History* (New York: Scribner's, 1980), which is presented in three thick volumes.

Useful textbooks, all of which contain ample bibliographies or source notes, include Mansel G. Blackford and K. Austin Kerr, *Business Enterprise in American History* (Boston: Houghton Mifflin, 3rd ed., 1994); Alfred D. Chandler, Jr., Thomas K. McCraw, and Richard S. Tedlow, *Management Past and Present: A Casebook on the History of American Business* (Cincinnati: South-Western, 1996); and Thomas K. McCraw, ed., *Creating Modern Capitalism: How Entrepreneurs, Companies, and Countries Triumphed in Three Industrial Revolutions* (Cambridge, MA: Harvard University Press, 1997), which covers Great Britain, Germany, and Japan as well as the United States.

Some important reference works are John N. Ingham, *Biographical Dictionary of American Business Leaders*, 4 vols. (Westport, CT: Greenwood Press, 1983); Thomas Derdak, ed., *International Directory of Company Histories*, 21+ vols. (Chicago: St. James Press, 1988–); and Susan Boyles Martin, ed., *Notable Corporate Chronologies*, 2 vols. (New York: Gale Research, 1995).

Standard Works

Because this book is restricted to the period 1920–2000, only a few standard works on business history can be mentioned here, and even for that period the following list cannot be complete, only representative. These works include three books by Alfred D. Chandler, Jr., a prolific scholar whose work redefined the field of business history: *Strategy and Structure: Chapters in the History of the American Industrial Enterprise* (Cambridge, MA: MIT Press, 1962); *The Visible Hand: The Managerial Revolution in American Business* (Cambridge, MA: Harvard University Press, 1977); and *Scale and Scope: The Dynamics of Industrial Capitalism* (Cambridge, MA: Harvard University Press, 1990). The standard book on strategic marketing is Richard S. Tedlow, *New and Improved: The Story of Mass Marketing in America* (Boston: Harvard Business School Press, 1996, first published in 1990). Indispensable on the production side is David A. Hounshell, *From the American System to Mass Production, 1800–1932: The Development of Manufacturing Technology in the United States* (Baltimore: Johns Hopkins University Press, 1984). A useful historiographical survey of the entire field of business history, taking as its point of departure the work of Chandler, is Richard R. John, Jr., "Elaborations, Revisions, Dissents: Alfred D. Chandler's *The Visible Hand* after Twenty Years," *Business History Review,* 71 (Summer 1997).

For a counterpoint to the "Chandlerian" emphasis on big business, see Philip Scranton, *Figured Tapestry: Production, Markets, and Power in Philadelphia Textiles, 1885–1941* (New York: Cambridge University Press, 1989) and the same author's *Endless Novelty: Specialty Production and American Industrialization, 1865–1925* (Princeton, NJ: Princeton University Press, 1997). A thoughtful discussion of small business with a thorough citation of relevant works may be found in Mansel G. Blackford, "Small Business in America: A Historiographic Survey," *Business History Review,* 65 (Spring 1991), pp. 1–26. See also Mansel G. Blackford, *A History of Small Business in American Life* (Toronto: Twayne, 1991); and Stuart Bruchey, ed., *Small Business and American Life* (New York: Columbia University Press, 1980). On social history, Olivier Zunz's *Making America Corporate, 1870–1920* (Chicago: University of Chicago Press, 1990), like Chandler's *Visible Hand* and Scranton's *Endless Novelty,* almost stops as it reaches the 1920s, where this book begins, but like them is important for its methodological contributions.

On government-business relations, which has received more coverage in the scholarly literature than it is possible to summarize in this book, a short list of standard works would include Ellis W. Hawley, *The New Deal and the Problem of Monopoly: A Study in Economic Ambivalence* (Princeton, NJ: Princeton University Press, 1966); Thomas K. McCraw, *Prophets of Regulation* (Cambridge, MA: Harvard University Press, 1984); Louis Galambos and Joseph Pratt, *The Rise of the Corporate Commonwealth: U.S. Business and Public Policy in the Twentieth Century* (New York:

Basic Books, 1988); Morton Keller, *Regulating a New Economy: Public Policy and Economic Change in America, 1900–1933* (Cambridge, MA: Harvard University Press, 1990); and Richard H. K. Vietor, *Contrived Competition: Regulation and Deregulation in America* (Cambridge, MA: Harvard University Press, 1994).

Theoretical evaluations of capitalism are explored in many books by economists, of which the following have unusual relevance to American business history: Joseph A. Schumpeter, *Capitalism, Socialism and Democracy* (New York: Harper, 1942, 3rd ed., 1950); Oliver E. Williamson, *The Economic Institutions of Capitalism: Firms, Markets, Relational Contracting* (New York: Free Press, 1985); Douglass C. North, *Institutions, Institutional Change, and Economic Performance* (Cambridge, MA: Cambridge University Press, 1990); and William Lazonick, *Business Organization and the Myth of the Market Economy* (Cambridge, MA: Cambridge University Press, 1991). Three influential works by Michael E. Porter provide practical guides to the analysis of business behavior: *Competitive Strategy* (New York: Free Press, 1980); *Competitive Advantage* (New York: Free Press, 1985); and *The Competitive Advantage of Nations* (New York: Free Press, 1990). The morphology of decision rights is ably analyzed in Michael C. Jensen, *Foundations of Organizational Strategy* (Cambridge, MA: Harvard University Press, 1998).

Selected Sources for Chapter One

The 1920s: Motor Vehicles and Modern Management

An invaluable collection of statistics and other primary materials is Alfred D. Chandler, Jr., comp. and ed., *Giant Enterprise: Ford, General Motors, and the Automobile Industry: Sources and Readings* (New York: Harcourt, Brace & World, 1964). See also the relevant portions of Chandler, *Strategy and Structure: Chapters in the History of the American Industrial Enterprise* (Cambridge, MA: MIT Press, 1962); Richard S. Tedlow, *New Improved: The Story of Mass Marketing in America* (Boston: Harvard Business School Press, 1996, first published in 1990); and David A. Hounshell, *From the American System to Mass Production, 1800–*

1932: The Development of Manufacturing Technology in the United States (Baltimore: Johns Hopkins University Press, 1984).

On the automobile industry in general, an excellent contemporary study is the Federal Trade Commission's *Report on the Motor Vehicle Industry* (Washington, DC: U.S. Government Printing Office, 1939). Other standard sources include James J. Flink, "Automobile," in Glenn Porter, ed., *Encyclopedia of American Economic History* (New York: Scribner's, 1980), pp. 1168–1193; Flink, *The Car Culture* (Cambridge, MA: MIT Press, 1975); John B. Rae, *The American Automobile* (Chicago: University of Chicago Press, 1965); Arthur J. Kuhn, *GM Passes Ford, 1918–1938: Designing the General Motors Performance-Control System* (University Park: Pennsylvania State University Press, 1986); and Daniel M. G. Raff, "Making Cars and Making Money in the Interwar Automobile Industry: Economies of Scale and Scope and the Manufacturing behind the Marketing," *Business History Review,* 65 (Winter 1991). The best introduction to the reasons behind the successful Japanese challenge later in the twentieth century is Michael A. Cusumano, *The Japanese Automobile Industry: Technology and Management at Nissan and Toyota* (Cambridge, MA: Harvard University Press, 1985).

The vast literature on Henry Ford includes several autobiographical statements, the most useful being two books Ford prepared in collaboration with Samuel Crowther, *My Life and Work* (Garden City, NY: Doubleday, 1923), and *Moving Forward* (Garden City, NY: Doubleday, 1931). A key associate of Ford's provided an alternative account in his own autobiography: Charles E. Sorensen with Samuel T. Williamson, *My Forty Years with Ford* (New York: Norton, 1956). A thorough company-sponsored history, with some but by no means all of the ugliness downplayed, is the three-volume study by Allan Nevins with the collaboration of Frank Ernest Hill: *Ford: The Times, the Man, the Company* (New York: Scribner's, 1954); *Ford: Expansion and Challenge 1915–1933* (New York: Scribner's, 1957); and *Ford: Decline and Rebirth 1933–1962* (New York: Scribner's, 1963).

Other useful studies include Keith Sward, *The Legend of Henry Ford* (New York: Holt, Rinehart and Winston, Inc., 1948); John B. Rae, ed., *Henry Ford* (Englewood Cliffs, NJ: Prentice-

Hall, 1960); Reynold M. Wik, *Henry Ford and Grass Roots America* (Ann Arbor: University of Michigan Press, 1972); David L. Lewis, *The Public Image of Henry Ford: An American Folk Hero and His Company* (Detroit: Wayne State University Press, 1976); and Stephen Meyer III, *The Five Dollar Day: Labor, Management, and Social Control in the Ford Motor Company, 1908–1921* (Albany: State University of New York Press, 1981).

The literature on Sloan is much less voluminous, partly because he wanted it that way. But see especially *Fortune,* "Alfred P. Sloan Jr.: Chairman," April 1938; Sloan in collaboration with Boyden Sparkes, *Adventures of a White Collar Man* (New York: Doubleday, 1941); and the very important Sloan, *My Years With General Motors* (New York: Doubleday, 1963).

Selected Sources for Chapter Two
Overview: The Financial System

The functional perspective for financial analysis is presented in Robert C. Merton, "The Financial System and Economic Performance," *Journal of Financial Services Research,* 4 (December 1990), pp. 263–300. For further explication, see Dwight B. Crane et al., *The Global Financial System: A Functional Perspective* (Boston: Harvard Business School Press, 1995), especially the chapters by Robert C. Merton and Zvi Bodie, Erik R. Sirri and Peter Tufano, and Dwight B. Crane.

Peter L. Bernstein, *Capital Ideas: The Improbable Origins of Modern Wall Street* (New York: Free Press, 1992) provides, among other insights, an excellent intellectual history of finance theory. Further theoretical explorations may be followed through current and back issues of numerous academic quarterlies, including the *Journal of Finance, Journal of Financial Economics, Journal of Accounting and Economics,* and *Journal of Accounting Research.* An informative historical survey is George David Smith and Richard Sylla, "Capital Markets," in Stanley I. Kutler, ed., *Encyclopedia of the United States in the Twentieth Century* (New York: Simon & Schuster, 1996), III, pp. 1209–1241.

For general accounts of Wall Street and securities markets, see New York Stock Exchange *Fact Book* (New York: NYSE, annual). Peter Wyckoff, *Wall Street and the Stock Markets: A Chronology, 1644–1971* (Philadelphia: Chilton, 1971); Charles R. Geisst, *Wall Street: A History* (New York: Oxford University Press, 1997); James Grant, *Money of the Mind: Borrowing and Lending in America from the Civil War to Michael Milken* (New York: Farrar Straus Giroux, 1992); Vincent P. Carosso, *Investment Banking in America: A History* (Cambridge, MA: Harvard University Press, 1970); Samuel L. Hayes et al., *Competition in the Investment Banking Industry* (Cambridge, MA: Harvard University Press, 1983); Jeremy J. Siegel, *Stocks for the Long Run* (New York: McGraw-Hill, 1998); and Richard Sylla, Jack W. Wilson, and Charles P. Jones, "U.S. Financial Markets and Long-Term Economic Growth, 1790–1989," in Thomas Weiss and Donald Schaefer, eds., *American Economic Development in Historical Perspective* (Stanford, CA: Stanford University Press, 1994). John Brooks, *Once in Golconda: A True Drama of Wall Street, 1920–1938* (New York: Harper & Row, 1969) is a sprightly account of doings and wrongdoings in the market during a crucial part of its history.

The nature of the capital markets changed significantly during the 1980s and 90s, eliciting a raft of new studies. Critical accounts of these events by influential journalists include Connie Bruck, *The Predators' Ball* (New York: Simon & Schuster, 1989); James B. Stewart, *Den of Thieves* (New York: Simon & Schuster, 1991); Jesse Kornbluth, *Highly Confident: The Crime and Punishment of Michael Milken* (New York: Morrow, 1992); and George Anders, *Merchants of Debt* (New York: Basic Books, 1993). A more favorable interpretation, which emphasizes the disciplinary effects of the capital markets on corporate management, may be found in Michael C. Jensen, "Eclipse of the Public Corporation," *Harvard Business Review,* 89 (September/October 1989).

Some of the statistics quoted in this overview chapter, especially for the 1990s, were compiled by Ken Kurson for "Money on the Mind," a collection of articles in the *New York Times Magazine,* June 7, 1998.

Selected Sources for Chapter Three
The 1930s: Depression, Consumers,
and the Case of Procter & Gamble

The Great Depression is the subject of a large academic literature, but scholars have not come to consensus about its causes. Two fundamental works are John Maynard Keynes, *The General Theory of Employment, Interest, and Money* (New York: Macmillan, 1936), and Milton J. Friedman and Anna Schwartz, *A Monetary History of the United States, 1867–1960* (Princeton, NJ: Princeton University Press, 1963). Other basic works include John Kenneth Galbraith, *The Great Crash: 1929* (Boston: Houghton Mifflin, 1972 edition); Charles P. Kindleberger, *The World in Depression: 1929–1939* (Berkeley: University of California Press, 1973); Robert M. Collins, *The Business Response to Keynes: 1929–1964* (New York: Columbia University Press, 1981); and Michael A. Bernstein, *The Great Depression: Delayed Recovery and Economic Change in America, 1929–1939* (New York: Cambridge University Press, 1987).

On films, see Jack C. Ellis, *A History of Film* (Boston: Allyn and Bacon, 4th ed., 1995); John Baxter, *Hollywood in the Thirties, 1929–1939* (New York: A. S. Barnes, 1968, 1980); and Martin Quigley et al., eds., *International Motion Picture Almanac* (New York: Quigley, annual), which contains detailed information on revenues, industry structure, theater attendance, and much else about the industry during the thirties and subsequent decades.

Good sources on Procter & Gamble include two articles published in *Fortune* during the 1930s: "Procter & Gamble," 4 (Dec. 1936), and especially "99-44/100% Pure Profit Record," 19 (April 1939). Alfred Lief, *"It Floats": The Story of Procter & Gamble* (New York: Rinehart, 1958), is a breezy informal history. A book put together by the editors of *Advertising Age,* entitled *Procter & Gamble: The House that Ivory Built* (Lincolnwood, IL, NTC Business Books, 1988), is a sympathetic and thorough analysis on which I have relied heavily; Alecia Swasy, *Soap Opera: The Inside Story of Procter & Gamble* (New York: Times Books, 1993) is a muckraker's account of the company's behavior in the 1980s and early 1990s.

Richard S. Tedlow's *New and Improved: The Story of Mass Marketing in America* (Boston, MA: Harvard Business School Press, 1996, first published in 1990) is superb on competitive marketing battles in several industries during the twentieth century; Susan Strasser, *Satisfaction Guaranteed: The Making of the American Mass Market* (New York: Pantheon, 1989) is excellent on P&G's initial Crisco marketing campaign, and more generally on the whole subject of mass marketing at the point where the consumer perceived the product. Insightful analyses of advertising include Daniel Pope, *The Making of Modern Advertising* (New York: Basic Books, 1983); Roland Marchand, *Advertising the American Dream: Making Way for Modernity, 1920–1940* (Berkeley: University of California Press, 1985); Michael Schudson, *Advertising, the Uneasy Persuasion: Its Dubious Impact on American Society* (New York: Basic Books, 1984); and Jackson Lears, *Fables of Abundance: A Cultural History of Advertising in America* (New York: Basic Books, 1994). Lizabeth Cohen's *Making a New Deal: Industrial Workers in Chicago, 1919–1939* (Cambridge: Cambridge University Press, 1990) is a wide-ranging analysis that includes a discussion of patterns of consumer behavior.

My brief treatment of brands in this chapter has been influenced by conversations with and presentations by my Harvard colleagues Alvin Silk, Nancy F. Koehn, and Susan Fournier. Useful published works include: Kevin Lane Keller, *Strategic Brand Management: Building, Measuring, and Managing Brand Equity* (Upper Saddle River, NJ: Prentice-Hall, 1998); David A. Aaker, *Building Strong Brands* (New York: Free Press, 1996); Jean-Noel Kapferer, *Strategic Brand Management* (New York: Free Press, 1992); Interbrand plc, *World's Greatest Brands: International Review* (New York: Wiley, 1992); Diane Crispell and Kathleen Brandenburg, "What's in a Brand?" *American Demographics,* 15 (May 1993); Paul Feldwick, "What is Brand Equity Anyway, and How Do You Measure It?", *Journal of the Market Research Society,* 38 (April 1996); and Susan Fournier and Julie L. Yao, "Reviving Brand Loyalty: A Reconceptualization within the Framework of Consumer-Brand Relationships," *International Journal of Research in Marketing,* 14 (December 1997). I have also relied on the textbook by Philip Kotler and Gary Armstrong entitled *Principles of Marketing,* (Upper Saddle River, NJ: Prentice-Hall, 7th ed., 1996), which contains an excellent discussion of brands. In addition, see Robert M. McMath and Thom Forbes, *What Were They Thinking? Lessons I've Learned from Over 80,000 New Product Innovations and Idiocies* (New York: Times Business, 1998).

Selected Sources for Chapter Four
Overview: Women in Business

The literature on women in business is not as voluminous as it is for political, social, and cultural topics involving women. It is stronger for the nineteenth century than the twentieth, and fuller for the early and late parts of the twentieth century than the middle. But scholarly work on the entire subject grew rapidly toward the close of the century, and the following items are especially useful: Angel Kwolek-Folland, *Incorporating Women: A History of Woman and Business in the United States* (New York: Twayne, 1998); Mary A. Yeager, ed., *Women in Business,* a three-volume collection of articles with a comprehensive introduction (Northampton, MA: Edward Elgar, 1999); Claudia Goldin, *Understanding the Gender Gap: An Economic History of American Women* (New York: Oxford University Press, 1990); Kathy Peiss, "'Vital Industry' and Women's Ventures: Conceptualizing Gender in Twentieth Century Business History," *Business History Review,* 72 (Summer 1998); Julia Kirk Blackwelder, *Now Hiring: The Feminization of Work in the United States, 1900–1995* (College Station: Texas A&M University Press, 1997); Charles W. Wootton and Barbara E. Kemmerer, "The Changing Genderization of Bookkeeping in the United States, 1870–1930," *Business History Review,* 70 (Winter 1996); Sharon Hartman Strom, *Beyond the Typewriter: Gender, Class, and the Origins of Modern Office*

Work, 1900–1930 (Urbana: University of Illinois Press, 1992); Rosabeth Moss Kanter, *Men and Women of the Corporation* (New York: Basic Books, 1977); Angel Kwolek-Folland, *Engendering Business: Men and Women of the Corporate Office, 1870–1930* (Baltimore: Johns Hopkins University Press, 1994); Caroline Bird, *Enterprising Women* (New York: Norton, 1986); Frank Stricker, "Cookbooks and Law Books: The Hidden History of Career Women in Twentieth Century America," in Nancy F. Cott, ed., *History of Women in the United States,* vol. 8: *Professional and White-Collar Employments,* part 2 (Munich: K. G. Saur, 1993); Wendy Gamber, *The Female Economy: The Millinery and Dressmaking Trades, 1860–1930* (Urbana: University of Illinois Press, 1997); Barbara J. Harris, *Beyond Her Sphere: Women and the Professions in American History* (Westport, CT: Greenwood Press, 1978); U.S. Department of Commerce, *The Bottom Line: Equal Enterprise in America: Report of the President's Interagency Task Force on Women Business Owners* (Washington, DC: Government Printing Office, 1978); Dawn-Marie Driscoll and Carol R. Goldberg, *Members of the Club: The Coming of Age of Executive Women* (New York: Free Press, 1993); Betsy Morris, "Tales of the Trailblazers: *Fortune* Visits Harvard's Women MBAs of 1973," *Fortune,* 138 (October 12, 1998); Ann Faircloth, Andrew Goldsmith, and Ann Harrington, "The Class of '83," ibid.

Some of the statistics about women in the workforce quoted in this overview chapter come from Andrew J. Cherlin, "By the Numbers," *New York Times Magazine,* April 8, 1998. There are many sources on the Estée Lauder and Mary Kay companies. Both entrepreneurs wrote autobiographies, and magazine coverage has been extensive; see, as examples, Sandra Mardenfeld, "Mary Kay Ash," *Incentive,* 170 (January 1996); and Nina Munk, "Why Women Find Lauder Mesmerizing," *Fortune,* 137 (May 25, 1998). For the earlier history of cosmetics and related industries, see Kathy Peiss, *Hope in a Jar: The Making of America's Beauty Culture* (New York: Metropolitan Books/ Henry Holt, 1998).

Selected Sources for Chapter Five
The New Deal and World War II:
Regulation and Decentralization

The literature on Franklin D. Roosevelt and the New Deal is vast. The standard analyses begin with Arthur M. Schlesinger, Jr.'s trilogy *The Age of Roosevelt* (Boston: Houghton Mifflin, 1957–60): *The Crisis of the Old Order, The Coming of the New Deal,* and *The Politics of Upheaval.* The best one-volume syntheses are William E. Leuchtenburg's thorough *Franklin D. Roosevelt and the New Deal, 1933–1940* (New York: Harper & Row, 1963), and Paul K. Conkin's brief interpretation, *The New Deal* (Wheeling, IL: Harlan Davidson, 3rd ed., 1992). For later analyses see Colin Gordon, *New Deals: Business, Labor, and Politics in America, 1920–1935* (Cambridge: Cambridge University Press, 1994), and Alan Brinkley, *The End of Reform: New Deal Liberalism in Recession and War* (New York: Knopf, 1995). See also the works by Ellis W. Hawley and Richard H. K. Vietor mentioned in the sources for Literature of the Field above. On securities regulation, see Chapter 5 of Thomas K. McCraw, *Prophets of Regulation* (Cambridge, MA: Harvard University Press, 1984); Michael E. Parrish, *Securities Regulation and the New Deal* (New Haven, CT: Yale University Press, 1970); and Chapters 2 and 3 of Joel Seligman, *The Transformation of Wall Street: A History of the Securities and Exchange Commission and Modern Corporate Finance* (Boston: Houghton Mifflin, 1982). On the Roosevelts' wartime roles, see Doris Kearns Goodwin, *Franklin and Eleanor Roosevelt: The Home Front in World War II* (New York: Simon and Schuster, 1994).

Otis L. Graham, Jr., *Toward a Planned Society: From Roosevelt to Nixon* (New York: Oxford University Press, 1976); and Paul A. C. Koistenen, *The Military-Industrial Complex: A Historical Perspective* (New York: Praeger, 1981) place the 1930s and 1940s in the wider frameworks implied by their titles. The same is true of two other excellent books that go beyond the chronological limits of this chapter: Robert D. Cuff, *The War Industries Board: Business-Government Relations During World War I* (Baltimore:

Johns Hopkins University Press, 1973); and Barry D. Karl, *The Uneasy State* (Chicago: University of Chicago Press, 1983). A useful summary discussion of the economic dimensions of American wars is Claudia D. Goldin, "War," in Glenn Porter, ed., *Encyclopedia of American Economic History* (New York: Scribner's, 1980), pp. 935–957. On mobilization for World War II, see the thorough compilation by the U.S. Department of Commerce, Bureau of the Budget, *The United States at War: Development and Administration of the War Program by the Federal Government* (Washington, DC: Government Printing Office, 1946); also Donald Nelson, *Arsenal of Democracy* (New York: Harcourt, Brace, 1946); Eliot Janeway, *The Struggle for Survival: A Chronicle of Economic Mobilization in World War II* (New Haven, CT: Yale University Press, 1951); Richard Polenberg, *War and Society: The United States, 1941–1945* (Philadelphia: J.B. Lippincott, 1972); John Morton Blum, *V Was for Victory: Politics and American Culture during World War II* (New York: Harcourt Brace Jovanovich, 1976); and Harold G. Vatter, *The U.S. Economy in World War II* (New York: Columbia University Press, 1985).

A provocative interpretation of the relationship between mobilization and economic recovery from the Great Depression is Robert Higgs, "Wartime Prosperity? A Reassessment of the U.S. Economy in the 1940s," *Journal of Economic History,* 52 (March 1992). See also Hugh Rockoff, "From Plowshares to Swords: The American Economy in World War II," National Bureau of Economic Research Historical Paper 77 (December 1995). For the social impact of the war as viewed by contemporaries, see the collection of articles edited by Richard Polenberg, *America at War: The Home Front, 1941–1945* (Englewood Cliffs, NJ: Prentice-Hall, 1968). On the control of prices, see Harvey C. Mansfield, *Historical Reports on War Administration: Office of Price Administration,* vol. XV of which is *A Short History of OPA* (Washington, DC: Government Printing Office, 1947); Andrew H. Bartels, "The Office of Price Administration and the Legacy of the New Deal, 1939–1946," *Public Historian,* 5 (Summer 1983), pp. 5–29; and Meg Jacobs, "'How About Some Meat?' The Office of Price Administration, Consumption Politics, and State Building from the Bottom Up," *Journal of American History,* 84 (December 1997). A brilliant cross-national analysis of all aspects of World War II, from economic and military mobilization to tactics and leadership, is Richard Overy, *Why the Allies Won* (New York: Norton, 1995).

On Ferdinand Eberstadt and the Controlled Materials Plan, see Robert C. Perez and Edward F. Willett, *The Will to Win: A Biography of Ferdinand Eberstadt* (New York: Greenwood Press, 1989); Jeffrey M. Dorwart, *Eberstadt and Forrestal: A National Security Partnership, 1909–1949* (College Station: Texas A&M University Press, 1991); "Ferdinand Eberstadt," *Fortune,* 19 (April 1939); and especially Calvin Lee Christman, "Ferdinand Eberstadt and Economic Mobilization for War, 1941–1943," Ph.D. dissertation (history), Ohio State University, 1971. A useful but in my judgment mistaken analysis by Hugh Rockoff entitled "The Paradox of Planning in World War II" and published as National Bureau of Economic Research Historical Paper 83 (May 1996), argues that the positive impact of the Controlled Materials Plan has been overrated, and that the mobilization miracle might more accurately be viewed as a "gold rush" by American business in response to lavish federal funding in a setting of controlled inflation. In my own interpretation of the Plan, I have relied on the other works mentioned, on conversations with Robert D. Cuff, and on his case study, "Organizational Capabilities and U.S. War Production: The Controlled Materials Plan of World War II," (Boston, MA: Harvard Business School Case #390166, 1997).

Statistics on American population movements, the growth of cities, employment, and consumption patterns may be found in *The Impact of the War on Civilian Consumption in the United Kingdom, the United States and Canada: A Report to the Combined Production and Resources Board from a Special Combined Committee on Nonfood Consumption Levels* (Washington, DC: Government Printing Office, 1945). See also Gerald D. Nash, *The American West Transformed: The Impact of World War II* (Bloomington: Indiana University Press, 1985); Jacob Vander Meulen, "World War II Aircraft Industry in the West," *Journal of the West,* 36 (July 1997), pp. 78–84) and Carl Abbott, *The New Urban*

America: Growth and Politics in Sunbelt Cities (Chapel Hill: University of North Carolina Press, 1981). A thorough analysis of the spread of defense-related industry during and especially after the war is Ann Markusen, Scott Campbell, Peter Hall, and Sabina Deitrick, *The Rise of the Gunbelt: The Military Remapping of Industrial America* (New York: Oxford University Press, 1991).

On the entry of women into the workforce outside the home, see Gregory Chester, *Women in Defense Work during World War II: An Analysis of the Labor Problem and Women's Rights* (New York: Exposition Press, 1974); Sherna Berger Gluck, *Rosie the Riveter Revisited: Women, the War, and Social Change* (Boston: Twayne, 1987); Ruth Milkman, *Gender at Work: The Dynamics of Job Segregation by Sex during World War II* (Urbana: University of Illinois Press, 1987); and D'Ann Campbell, *Women at War with America: Private Lives in a Patriotic Era* (Cambridge, MA: Harvard University Press, 1984).

On the evolution of the federal tax system, see W. Elliot Brownlee, *Federal Taxation in America: A Short History* (New York: Cambridge University Press, 1996); and Carolyn C. Jones, "Class Tax to Mass Tax: the Role of Propaganda in the Expansion of the Income Tax during World War II," *Buffalo Law Review*, 37 (Fall 1988/89).

The experience of individual industries and companies during the war may be traced in specialized books and articles. Representative of this large literature are William M. Tuttle, Jr., "The Birth of an Industry: The Synthetic Rubber 'Mess' in World War II," *Technology and Culture*, 22 (January 1981); and, for the aluminum industry, which the war changed from a monopoly to a three-firm oligopoly of Alcoa, Kaiser, and Reynolds, George David Smith, *From Monopoly to Competition: The Transformations of Alcoa, 1888–1986* (New York: Cambridge University Press, 1988). On the remarkable achievement in producing ships, see Frederic C. Lane, *Ships for Victory: A History of Shipbuilding under the U.S. Maritime Commission in World War II* (Baltimore: Johns Hopkins University Press, 1951).

For statistics and other information on aircraft procurement, see I. B. Holley, Jr.'s thorough *Buying Aircraft: Materiel Procure-*

ment for the Army Air Forces (Washington, DC: Government Printing Office, 1964). An outstanding analysis of business-government interplay in this industry is Robert D. Cuff, "Organizing U.S. Aircraft Production for War, 1938–1944: An Experiment in Group Enterprise," in Jun Sakudo and Takao Shiba, eds., *World War II and the Transformation of Business Systems* (Tokyo: University of Tokyo Press, 1994). See also Tom Lilley et al., *Problems of Accelerating Aircraft Production during World War II* (Boston: Harvard University Graduate School of Business Administration, 1947); and Jonathan Zeitlin, "Flexibility and Mass Production at War: Aircraft Manufacture in Britain, the United States, and Germany, 1939–1945," *Technology and Culture,* 36 (January 1995).

On aviation more generally, see Roger E. Bilstein, *The American Aerospace Industry: From Workshop to Global Enterprise* (New York: Twayne, 1996); John B. Rae, *Climb to Greatness* (Cambridge, MA: MIT Press, 1968); Michael S. Sherry, *The Rise of American Air Power: The Creation of Armageddon* (New Haven, CT: Yale University Press, 1987); Jacob Vander Meulen, *The Politics of Aircraft: Building an American Military Industry* (Lawrence: University Press of Kansas, 1991); and Ronald Shaffer, *Wings of Judgment: American Bombing in World War II* (New York: Oxford University Press, 1985).

Data on the aircraft companies discussed in this chapter come from a variety of sources, including the works cited above plus the corporate and biographical reference books mentioned for Literature of the Field above. See also René J. Francillon, *McDonnell Douglas Aircraft since 1920* (London: Putnam Aeronautical Books, 1979); Peter M. Bowers, *Boeing Aircraft since 1916* (London: Putnam Aeronautical Books, 1989); Harold Mansfield, *Vision: A Saga of the Sky* [Boeing] (New York: Duell, Sloan and Pearce, 1956); *Pedigree of Champions: Boeing Since 1916* (The Boeing Co., 4th ed., 1977); Robert J. Serling, *Legend and Legacy: The Story of Boeing and Its People* (New York: St. Martin's Press, 1992); H. P. Willmott, *B-17 Flying Fortress* (New York: Prentice-Hall, 1983); and Jacob Vander Meulen, *Building the B-29* (Washington, DC: Smithsonian Institution Press, 1995).

Selected Sources for Chapter Six
Overview: African Americans in Business

Scholarly work on African Americans and business began to grow rapidly toward the close of the century. The following items provide a good introduction: Juliet E. K. Walker, *The History of Black Business in America: Capitalism, Race, Entrepreneurship* (New York: Macmillan, 1998), which is a thorough analysis covering the colonial period to the middle 1990s; Timothy Bates, "Black Business Community," in Jack Salzman, David Lionel Smith, and Cornel West, eds., *Encyclopedia of African-American Culture and History* (New York: Simon & Schuster Macmillan, 1996), pp. 332–346; Juliet E. K. Walker, ibid., "Banking," pp. 246–250, and "Entrepreneurs," pp. 897–909; Ronald W. Bailey, ed., *Black Business Enterprise: Historical and Contemporary Perspectives* (New York: Basic Books, 1971); John Ingham and Lynne Feld-man, eds., *African American Business Leaders: A Biographical Dictionary* (Westport, CT: Greenwood Press, 1994); John Sibley Butler, *Entrepreneurship and Self-Help among Black Americans: A Reconsideration of Race and Economics* (Albany: State University of New York Press, 1991); Shelley Greene and Paul Pryde, *Black Entrepreneurship in America* (New Brunswick, NJ: Transaction Publishers, 1990); Timothy Bates, *Black Capitalism: A Quantitative Analysis* (New York: Praeger, 1973), which is especially concerned with the issue of whether black patronage of black businesses was on balance a helpful or limiting phenomenon, as is Russ Rymer, "Integration's Casualties: Segregation Helped Black Business, Civil Rights Helped Destroy It," *New York Times Magazine,* November 1, 1998. See also Paula Mergenhagen, "Black-owned Businesses," *American Demographics,* 18 (June 1996); and any issue of *Black Enterprise,* a periodical established in 1970.

On insurance, see Walter A. Friedman, "Insurance Companies," in *Encyclopedia of African-American Culture and History,* pp. 1365–1369; Robert Weems, *Black Business in the Black Metropolis* (Bloomington: Indiana University Press, 1996), which examines the Chicago Metropolitan Assurance Company; Alexa Henderson, *Atlanta Life Insurance Company: Guardian of Black Economic Dignity* (Tuscaloosa: University of Alabama Press, 1990); and Walter Weare, *Black Business in the New South: A Social History of the North Carolina Mutual Life Insurance Company* (Urbana: University of Illinois Press, 1973).

On the intersection of politics and minority business, see George R. LaNoue, "Split Visions: Minority Business Set Asides," *Annals of the American Academy of Political and Social Science,* 523 (September 1992); and Dean Kotlowski, "Black Power—Nixon Style: The Nixon Administration and Minority Business Enterprise," *Business History Review,* 72 (Autumn 1998). On black managers and the corporate ladder, see David A. Thomas and John J. Gabarro, *Breaking Through: The Making of Minority Executives in Corporate America* (Boston: Harvard Business School Press, 1999).

Selected Sources for Chapter Seven
Toward a Peak of Prosperity, 1945–1973:
RCA and Color TV

On the performance of the American economy during these years, see *Historical Statistics of the United States* (1970) and the annual updates in *Statistical Abstract of the United States.* A concise analysis and interpretation of postwar America prosperity is Richard H. K. Vietor, "Economic Performance," in Stanley I. Kutler, ed., *Encyclopedia of the United States in the Twentieth Century,* III, pp. 1155–1181. Also in this volume, see the following essays: Alfred D. Chandler, Jr., "Industrial Production," pp. 1127–1154; Susan Strasser, "Consumption," pp. 1017–1035; and William R. Childs, "Infrastructure," pp. 1331–1355. I have also relied on two other essays, which appear in Volume II of the encyclopedia: David A. Hounshell, "Industrial Research and Manufacturing Technology," pp. 831–857; and Steven W. Usselman, "Computer and Communications Technology," pp. 799–829. All of these essays themselves contain ample bibliographies.

A general overview of American manufacturing may be found in Alfred D. Chandler, Jr., "The Competitive Performance of U.S.

Industrial Enterprises since the Second World War," *Business History Review,* 68 (Spring 1994). On the evolution of air conditioning, see Raymond Arsenault, "The End of the Long Hot Summer: The Air Conditioner and Southern Culture," *Journal of Southern History,* 50 (November 1984); and Gail Cooper, *Air-conditioning America: Engineers and the Controlled Environment, 1900–1960* (Baltimore: Johns Hopkins University Press, 1998).

On research and development during World War II, see Ronald Kline, "R&D: Organizing for War," *IEEE Spectrum,* November 1987, a cross-national study. On the origins and early development of radio, the standard source is Hugh G. J. Aitken, *The Continuous Wave: Technology and American Radio, 1900–1932* (Princeton, NJ: Princeton University Press, 1985), which has excellent material on the formation of RCA. For a cultural historian's approach, see Susan Smulyan, *Selling Radio: The Commercialization of American Broadcasting* (Washington, DC: Smithsonian Institution Press, 1994). Michele Hilmes, *Radio Voices: American Broadcasting, 1922–1952* (St. Paul: University of Minnesota Press, 1998) examines the intersection of technology, advertising, and program content. An outstanding introduction to the nature of the electronics industry and its history through the 1950s and into the early 1960s is Stanley S. Miller et al., *Manufacturing Policy: A Casebook of Major Production Problems in Six Selected Industries* (Homewood, IL: Irwin, 1957; 2d ed., 1964); the materials in this book on television and the rest of the electronics industry were written by my Harvard Business School colleague Richard S. Rosenbloom, and I have made liberal use of these materials in addition to benefiting from conversations with Professor Rosenbloom. Another important study of R&D is Stuart W. Leslie, *The Cold War and American Science* (New York: Columbia University Press, 1993), which focuses on Stanford University and MIT.

The best source on the career of David Sarnoff is Kenneth Bilby, *The General: David Sarnoff and the Rise of the Communications Industry* (New York: Harper & Row, 1986); Bilby was a close associate of Sarnoff and himself a high-ranking RCA executive, and I have leaned heavily on his book in my interpretation of Sarnoff and RCA. See also David Sarnoff, *Looking Ahead: The Papers of David Sarnoff* (New York: McGraw-Hill, 1968); Carl

Dreher, *Sarnoff: An American Success* (New York: Quadrangle, 1977), written by a technical expert with a long association with Sarnoff and RCA; Eugene Lyons, *David Sarnoff: A Biography* (New York: Harper & Row, 1966), a hagiographic account; and Tom Lewis, *Empire of the Air: The Men Who Made Radio* (New York: HarperCollins, 1991), which covers the careers of Sarnoff, Lee de Forest, Howard Armstrong, and other industry pioneers. Additional sources on RCA include Margaret B. W. Graham, *RCA and the VideoDisc: The Business of Research* (Cambridge: Cambridge University Press, 1986), an especially insightful analysis; Robert Sobel, *RCA* (New York: Stein and Day, 1986), which contains some useful statistics; and *Fortune*'s frequent articles on RCA and the electronics industry from the 1930s to the 1980s, among which I found the following particularly useful: "RCA's Television," *Fortune*, September 1948; Lawrence P. Lessing, "The Electronics Era," *Fortune*, July 1951; "C.B.S. Steals the Show," *Fortune*, July 1953; David Sarnoff, "The Fabulous Future," *Fortune*, January 1955, which contains examples of Sarnoff's sometimes overblown rhetoric; William B. Harris, "R.C.A. Organizes for Profit," *Fortune*, August 1957; Walter Guzzardi, Jr., "R.C.A.: The General Never Got Butterflies," *Fortune*, October 1962; Bro Uttal, "How Ed Griffiths Brought RCA into Focus," *Fortune*, December 31, 1978; Peter Nulty, "A Peacemaker Comes to RCA," *Fortune*, May 4, 1981; and "The Colossus of Conglomerates [General Electric] Moves Away from Smokestacks by Buying RCA," *Fortune*, January 1, 1986.

Coverage of the many aspects of TV's influence on American culture lies beyond the scope of this book, but the interested reader is referred to the following sample of works: Erik Barnouw, *Tube of Plenty: The Evolution of American Television* (New York: Oxford University Press, 1970); Jerry Mander, *Four Arguments for the Elimination of Television* (New York: Quill, 1978); George Comstock et al., *Television and Human Behavior* (New York: Columbia University Press, 1978); Carl Lowe, ed., *Television and American Culture* (New York: H. W. Wilson Co., 1981); and Joseph Turow, *Breaking Up America: Advertisers and the New Media World* (Chicago: University of Chicago Press, 1997).

The theme of American industrial arrogance and consequent decline, exemplified in this chapter through the story of RCA, is set forth in numerous books published during the 1980s. A good example of this literature is Robert C. Hayes, Steven C. Wheelwright, and Kim B. Clark, *Dynamic Manufacturing: Creating the Learning Organization* (New York: Free Press, 1988). There is also a plethora of works on the Japanese challenge in electronics and other industries, examples of which include Thomas K. McCraw, ed., *America Versus Japan: A Study in Business-Government Relations* (Boston: Harvard Business School Press, 1986); Philip J. Curtis, *The Fall of the U.S. Consumer Electronics Industry: An American Trade Tragedy* (Westport, CT: Quorum Books, 1994); and David Schwartzman, *The Japanese Television Cartel: A Study Based on Matsushita vs. Zenith* (Ann Arbor: University of Michigan Press, 1993). See also MIT Commission on Industrial Productivity, Commission Working Group on the Consumer Electronics Industries, "The Decline of U.S. Consumer Electronics Manufacturing: History, Hypotheses, and Remedies," in *Working Papers of the MIT Commission on Industrial Productivity*, Vol. 1 (Cambridge, MA: MIT Press, 1989); and Richard Rosenbloom and William Abernathy, "The Climate for Innovation in Industry: The Role of Management Attitudes and Practices in Consumer Electronics," *Research Policy*, 11 (1982). A readable account of the consumer-electronics story from the Japanese side may be found in Akio Morita, *Made in Japan* (New York: Dutton, 1986), written by the co-founder and longtime CEO of Sony.

Selected Sources for Chapter Eight

Overview: Industrial Chemicals and Pharmaceuticals

For the chemical industry and the morphology of industrial research, see David A. Hounshell and John Kenly Smith, *Science and Corporate Strategy: Du Pont R&D, 1902–1980* (New York: Cambridge University Press, 1988), which ably analyzes the theme of centralization versus decentralization in industrial R&D. Alfred D. Chandler, Jr., "The Competitive Performance of U.S. Industrial Enterprises since the Second World War," *Business His-*

tory Review, 68 (Spring 1994), contains an insightful account of the chemical and pharmaceutical industries. Some other information on chemical companies discussed in this chapter comes from Thomas Derdak, ed., *International Directory of Company Histories* (Chicago: St. James Press, 1988–).

On pharmaceuticals, see David Schwartzman, *Innovation in the Pharmaceutical Industry* (Baltimore: Johns Hopkins University Press, 1976); Peter Temin, *Taking Your Medicine: Drug Regulation in the United States* (Cambridge, MA: Harvard University Press, 1980); and National Research Council, *The Competitive Status of the U.S. Pharmaceutical Industry: The Influences of Technology in Determining International Industrial Competitive Advantage* (Washington, DC: National Academy Press, 1983). See also the *Annual Survey Report* of the Pharmaceutical Manufacturers Association (Washington, DC: the Association, annual), and the same association's *Fact Book,* also issued annually. The industry can be followed through other trade publications as well, such as *Pharmacy in History, Drug Topics,* and *Chemist and Druggist.* One of the best company histories is Louis Galambos with Jane Eliot Sewell, *Networks of Innovation: Vaccine Development at Merck, Sharp & Dohme, and Mulford, 1895–1995* (New York: Cambridge University Press, 1995).

Selected Sources for Chapter Nine
1973–2000: Slower Growth, Franchising,
and the Case of McDonald's

General sources for macroeconomic performance are the same as listed for Literature of the Field, especially the annual *Economic Report of the President* (Washington, DC: Government Printing Office), and *Statistical Abstract of the United States* (Washington, DC: Government Printing Office). See also Richard H. K. Vietor, "Economic Performance," in Stanley I. Kutler, ed., *Encyclopedia of the United States in the Twentieth Century,* III, pp. 1155–1182.

For discussions of the distribution of wealth and income, see James T. Patterson, "Wealth and Poverty," in ibid., pp. 1067–1090; Edward Wolff, "Trends in Household Wealth in the United States,

1962–83 and 1983–89," *Review of Income and Wealth,* 40, No. 2 (1994); "How the Pie is Sliced," *The American Prospect* (Summer 1995); Steven Sass, "Passing the Buck: The Intergenerational Transfer of Wealth," Federal Reserve Bank of Boston *Regional Review* (Summer 1995); and Lee Soltow, "Distribution of Income and Wealth," in Glenn Porter, ed., *Encyclopedia of American Economic History,* pp. 1087–1119. See also Andrew Hacker, *Money: Who Has How Much and Why* (New York: Scribner & Sons, 1997), an insightful and broad-ranging analysis; James K. Galbraith, *Created Unequal: The Crisis in American Pay* (New York: Free Press, 1998); John McNeil, "Changes in Median Household Income: 1969 to 1996," U.S. Bureau of the Census, Special Studies P. 23–196, July 1998; Edward N. Wolff, *Top Heavy: The Increasing Inequality of Wealth in America and What Can Be Done About It* (New York: The New Press, 1996); and the articles in The *New York Times Magazine,* June 12, 1998, collectively entitled "Money on the Mind." On corporate executives' pay, see also Jennifer Carpenter and David Yermack, eds., *Executive Compensation and Shareholder Value* (New York: Kluwer Academic Publishers, 1998); and Michael M. Weinstein, "Why They Deserve It," *New York Times Magazine,* November 19, 1995, citing a study by Graef Crystal. *Business Week* publishes annual statistical surveys of executive compensation. See, for example, "Is Greed Good?" *Business Week,* April 19, 1999, pp. 72–118. Reasons for rising inequality are primarily technological in nature, according to a poll by economists; see *Economic Report of the President* (Washington, DC, 1997), Box 5–3, p. 175.

The standard historical analysis of franchising is Thomas S. Dicke, *Franchising in America: The Development of a Business Method, 1840–1980* (Chapel Hill: University of North Carolina Press, 1992). See also Scott Partridge, "The Origins and Development of Modern Franchising," doctoral thesis, Harvard Business School, 1970; and Charles L. Vaughn, *Franchising: Its Nature, Scope, Advantages, and Development* (Lexington, MA: Lexington Books, 2nd ed., 1979). A major source listing numerous articles is B. Elango and Vance H. Fried, "Franchising Research: A Literature Review and Synthesis," *Journal of Small Business Management,* 35 (July 1997). See also the following annual publications:

Franchising in the Economy; The Franchise Annual; The Franchise Opportunities Handbook; Bond's Franchise Guide; Proceedings of the Society of Franchising, and *The Source Book of Franchise Opportunities.* An annual survey of franchising by the magazine *Entrepreneur* has been conducted since the early 1980s, containing information on *Entrepreneur*'s "Franchise 500." See also current issues of *Nation's Restaurant News, Franchising World, Restaurant Business, American Journal of Small Business, Women in Franchising,* and *Pizza Today.* Bill Carlino, "75 Years: The Odyssey of Eating Out," *Nation's Restaurant News,* Special Commemorative Issue, January 1994, is a breezy survey full of anecdotes and other information not only on franchising but on restaurant dining in general. In addition, see Patrick J. Kaufmann and Rajiv P. Dant, eds., *Franchising: Contemporary Issues and Research* (Binghamton, NY: Haworth Press, 1995); Robert Dahlstrom, "Franchising: Contemporary Issues and Research," *Journal of Public Policy & Marketing,* 15 (Spring 1996); Robert Emerson, *Fast Food: The Endless Shakeout* (New York: Lebhar-Friedman, 1982); and Robert Emerson, *The New Economics of Fast Food* (New York: Van Nostrand Reinhold, 1990).

Economic analyses include Richard E. Caves and William F. Murphy II, "Franchising: Firms, Markets, and Intangible Assets," *Southern Economic Journal,* 42 (April 1976); Paul H. Rubin, "The Theory of the Firm and the Structure of the Franchise Contract," *Journal of Law & Economics,* 21 (April 1978); Benjamin Klein and Lester F. Saft, "The Law and Economics of Franchise Tying Contracts," *Journal of Law & Economics,* 28 (May 1985); and Alan Krueger, "Ownership, Agency, and Wages: An Examination of Franchising in the Fast-Food Industry," *The Quarterly Journal of Economics* (February 1991); see also John F. Preble and Richard C. Hoffman, "Franchising Systems around the Globe: A Status Report," *Journal of Small Business Management,* 33 (April 1995).

John Love, *McDonald's: Behind the Arches* (New York: Bantam, 1986, revised ed., 1995) is by far the most informative single source on the company, and I am much indebted to it in my account of McDonald's. Robin Leidner, *Fast Food, Fast Talk: Ser-*

vice Work and the Routinization of Everyday Life (Berkeley: University of California Press, 1993) is a sociologist's first-hand account of working conditions, especially strong in its evocation of life inside a McDonald's restaurant. James L. Watson, ed., *Golden Arches East: McDonald's in East Asia* (Stanford, CA: Stanford University Press, 1997) is an insightful analysis by anthropologists of the McDonald's experience in Beijing, Hong Kong, Taipei, Seoul, and Tokyo. Ray Kroc with Robert Anderson, *Grinding It Out: The Making of McDonald's* (Chicago: Henry Regnery, 1977) is a brief autobiography, characteristically unpretentious. Lisa Bertagnoli, "McDonald's: Company of the Century," *Restaurants and Institutions,* 99 (July 10, 1989) and the same author's "Inside McDonald's," *Restaurants and Institutions,* 99 (August 21, 1989) are excellent surveys containing useful information about employment of women and minorities. For analyses of McDonald's problems toward the close of the century, see Shelly Branch, "What's Eating McDonald's?", *Fortune,* October 13, 1997; and David Leonhardt, "McDonald's: Can It Regain its Golden Touch?", *Business Week,* March 9, 1998.

An especially valuable analysis of "plural" franchise systems involving company-owned stores, master franchisees, and individual franchisees is Jeffrey Bradach, *Franchise Organizations* (Boston: Harvard Business School Press, 1998). See also Maxwell Boas, *Big Mac: The Unauthorized Story of McDonald's* (New York: New American Library, 1977); Stan Luxenberg, *Roadside Empires: How the Chains Franchised America* (New York: Penguin, 1985); Timothy Bates, "Analysis of Survival Rates among Franchise and Independent Small Business Startups," *Journal of Small Business Management,* 33 (April 1995); and Eric Schlosser, "Fast Food Nation: The True Cost of America's Diet," *Rolling Stone,* September 3, 1998. On motels and franchising, see John A. Jakle, Keith A. Sculle, and Jefferson S. Rogers, *The Motel in America* (Baltimore: Johns Hopkins University Press, 1996), Chapters 6 and 7.

The seminal article on agency theory is Michael C. Jensen and William H. Meckling, "Theory of the Firm: Managerial Behavior, Agency Costs, and Ownership Structure," *Journal of Financial*

Economics, 3 (1976). For a more thorough explanation, see Michael C. Jensen, *Foundations of Organizational Strategy* (Cambridge, MA: Harvard University Press, 1998).

Selected Sources for Chapter Ten
Overview: Computers and Silicon Valley

For an excellent introduction, see Steven W. Usselman, "Computer and Communications Technology," in Stanley I. Kutler, ed., *Encyclopedia of the United States in the Twentieth Century* (New York: Simon & Schuster, 1996), II, pp. 799–829. Good sources on the history of information technology include JoAnne Yates, *Control Through Communication: The Rise of System in American Management* (Baltimore: Johns Hopkins University Press, 1989); James W. Cortada, *Before the Computer: IBM, NCR, Burroughs, and Remington Rand and the Industry They Created, 1865–1956* (Princeton: Princeton University Press, 1993); James R. Beniger, *The Control Revolution: Technical and Economic Origins of the Information Society* (Cambridge, MA: Harvard University Press, 1986); Ernest Braun and Stuart Macdonald, *Revolution in Miniature: The History and Impact of Semiconductor Electronics* (New York: Cambridge University Press, 1978); Kenneth Flamm, *Targeting the Computer: Government Support and International Competition* (Washington, DC: Brookings Institution, 1987); and Flamm, *Creating the Computer: Government, Industry, and High Technology* (Washington, DC: Brookings Institution, 1988). On IBM, see Emerson W. Pugh, *Building IBM: Shaping an Industry and Its Technology* (Cambridge, MA: MIT Press, 1995); and Thomas J. Watson, Jr., and Peter Petre, *Father, Son & Co.: My Life at IBM and Beyond* (New York: Bantam, 1990), the extraordinary autobiography of IBM's second CEO.

For other first-hand accounts, see David Packard, *The H-P Way: How Bill Hewlett and I Built Our Company* (New York: Harper Business, 1995), an oddly disembodied book; the livelier works are by Intel's Andrew S. Grove, *Only the Paranoid Survive: How to Exploit the Crisis Points that Challenge Every Company and Career* (New York: Currency Doubleday, 1996); and Bill

Gates with Nathan Myhrvold and Peter Rinearson, *The Road Ahead* (New York: Penguin, 1996). On the leading software firm, see Randall E. Stross, *The Microsoft Way* (Reading, MA: Addison-Wesley, 1996); and Michael A. Cusumano and Richard W. Selby, *Microsoft Secrets: How the World's Most Powerful Software Company Creates Technology, Shapes Markets, and Manages People* (New York: Free Press, 1995).

A good overview of Silicon Valley may be found in a special 20-page survey by John Micklethwait, "Silicon Valley: The Valley of Money's Delight," *The Economist,* March 19, 1997. Carolyn Caddes, *Portraits of Success: Impressions of Silicon Valley Pioneers* (Palo Alto, CA: Tioga, 1986), is a photographs-with-text coverage of numerous participants in the creation of Silicon Valley firms. AnnaLee Saxenian, *Regional Advantage: Culture and Competition in Silicon Valley and Route 128* (Cambridge, MA: Harvard University Press, 1994), is a good comparative study that also contributes to the theoretical literature on industry clusters, a subject discussed for several countries in Michael E. Porter's *The Competitive Advantage of Nations* (New York: Free Press, 1990). A direct examination of this phenomenon as it relates to Silicon Valley is Stuart W. Leslie and Robert H. Kargon, "Selling Silicon Valley: Frederick Terman's Model for Regional Advantage," *Business History Review,* 70 (Winter 1996). Other useful works include Robert X. Cringely, *Accidental Empires: How the Boys of Silicon Valley Make Their Millions, Battle Foreign Competition, and Still Can't Get a Date* (Reading, MA: Addison-Wesley, 1992); Michael Malone, *The Big Score: The Billion-Dollar Story of Silicon Valley* (Garden City, N.Y.: Doubleday, 1985); and Everett Rogers and Judith K. Larsen, *Silicon Valley Fever: Growth of High-Technology Culture* (New York: Basic Books, 1984).

The relationship between computerization and productivity is addressed in Shoshana Zuboff, *In the Age of the Smart Machine* (New York: Basic Books, 1988); and Daniel E. Sichel, *The Computer Revolution: An Economic Perspective* (Washington, DC: Brookings Institution Press, 1997). Analytical approaches to organized R&D may be found in Richard S. Rosenbloom and William J. Spencer, eds., *Engines of Innovation: U.S. Industrial Research at the End of an Era* (Boston: Harvard Business School Press, 1996), which contains wide-ranging essays by both scholars and practitioners and includes thorough bibliographies. The periodicals *Datamation, Wired, Internet World,* and *Interactive Age* also provide a wealth of data.

Statistics about Internet usage and other developments may be traced through online reports by The Internet Council and The Internet Almanac. On the history of the Internet, see Debora L. Spar, "Lost in (Cyber)space: The Private Rules of Online Commerce," Chapter 2 of A. Claire Cutler, Virginia Haufler, and Tony Porter, eds., *Private Authority and International Affairs* (Albany: State University of New York Press, 1999); Thomas P. Hughes, "Networking: ARPANET," Chapter VI of *Rescuing Prometheus* (New York: Pantheon, 1998); and especially Janet Abbate, *Inventing the Internet* (Cambridge, MA: MIT Press, 1999); and Robert H. Reid, *Architects of the Web: 1,000 Days that Built the Future of Business* (New York: Wiley, 1997).

ACKNOWLEDGEMENTS

During 25 years of teaching at the Harvard Business School, I have benefited from the rich insights of my students, colleagues, friends, and research associates, and of members of Harvard's ongoing Business History Seminar. I am exceedingly grateful for their help. For advice and assistance with this book I am especially indebted to Sven Beckert, Jeffrey Bernstein, Larry Block, Laura Bureš, Fred Carstensen, Alfred Chandler, Bob Cuff, Alexander Dyck, Tom Eisenmann, Lei Feng, Walter Friedman, Max Hall, Nayantara Hensel, Rob Huckman, Nancy Koehn, George Lodge, Lisa McGirr, David Moss, Margaret Murphy, David Nickles, Rowena Olegario, Forest Reinhardt, David Rice, Dick Rosenbloom, Julio Rotemberg, Richard Tedlow, David Thomas, Peter Tufano, Dick Vietor, Lou Wells, Wyatt Wells, Felice Whittum, Mary Yeager, and Andy Zelleke. As always, Susan McCraw, who is the most generous person I know, gave me indispensable editorial and organizational advice. For any remaining errors and infelicities, I alone am responsible.

INDEX

American Business, 1920–2000: How It Worked
Developmental editor and copy editor: Andrew J. Davidson
Production editor: Lucy Herz
Proofreader: Claudia Siler
Indexer: Fred Liese
Printer: Versa Press, Inc.